William J. V. Neill and Hanns-Uve Schwedler (*editors*)
URBAN PLANNING AND CULTURAL INCLUSION
Lessons from Belfast and Berlin

Howard Williams, Colin Wight and Norbert Kapferer (*editors*)
POLITICAL THOUGHT AND GERMAN REUNIFICATION
The New German Ideology?

Anglo-German Foundation
Series Standing Order ISBN 0–333–71459–8
(*outside North America only*)

You can receive future titles in this series as they are published by placing a standing order. Please contact your bookseller or, in case of difficulty, write to us at the address below with your name and address, the title of the series and the ISBN quoted above.

Customer Services Department, Macmillan Distribution Ltd, Houndmills, Basingstoke, Hampshire RG21 6XS, England

Urban Planning and Cultural Inclusion

Lessons from Belfast and Berlin

Edited by

William J. V. Neill
Reader in Urban Planning
Queen's University of Belfast
Northern Ireland

and

Hanns-Uve Schwedler
Managing Director of the European Academy of the Urban Environment
Berlin
Germany

First published 2001 by
PALGRAVE
Houndmills, Basingstoke, Hampshire RG21 6XS and
175 Fifth Avenue, New York, N. Y. 10010
Companies and representatives throughout the world

PALGRAVE is the new global academic imprint of
St. Martin's Press LLC Scholarly and Reference Division and
Palgrave Publishers Ltd (formerly Macmillan Press Ltd).

ISBN 0–333–79368–4

This book is printed on paper suitable for recycling and
made from fully managed and sustained forest sources.

A catalogue record for this book is available
from the British Library.

Library of Congress Cataloging-in-Publication Data
Urban planning and cultural inclusion : lessons from Belfast and
Berlin / edited by William J.V. Neill and Hanns-Uve Schwedler.
          p. cm.
Includes bibliographical references and index.
ISBN 0–333–79368–4
      1. City planning—Northern Ireland—Belfast. 2. City planning–
–Germany—Berlin. 3. Multiculturalism—Northern Ireland–
–Belfast. 4. Multiculturalism—Germany—Berlin. I. Neill, William
J. V. II. Schwedler, Hanns-Uve.
      HT169.G72 B4948 2000
      307.1'216'094167—dc21
                                                            00–066575

10   9   8   7   6   5   4   3   2   1
10   09 08 07 06 05 04 03 02 01

Printed in Great Britain by Antony Rowe Ltd, Chippenham, Wiltshire

Contents

List of Figures and Table

Table

List of Maps

Acknowledgements

Translations

Jenny Johnson; Michael LaFond

All quotations derived from German-language sources have been translated into English; the accuracy of the rendition is guaranteed by the joint editors, not by the individual authors.

Illustrations

All the illustrations and pictorial material were kindly provided by the authors. The joint editors would like to express their thanks for permission to use illustrations to the Berlin Ministry for Urban Development (*Land Berlin*), for Maps 2.1, 4.1, 4.2, 4.3, 4.4; to Manuela Preuss for Fig. (photo) 11.1; to Partner für Berlin, Gesellschaft für Hauptstadtmarketing, for Figs. (photos) 11.2, 11.3, 11.4, 11.5; to Professor F.W. Boal for Map 3.2; to the Laganside Corporation for Figs. (map) 12.1, (photos) 12.2, 12.3, 12.4, 12.5 and to Chris Hill Photographic for Figs. (photos) 13.2 and 13.4.

Foreword

Cities which are divided along ethnic and cultural lines are nothing new. From a historical point of view entire societies were constructed on the basis of urban segregation. This structuring was, for example, both a constitutive and conflict-regulating element in Middle-Eastern city-states. It provided collective strength and social certainty, upheld despotic rule and was accepted in society.

But nowadays in democratic constitutional countries urban segregation is perceived rather as a threat, in any event as ambivalent and as a source of conflict. The Federal Republic of Germany may be cited as an example of this. For many years (and for many people probably still today) integration of foreigners meant not only learning to speak the German language, but also learning 'to be' German: if you want to live here, then you must become one of us! However, this could only mean for recipients negating their own identity and assuming a strange one.

Be this as it may, the co-editors of the present work have taken as their starting point the belief that if cities wish to survive in competition with one another and not be submerged in tensions, they need to identify, create and maintain some kind of a shared identity amongst their inhabitants. But of course this does not mean negating the many and varied identities amongst urban population groups which also express themselves in spatial terms. On the contrary, what is at issue is how urban planning and city management can take these identities on board constructively and can assist them without allowing the city to deteriorate into a disconnected, hostile conglomeration of many and varied places to live.

Belfast and Berlin are currently in the process of responding to this challenge. Since the Berlin Wall came down and Germany was reunited, two cities with a combined population of 3.5 million are fusing together in the Federal capital. What are the implications of this for urban planning? How do the planners approach their task? Since the 'Good Friday Agreement', in the Northern Irish capital, town planners are now required to confront the question of whether their activities contribute towards bringing together Catholic and Protestant Belfast and how they can physically deal with these two urban cultures which have been diametrically opposed for such a long time.

Questions of this nature formed the central focus of a symposium organised early in 1999 by the European Academy of the Urban Environment and The Queen's University of Belfast, School of Environmental Planning. To a large extent the present publication is based on this conference.

The symposium was made possible at the time thanks to funding support from the Anglo-German Foundation for the Study of Industrial Society and the Ministry for Urban Development of the Federal State (*Land*) of Berlin. For their support we would like to express our thanks. In addition – last but not least – we would like to thank the authors of the individual chapters here brought together, as well as other participants at the symposium. Many of the ideas which are now formulated are based on discussions in which we all shared. Jenny Johnson and Michael LaFond translated the German chapters into English. Our thanks to them. Our thanks also to David Houston, Irene Watson and Catherine Moore for their invaluable assistance with the text. Finally, we would both like to thank the authors and the institutions which they represent for enabling us to use photographic and graphic material which they have provided.

WILLIAM J.V. NEILL   HANNS-UVE SCHWEDLER

Notes on the Contributors

Kyle Alexander is a professional urban planner and is Director of Development of the Laganside Corporation in Belfast.

Sir Charles Brett is a former Chairman of the Northern Ireland Housing Executive and Chair of the International Fund for Ireland. He is President and founder member of the Ulster Architectural Heritage Society.

Frank Gaffikin, PhD, is Co-Director of the Urban Institute, a research and consultancy unit of the University of Ulster. He has been involved in community development and urban regeneration for a number of years and is the author of several books on the theme of urban regeneration.

Simone Hain, PhD, trained in fine arts, now works freelance in Berlin as a writer and historian of urban planning. Her principal study and publishing fields are the history of architecture in the twentieth century, history of building in the GDR, post-war reconstruction planning and architecture in East Berlin and monument conservation for buildings of the modern period.

Peter Heine, PhD, is Professor of Islamic Studies in the non-Arab world at the Humboldt University of Berlin. His principal research emphases include the history of the Islamic world and culture, conflicts between the Sunni and Shiite sects, the Islamic religion in the 'diaspora', especially in Germany and in the Indian sub-continent.

Malachy McEldowney is a town planner with an architectural background and a planning academic. He worked for Leicester City Council in the 1970s and for De Montfort University in the early 1980s. Since 1981 he has been a lecturer/senior lecturer in the School of Environmental Planning at Queen's University of Belfast. He has been Head of School since 1993 and Professor of Town and Country Planning since 2000.

Bill Morrison is an architect-planner and is chief planner with responsibility for the city of Belfast.

Mike Morrissey, PhD, is Co-Director of the Urban Institute in Belfast. He has worked in the Northern Ireland Polytechnic and the University of Ulster since 1975. His main interests are in local labour markets and local economic development. Recent publications include (with Frank Gaffikin) *The New Unemployed: Joblessness and the Market Economy* (1992) and *A Tale of One City* (1996).

Renate Müller, geographer, is a research and teaching assistant in the Institute of Geography at the Free University of Berlin. Her fields of interest include socio-spatial development in the Berlin urban area.

William J.V. Neill, PhD, is Reader in Urban Planning in the Queen's University of Belfast. He worked for many years as an urban planner in the United States and has published widely in the field of urban identity and city marketing.

Bernhard Schneider is a freelance architect and consultant. He works for various Berlin Ministries as well as 'Partner für Berlin GmbH. His published works deal with questions of public space and of museum architecture. He has been in addition fundamentally involved in setting up the Berlin urban consultation process known as 'Stadtforum'.

Hanns-Uve Schwedler, PhD, is a geographer by training and managing director of the European Academy of the Urban Environment in Berlin. His publications include works on urban development questions, in particular dealing with socio-spatial segregation in the Middle East.

Mike Smith is a professional urban planner and chartered surveyor. He is Chief Executive of the Laganside Corporation in Belfast.

Ken Sterrett, PhD, is a lecturer in the School of Environmental Planning at Queen's University in Belfast. His main research interests are in the sociology of design and aesthetics and in community involvement in planning. Before joining the School at Queen's, he worked as a senior planner with the Department of the Environment for Northern Ireland.

Wolfgang Süchting, town planner and architect, is a civil servant in the Berlin Ministry of Urban Development, where he heads the project group dealing with 'Planwerk Innenstadt'.

Patrick Weiss, town planner, works as a civil servant in the Berlin Ministry of Urban Development. He coordinates the section dealing with the historical city centre 'Historisches Zentrum' in the 'Planwerk Innenstadt' project group.

Part I
Introduction

1

Memory, Spatial Planning and the Construction of Cultural Identity in Belfast and Berlin – an Overview

William J.V. Neill

Berlin, a central European metropolis of 3.5 million people, 12 per cent of whom are foreigners from no less than 184 countries,[1] became in 1999, with the move of the most important federal government functions from Bonn, the new functioning German capital. It is the beginning of the Berlin Republic as some have called it. What could Berlin possibly have in common with Belfast, a city of around half a million people of predominantly two ethnic backgrounds on the European Atlantic fringe? Why is a comparison, a sharing of urban planning experiences, of interest and value?

Of course, both cities have been and Belfast continues to be scarred by physical walls of division. But, whereas the Berlin Wall represented competing and mutually exclusive political ideologies, the Belfast so called 'peace walls' represent the extreme form of competing and until recently seemingly mutually exclusive cultural identities. And it is the coming to terms with developing a new place identity that provides the common ground where it is beneficial, I think, to compare recent spatial planning developments in Belfast and Berlin. Both cities facing historical fresh starts throw into sharp relief the questions of what it means now to be German, of what it means now to be Irish and/or British in Ireland and how this struggle and contestation of identity is constituted in the built fabric of the distinctive places which are Belfast and Berlin. This book shares experience over how cultural identity issues enter into urban planning discourse and action in both cities. How does the self-understanding of collective identities (Ossies, Wessies, Berliners, Germans, Turks living in Germany ... Irish nationalists, Ulster unionists, Belfasters ...) defined by characteristics of difference from other identities work themselves out and seek their necessary expression in the concrete and symbolic landscapes of the city? In an environment of contested identities and cultural diversity can all the city's inhabitants be made to feel at home and to identify with the city whilst at the same time an attractive image and ambience is presented to potential tourists and investors? Of course, an inclusive civic and political culture and the importance of people having an economic stake in the city are crucial to a sense of 'belonging'. But our focus is primarily on the physical environment and the meaning which people from diverse backgrounds invest in it. We should not be naïve about this. As Professor Barbara Jakubeit, a recent Berlin Building Director (Senatsbaudirektor), has pointed out in relation to the building of the new federal government quarter in Berlin, the fact, for example, that we use transparent building materials does not necessarily mean that we have a transparent open democracy. That depends on people.[2] However, we should not forget either that the built environment is an important constitutive and enduring element in people's sense of themselves, their identity. Before giving an overview and raising some questions about specific aspects of place in relation to cultural diversity and difference in Belfast and Berlin, it is worthwhile to consider more exactly what we mean by cultural identity, why collective memory is so bound up with this and why identity issues are so much to the fore at the turn of the millennium.

Memory and identity in the city – some theoretical considerations

Whilst Jenkins in his recent book on the social construction of identity cautions against the use of the term 'cultural' identity because of the multiplicity of contested meanings to which the word culture is attached,[3] other writers have less hesitancy in using the term.[4] Individual identity is to a considerable extent 'a customised collage of collective identifications'.[5] Collective identities, in turn, as Castells points out, must be distinguished from what sociologists have traditionally called 'roles' in that identities are stronger sources of meaning for the social actors involved.[6] The social construction of collective identities, according to Castells, always taking place in a context marked by power relationships, 'uses building materials from history, from geography, from biology, from productive and reproductive institutions, from collective memory and from personal fantasies, from power apparatuses and religious revelations'.[7] Cultural identities may be considered as particularly meaningful collective identities of overarching common significance to people who may be otherwise socially diversified in terms of experience. Such cultural identities may take an ethnic, religious or national form, for example. These cultural identities may be what Castells calls 'primary identities', identities which for most social actors have a primary role in the organisation of meaning and which frame other identities which people have.[8]

Of central importance to urban planning practice which is sensitive to ongoing cultural identity formation, contestation and negotiation is an appreciation of the centrality of collective memory to identity constitution and the implications of this for place making and the built fabric of the city. Identity requires the positing of a meaningful past, a narrative of continuity. In relation to the invocation and shaping of memory in the construction of national narratives Easthope makes the following useful distinction between history and the collective memory wrapped up in narratives:

> 'In conventional history writing it is generally accepted that 'past events' are interpreted in the present according to a subject/object relation consistent with knowledge; thus an event, period or epoch is conceived as an object separate from other historical objects and separated from the subject who interprets it. National narrative is also interpreted in the present but differs from conventional history-writing in two respects: the historical events of the national narrative are not considered to the same degree as separate from each other since they form, as it were, diamonds on a single string; second, the pull towards present needs means that the national narrative forgoes a sense of subject/object consistent with a discourse of knowledge in favour of a subject/object relation appropriate to the formation of identity'.[9]

Samuel reminds us that in society memory is not something abstract like history, that it cannot exist outside those people who do the remembering and that in this context memory is not to be regarded as 'a passive receptacle or storage system, an image bank of the past'. Rather 'memory is historically conditioned changing colour and shape according to the emergencies of the moment...'.[10] Collective remembering can take various institutionalised, cultural and ritualised forms. It is also constituted spatially and, therefore, of major significance for urban planning.

Place and identity: dwelling in the city
Bouchet has recently reminded us that despite the supposed possibilities opening up for the forging and reinforcement of new identities in

cyberspace a strong sense of identity is both corporal and spatial.[11] Individual identity is always embodied, having the possibilities for seeing, feeling and smelling the other, for example, not provided by the Internet.[12] Likewise in terms of identification of the self, identity has always been related to a physical space, the German word for being alive, *Dasein*, for example, literally meaning 'being there'.[13] Experience, 'being there' in the city, provides many opportunities and spaces for individual and collective identity formation and affirmation. Urban material and cultural consumption in restaurants, museums, art galleries, boutiques, flea markets and so forth all play their part in the construction of identity and difference.[14] In various combinations consumption and lifestyle patterns can bestow distinctive place identities on cities. The cultural consumption in Berlin differs from that of Belfast. In fact, market-driven postmodern architecture and planning in cities for some time now have been seeking a re-enchantment of place in order 'to restore identity to local cultures swamped, hitherto, by the austere universalism of modernist aesthetics'.[15] That this can often appear superficial resonates with Sennett's argument that western urban planners are in the grip of a Protestant ethic of space. This regards the inner life as the most important and, which being fearful of the pleasures, differences and distractions of the 'outside', has had a controlling and neutralising effect on the environment.[16] It is in Christian cities that Sennett[17] finds the root of the desire for legibility and the organisation of difference celebrated as desirable by Kevin Lynch. In his book *The Image of the City*[18] Lynch argued, based on interview analysis, that people hold in their minds an image of the city essential to their experience and interaction with it. This image of the city was based around physical forms and landmarks and as Neuman argues, while having its shortcomings later recognised by Lynch himself, did liberate planners from abstract models of the city based on plans and land use classifications and 'injected the very real sense of the way people experienced cities'.[19] It was Lefebvre who perhaps more than anyone else extended the approach developed by Lynch to incorporate an awareness of the symbolic aspects of people's imagery of the city alongside the physical dimensions.[20] Lefebvre distinguishes between the 'representations of space' engaged in by professional planners and cartographers which often lacks a critical sensitivity to the everyday 'spatial practices' of people and to the meaning wrapped up in these and to 'representational spaces' in cities which are loaded with important symbolic meanings.[21] The latter draw on shared experiences and interpretations at a profound level. Making space is therefore very much a way of making meaning. In the city which, as theatre for social action, depends on memories, signifying practices are constantly involved in the making and changing of meaning. A key question for urban design thus becomes how meaning is working at particular sites. And importantly, signification should not be thought of as what 'the thing' communicates but as the readings that, within a given culture, may be produced out of it.[22]

In focusing on the socially produced symbolic landscapes of the city alongside the concrete ones one becomes better able to study the relationship between place and the constitution, contestation and negotiation of major cultural identity narratives as played out in cities. In cities the narrative of identity is constituted spatially and is made palpably real. Here it is helpful, as Harvey points out, drawing on the work of Norberg-Schulz, to talk in terms of contestation over the 'genius loci' where the latter 'spirit of place' is defined as the 'meanings which are gathered by a place'.[23] The absence of active political controversy over the genius loci can be seen as a sign of the domination of some hegemonic power, a situation which does not totally pertain in either Belfast or Berlin. This is a contest which is important because 'to release a different imaginary concerning the past is to release a different imaginary as to possibilities in the future'.[24] The power of symbolic places in cities holds major sway over the imagination and, therefore, can be sites of struggle in the same way that images representing the city as a whole can be disputed because of the power which they bestow.[25] The notion of genius loci in turn can be linked back to Heidegger's concept of 'dwelling'. With acknowledgement to Heidegger, Norberg-Schulz defines 'dwelling' and existential foothold as synonymous:

> Man dwells when he can orientate himself within and identify himself with an environment, or, in short, when he experiences the environment as meaningful.[26]

This goes beyond Lynch's notion of legibility in the built environment, important as that is for emotional well-being. Having roots in a place, belonging to a place, grounding oneself in the everyday meaningful world of significance keeps at bay the ultimately unsettling groundlessness of experience or 'Dasein' in Heidegger's terminology. Likewise, drawing on Heidegger, Casey accords to place a position of respect. Recognising that in late modern times the world is becoming increasingly placeless, a matter of mere sites instead of lived places, place is due respect because of 'its power to direct and stabilise us, to memorialise and identify us, to tell us who we are in terms of *where we are* (as well as where we are *not*)'.[27] It is the 'bedrock of our being-in-the world'.[28] In short, place protects us from the void. Here Abel's characterisation of architecture and implicitly urban planning as a way of being-in-the world is insightful:

> We do not *have* architecture, therefore, but rather, a part of us *is* architecture. Architecture is a way of being, just as science, art and the other major culture-forms are ways of being. So when we come to define the true and deeper functions of architecture, we will not be simply describing the production of a certain type of artefact, but explaining one of the original ways in which we know ourselves.[29]

Memory and identity: Berlin

Issues of cultural identity loom large for us at the millennium. The twentieth century has shaken our confidence in universals, in big narratives, in progress, in reason itself. Yet we still need to find meaning in something, to belong to some enterprise and community bigger than ourselves. Castells talks here of the paradox of an increasingly local politics as people strive to create meaning in a world structured by increasingly global processes. People can create defensive identities as they struggle to protect their city, their environment, their community, their tree.[30] In Europe, we have the reassertion of national identities after the collapse of the attempt to create new identities under the umbrella of a Soviet hegemony. A pan-European identity project driven by the economic imperatives for a single market but also by the legacy of the Second World War seems as yet a pale substitute for the very much alive national narratives of existing and aspiring nation states. As expressed by Easthope 'within the unprecedented alienations of modernity the nation-state promises a new form of community to replace the old, and so, with modernity, collectivity as nation has spread across the world so it now approaches the condition of universality'.[31] While Germans, therefore, when they spend Euros instead of Deutschmarks may think of themselves as more European, the rupture in the German national narrative represented by the Third Reich and the Holocaust remains undiminished and unresolved. Nowhere is this more acute than in Berlin. The negotiation and renegotiation of the 'national story' which in the German case has been more ethnic and cultural rather than political and institutional, continues. To be German now means being involved in a debate over what to emphasise or de-emphasise in national identity, a debate which is at least nominally equivalent to debates on 'Germanness' in 1938, 1916 or 1871.[32] Central to the contestation over present German identity is what Kramer has referred to as the effort by Germans to try 'to talk their way out of an unutterable past and back into what they like to call History'.[33] Whereas it is possible to drop the behaviour of Oliver Cromwell in Drogheda, for example, from the English national narrative,[34] it is not so easy to drop Auschwitz from the German narrative of shared identity, of being a people. In reconstructing the German national narrative, as Habermas has pointed out, much is at stake in the politics of memory.[35] Thus while ex-Chancellor Kohl was keen to see reunification in 1989 as a return to normality and normal history in Germany, Habermas argues that 'violence' is done to memory involving inadequate learning from the past, if 1945 is not regarded as the more significant date in German history after which the political mentality in the Federal Republic grew unmistakably more liberal. The latter date represents a rupture in the national narrative but with the chance provided of a new beginning. Habermas has consistently intervened where he observes attempts to paper over the Third Reich and restore a sense of normal continuity from Bismarck to Kohl. Rather, Habermas argues, Germany shows up the failure of ethnic nationalism which resulted in the Holocaust, with 1945 seen as a crucial turning point in German history when West Germany's political culture took in the ideas of the European Enlightenment.[36] It is a view which contrasts, for example, with that of the French philosopher Jean-François Lyotard who points to an insidious relationship between enlightenment modernity itself and Auschwitz. In this view National Socialism is a singular, but not unique case in which the narcissistic fantasies of omnipotence and superiority that haunt Western modernity have come to the surface with post-modernist thought providing a much-needed ethical antidote with its emphasis on others as others with their own histories and aspirations.[37] In contradistinction Habermas refers to West Germans after 1945 as being in a process of rediscovering 'the muted legacy of humanism and the Enlightenment in their own tradition'.[38] The 'completely unspeakable breach in civilisation associated with the name Auschwitz'[39] is related to the irrational subterranean stream of the German tradition with which Heidegger, a supporter of the 'Nazis', is associated. The search for 'misleading continuities of long since questionable aspects' of the German tradition is regarded as dangerous given the fear of sinking 'back into the fetid German swamp'.[40]

In contrast to the view of Habermas and former President of the Federal Republic Richard von Weizsäcker that 8 May 1945 – *Null-Stunde* – was the only possible beginning for Germany in the construction of a new narrative of Germanness,[41] Ex-Chancellor Kohl, while given credit by Habermas for his commitment to European unification, has been associated with intellectual voices in Germany which see 1989 as a return to normality with Germany again a major political power in Europe.[42] Here Chancellor Kohl's project has been described as settling the past 'by turning defeat into liberation and Nazi Germany into the Germany that Hitler seized'.[43] In this view which regards it as unhealthy to mistake the tributaries of Germany's bad moments for the 'mighty current' of present-day Germany, the Nazi past becomes something that happened to 'victim Germany'. The year 1989 marks the return of a common past to East and West Germans with Kohl's new German Historical Museum in Berlin showing this history by taking the Germany pieced together by Bismarck in 1871 and giving it a coherence, continuity and nobility going back centuries.[44] Within this grand narrative the Holocaust can be symbolically objectified. Monuments, memorials and commemorative sites can take memory and deposit it in the landscape where 'it can be visited at appropriate ceremonial moments, but where it does not interfere unduly with the business of life at hand'.[45]

The significant rise of interest in Jewish issues in a wider West German public involving especially the commemorating of the Shoah and the anniversary of the Kristallnacht, can be dated to 1978. Here Bodemann refers to how Allied interventions and the 'justice of the victors' thwarted to a degree a post-war German national discourse on the Holocaust.[46] This, of course, did not prevent major cultural reverberations in West Germany. Thus, Ingrid Caven, wife of Werner Fassbinder, emphasises the importance of German identity to the filmmaker's work:

> In his films, and in his life, until the most tearing and aggressive moments, he was looking for a form, for a beauty and joy based on the ruins of a Germany drained of life and soul.[47]

Likewise Wim Wenders, another German filmmaker, in having one of his characters in *Kings of the Road* say that 'the Americans have colonised our subconscious' alludes to how in Germany one way of remembering and forgetting fascism has been an involvement with other cultures.[48] It would be surprising indeed, if making space is in fact a way of making meaning, if such major cultural tensions did not also find expression in urban planning discourse and practice. The centre place given to the Sony Centre in the new Potsdamer Platz seems especially pertinent here.

Bodemann in dating the more active public invocation of Holocaust memory in West Germany singles out in particular a state ceremony in 1978 in the Cologne Synagogue and the commemoration of the Kristallnacht shortly before the airing of the American television series *Holocaust*. Bodemann also comments importantly:

> Only when the bulk of the first post-war generation of politicians had begun to leave the political arena with their retirement (politicians who built their careers under Hitler, who were implicated in Nazism and continued under Adenauer, who were at least thirty years old in 1945), only when they began to withdraw from the political scene in the mid-seventies, could the commemoration take on a broader political frame of reference and became an act of state, most visibly first in the Cologne synagogue ceremony in 1978 with Chancellor Schmidt and President Scheel.[49]

The *Holocaust* series and its media manufacture of raw material and discursive threads for the construction of memory and identity was watched by over 20 million Germans in 1979.[50] Commenting in *Der Spiegel* one commentator wrote:

> an American TV series, made in a trivial style, produced more for commercial than for moral reasons, more for entertainment than for enlightenment, accomplished what hundreds of books, plays, films ... documents and the concentration camp trials themselves have failed to do in the three decades since the end of the war: to inform Germans about crimes against Jews committed in their name so that millions were emotionally touched and moved.[51]

The West German television series *Heimat* broadcast in 1984 to an equally mass audience was conceived by its creator Edgar Reitz as a German 'answer' to the American Holocaust series which he argued had 'stolen our history ... taken narrative possession of our past'.[52]

The debate over memory and representation of the German past wrapped up as it is with the politics of identity in Germany and the spatial manifestation of this was, therefore, picking up pace even before the fall of the Berlin Wall in 1989. After a hasty reunification, which missed the chance in Habermas's opinion of a republican refounding of the Federal Republic based on a new national self-understanding, the negotiation of a new German past and identity has assumed greater urgency.[53] With the move of the federal government to Berlin in 1999, the reinstated German capital has become, it can be argued, an intensified theatre of memory forming a stage for the contesting plays of collective memory. Here Wenders reminds us in his 1987 film *The Sky over Berlin* that the tangibility of experience even in places with a tortured genius loci is preferable to the erasure of memory and floating placelessness.

Urban planning and identity reverberations: Berlin

Reverberations from the burden of Germany's recent history of extreme cultural exclusion and how to deal with this memory resonate in the rebuilding of the new German capital and are reflected in contributions to this volume. This seems acutely to the fore in the debate over the Planwerk Innenstadt (plan for the inner city), the subject of the paper by Süchting and Weiss, the whole concept being passionately opposed in the following contribution by Hain. The 'official' argument in the paper by Süchting and Weiss is that the new German capital, in urban design terms, should return to the architectural principles and urban ground plan of Berlin as a European city in the nineteenth and early twentieth centuries. The architectural principles are incorporated in the notion of 'critical reconstruction' strongly advocated and implemented by Berlin's former Building Director, Hans Stimmann. The Planwerk Innenstadt produced by the Berlin Ministry of Urban Development and Environmental Protection proposes to use design to suture together both parts of the previously divided city through the invocation of a history common to both west and east. In this view 1989 would seem to represent a return to German normality. The paper by Hain, written from the perspective of an engaged East Berliner, raises difficult questions which refuse to go away. What does design suture say about how Germans see their identity? Are true historical discontinuities which cry out for a place in collective memory being sacrificed at the altar of aesthetics? How are 40 years of Communism remembered or forgotten in the fabric of the city? How sensitive is the development and design plan to East Berlin experience and identity? Hain mentions the future of the representational space, in Lefebvre's terms, of the Palast der Republik, home of the former DDR Volkskammer which seems totemic in indicating how memory or forgetting will be incorporated into the fabric of Berlin. The Palast now seems to be losing the battle to remain as an acknowledgement to the post-Fascist, communist period of Berlin and East German history during which a distinctive identity did grow up in the East. We may even see constructed on the site a rebuilt Stadtschloss, Berlin residence of the Hohenzollerns.[54] Will this in the name of aesthetics connect Berlin back to 'real' history? It is the 'presence of the absence'[55] in these papers of explicit mention of the Fascist period in real Berlin history that might astonish a foreign reader. It was after all Albert Speer, Hitler's architect and urban planner, who formulated the last master plan for the centre of a united Berlin giving expression to an ideology of the most extreme form of cultural exclusion. The reader might rightly sense, however, that awareness of this aspect of Berlin's genius loci lurks in the background of most discussion of urban planning concepts for Germany's reinstated capital city. The non appearance by Eberhard Diepgen, Berlin's Governing Mayor, at the dedication ceremony on 27 January 2000 (the 55th anniversary of the liberation of Auschwitz) for a Holocaust memorial in the city undoubtedly reflects unease associated with the explicit acknowledgement, so close to the heart of the government quarter, of this episode in the city's real history. The transparent dome of the new Reichstag which looks down over the nearby memorial site symbolises the hopes, rising above the legacy of the past, for a constitutional as opposed to ethnic patriotism necessary to build a pluralistic and sustainable German democracy. In some senses, to the outside observer the debate over the Planwerk Innenstadt can seem like a proxy discussion over what to do with a genius loci disturbed by recent and unspeakable real events which will not easily be erased from memory.

The chapters in this volume by Heine and Müller deal with urban planning and issues of cultural inclusion in relation to Berlin's present Turkish population. Do Berlin Turks feel a civic and inclusionary identification with the new Reichstag cupola? The paper by Heine discusses the spatial manifestations of Turkish cultural difference in relation to worship and burial. It explores how this comes into sharp conflict with accepted German urban design and domiciliary norms for both the living and the dead. Certainly a British reader, familiar with the domes and minarets of mosques in, say, Birmingham or Bradford would be surprised at the extent to which cultural pluralism still has to take root in Berlin through the acceptance of Muslim architectural design features as part of the city's skyline. The paper by Müller in charting the growth of Turkish small businesses in Berlin and

Kreuzberg, in particular, reveals how a market-led organic approach to urban development can create quarters in the city of cultural distinctiveness and opportunities for contact across cultural divides. Not everything needs to be planned but places of cultural difference need to be respected and protected. Within a paper endorsing the notion of the pluralist city, the reader may still find it strange that the author starkly refers to Turks in Berlin with a rigid cultural dividing line between Turks and Germans, seemingly making the notion of a Berlin Turk impossible. But this judgement is perhaps too harsh. Berlin does have a history of positive pluralism and has long been a focus for the European cultural avant-garde. In the Berlin Love Parade, dismissed by some as the globalisation of urban spatial practices in the form of parades, we have seen the creation of a new culturally inclusive tradition in the past decade.

The final German paper by Bernhard Schneider, a representative of the Berlin promotional agency Partner für Berlin, considers the identity of Berlin in the context of city marketing. These days cultural identity is not just about being yourself but selling yourself. Schneider argues that places should dare to be different but that broad brush strokes are needed to project the image and identity of a place to outsiders. Whether the introspective navel-gazing over the minutiae of identity in Berlin which Schneider describes is, as claimed, only of interest to the Berlin cognoscenti must, however, remain a matter of some dispute.

Memory and identity: Belfast

In Berlin, acceptance of cultural diversity ultimately depends on how one dominant group (West Berliners and Germans) defines itself in relation to a narrative of belonging and what possibilities it holds out to others for a shared future. In Belfast, however, two cultural identities are locked in what sometimes seems like a 'zero sum' struggle with the ideal of cultural pluralism easier to evoke than to concretely realise. At the heart of the political peace process in Northern Ireland has been the issue of how the identity of the nationalist Catholic population can be given agreed and officially legitimised forms of expression. This particular Irish identity which was forged through the historical experience of British colonialism and constituted in mythology, poetry, music, sport, religious practices, values, beliefs and so forth demands expression in the institutions of the state. Since identities have a relationship to place, this is also a spatial planning issue. Here nationalist cultural identity comes up against the Protestant unionist cultural identity of 'the other', where memory is spatially constituted in quintessential form in the representational space of the Parliament Building at Stormont in Belfast. The remainder of this chapter considers what this building conjures up in memory and has meant to both ethnic identities in Northern Ireland. This introduction to identity conflict in Belfast and Northern Ireland, through the examination of this particular urban planning issue, sets the context for an overview of the Belfast contributions to this volume.

An official government publication introduces Stormont thus:

> The Northern Ireland Parliament Building stands on an elevated site at Stormont, about 5 miles from the centre of Belfast. The main approach to the building is by a broad processional avenue three-quarters of a mile long and rising some 180 feet, planted on either side with a double row of lime trees, and running through well-tended grounds of 300 acres. At the top of the avenue, a staircase of granite steps 90 feet wide leads up to the building itself, 365 feet long, 164 feet wide and 70 feet high, rising to 92 feet at the centre of the main façade.[56]

Fig. 1.1 Parliament Buildings at Stormont, Belfast

In a similar neutral style, employing the detached language of aesthetics, Belfast's leading architectural historian describes the Parliament Buildings, designed in the 1920s by Arnold Thornley from Liverpool, as 'one of the most outstanding architectural sites in Ireland'. With a 'very dignified exterior', designed in the Greek classical tradition with a grand Ionic temple front, the building, opened in 1932, 'enjoys a magnificent and commanding situation to the east of the city'.[57] With a façade of Portland stone above a plinth of granite from the local Mourne Mountains, Stormont looks down upon what two urban conservationist writers have described as 'one of the most impressive man-made vistas in the Province'. This 'show piece of the local conservation movement', it is suggested, could have a role in the creation of an 'image for Belfast'.[58] It remains to be seen, however, if such a contentious image can ever gain general acceptance.

A closer examination of Stormont reveals that its construction was constitutive of a partially successful unionist project. It symbolised that while Southern Ireland had, against Protestant opposition, left the Union with Britain, nevertheless, the division of Ireland had given recognition and legitimacy to the unionist position of maintaining the link with Britain. The building, in short, has symbolised unionist self-assertion and the will to preserve their British cultural identity against the nationalist 'other'. From the top of Stormont, a large statue of Britannia, flanked by two guardian lions, looks out over Belfast's eastern suburbs. On the pediment below her, another group of statues 'represents Ulster presenting the golden flame of loyalty to Britain and the Commonwealth'.[59] This loyalist ensemble, firmly expressing unionism in terms of a British identity, in turn looks down upon a large bronze monumental sculpture of Northern Ireland's founding father, Lord Edward Carson, who rises up on a granite plinth at the endpoint of the processional avenue. The depiction of the unionist leader 'galvanised in rhetorical declaration' has been described as the 'expressive personification of the challenge which was mounted to an ascendant Irish nationalism'.[60] Panels around the base of the statue invoke memory by depicting various scenes in the history of early Ulster unionism, including the signing of the Ulster Covenant in September 1912 when 400 000 or so loyalists pledged themselves, sometimes in their own blood, to use 'all means which may be found necessary to defeat the present conspiracy to set up a Home Rule Parliament in Ireland.' Stormont was deliberately conceived to physically constitute a grand symbolic demarcation of difference and was actually, impressive as it is, scaled back on financial grounds from a more grandiose building with a grand dome. However, it continues 'to soar over the North'[61] having in the past been an important place of unionist pilgrimage.

The completion of Stormont, in the words of Hugh Pollock, a government unionist spokesman of the time, was the outward and visible proof of the permanence of our institutions; that for all time we are bound indissolubly to the British Crown.[62] Almost 70 years on, and in the wake of the Anglo-Irish Agreement of 1985, the Downing Street Declaration of 1993 and the Good Friday Agreement of 1998 which explicitly recognise the legitimacy of two ethnic identities in Northern Ireland and contemplate Irish unity under certain circumstances, the indissolubility of the link to the British crown is precisely at risk in unionist eyes. Against this background, issues of representational space go to the centre of unionist cultural insecurity in Northern Ireland. This makes the taking root of a new political settlement presently very difficult along with any meaningful notion of a place vision for Belfast. In an astute observation by Graham, the implications of which have not been taken on board by planners in Northern Ireland, it has been pointed out that the single most important weakness of the unionist cause 'arguably lies in its failure to develop – through the creation of a specific heritage – a separate place consciousness'.[63] Stormont, at the apex of Protestant representational space, was intended as a symbol of defiance against Irish Catholic nationalism, not as an icon of Ulster Protestant nationalism. No attempt has been made to produce a robust Protestant historic foundation myth. The greatness of the British past was sufficient substitute. In the words of Graham:

> British Ulster demonstrates the weakness and futility of a place in which the imaginary and symbolic world of identity is external to itself. The Unionist failure to recognise the centrality of laying claim and giving meaning to the landscape of Ulster, as distinct from grabbing territory, is part and parcel of the nationalist claim to the rhetorical high ground of moral advantage against the putative descendants of their oppressors.[64]

Absent an adequate representational landscape imbued with legitimising memory and involving the construction of identity in symbolic spatial terms, northern Protestant unionists live to an extent in a state of embattled planter or settler insecurity. With the present increase in regional consciousness and political autonomy in other parts of the United Kingdom and with the very notion of a British identity under threat, 'identity work' within the unionist community seems a matter of urgency.

From the perspective of the other ethnic identity in Northern Ireland, Stormont is a place which has always been anathematised by republicans and jars with the orientation to a different symbolic order on the part of more moderate Catholic nationalists. Brian Faulkner, a past Northern Ireland Prime Minister, has described how questions of symbolism were important to the Catholic SDLP party in formulating the operational practices in 1973 of Northern Ireland's last elected Assembly with executive responsibility. For example, the SDLP wanted the Assembly to meet not at Stormont but in Ireland's ecclesiastical capital Armagh. Westminster trappings and references to the Queen in procedures were disputed. Going to the heart of the matter, Faulkner writes: 'It was an argument over symbols and to many Irish politicians symbols are the central issue in politics.'[65] While the experience of 75 years of Irish partition and nearly 30 years of civil conflict have forged a discernibly northern Catholic identity,[66] nationalists still tap into a Gaelic Catholic Irish identity from which exclusivity northern Protestants feel alienated to the point of denying their own Irishness. As Graham points out: 'de Valera's vision of Ulster was also shrouded in Celtic mists and populated with warrior heroes'.[67] It is a place vision which, while waning in the Republic of Ireland, leaves little place for Protestant attachment to the legacy of the Victorian industrial city of Belfast.

From Stormont, at the apex of contested representational space in Belfast, with its stone solidity and classical claims constituting in physical terms unionist legitimacy for the division of Ireland, other spatial reverberations flow which can be traced through the various Belfast contributions to this book.

Urban planning and identity reverberations: Belfast

The paper by Brett argues for the preservation of the Victorian and Edwardian legacy of Belfast's inner city or at least what remains of it. In its appeal to the notion of the city as an aesthetic composition, where new development should have the good manners to respect the built heritage of what has gone before, the paper parallels the Berlin contribution by Süchting and Weiss which argues for design as a suturing cultural force. In recent years, however, it has often been third-rate market-led 'neutral' post-modernist architecture which has been politically blessed for its contribution to cultural suturing in Belfast. The reasons for this are explored in the paper by McEldowney and Sterrett which, strongly echoing the Berlin paper by Hain, makes clear that Belfast's built environment is not just an aesthetic composition but is strongly impregnated with symbolic meaning. That the Victorian and Edwardian legacy can be a locus for common identification is disputed; the situation is more ambivalent. While Belfast city centre is hailed as neutral ground, for example, at least in functional terms, references to Catholic nationalism and identity are as palpably absent as they are palpably present in Dublin. In Belfast's public realm a memorialising process draws largely on links to the British Crown and Queen Victoria in particular which is occasionally punctuated by rather insipid public art. However, insipidness can have its advantages. At one important junction in the city the plinth for a statue of a nineteenth-century Protestant anti-home rule spokesman, the Reverend Hugh Hanna, stands empty, its provocative occupant having been blown up as a casualty of the euphemistically termed 'Troubles'. Even the language of extreme cultural conflict is not neutral. The built environment in Belfast, in other words, can be symbolically charged, an arena of cultural conflict rather than a canvas for artistic contemplation. Nowhere is cultural difference more spatially vivid through wall murals and street signage than in many of Belfast's de facto 'cultural quarters'. Here the paper by Gaffikin *et al.* complements the Berlin contributions dealing with the problems and potential of Turkish difference in Kreuzberg. The authors in the Belfast context point to the cultural vitality of the city and explore ways whereby this could be more creatively tapped and harnessed to economic development ends. The problem is not an easy one. Catholic West Belfast, for example, without official planning, is arguably the most distinctive de facto cultural quarter in the city. With a strong nationalist culture and ethos, having extended on the part of some to an armed prosecution of a claim to place, West Belfast possesses a unique place identity almost as a city within a city. This identity has found growing expression since 1988 in the annual staging of a People's Festival (Féile an Phobail), claimed to be the largest in Ireland. Intended to project a positive image and to provide an outlet for expressions of collective identity this has obvious tourism potential, but limited funding in recent years from Belfast City Council and the Northern Ireland Tourist Board has been contested by unionists given the festival's close association with Sinn Fein and its threatening wider place vision for Ireland. Likewise agreement between unionists and nationalists has not yet been possible on the appropriate form of a Saint Patrick's Day parade in the city with the former complaining that the event is too closely associated with the trappings of nationalist cultural identity. On the other hand, Protestant marches around the Twelfth of July commemorating the Battle of the Boyne, where in 1690 Protestant King William III defeated Catholic King James II, do not project the air of a unionist Mardi Gras and are read by some nationalists as still communicating a certain hostile triumphalism. With the old assurances of Stormont symbolism gone, such parades can increasingly be read as affirming the right of a British cultural identity to exist in Ireland but in any case such spatial practices sit uncomfortably with the job of official place promotion. The final Belfast chapters deal with urban planning and the 'selling of the city'. Set alongside the paper by Schneider on place promotion in Berlin we see two cities grappling with questions of cultural identity and pluralism and desperately seeking 'normality' in presenting themselves to an international audience. The contribution by Alexander and Smith of the Laganside Corporation in Belfast displays the not inconsiderable physical results of a flagship development agency endeavouring to create shared cultural spaces on Belfast's waterfront. The appeal seems often to a transcendent 'loft living' lifestyle emphasising youth culture and a cosmopolitan outlook. A pessimist might reflect that a cosmopolitan outlook in parts of former Yugoslavia did not dispel deeper cultural and ethnic tensions there. A final Belfast chapter by the city's chief planner is a call to realism and a call to positively plan with an ethic of cultural inclusion in mind. Despite major cultural frictions a common Belfast civic identity is supported where, it is argued, sensitive urban planning can make a difference. Let us hope so.

Notes

1 Federal State of Berlin, *Berlin in Brief* (Berlin: Presse- und Informationsamt, 1995), p. 21.
2 B. Jakubeit, in A. Burg and S. Redecke (eds), *Chancellery and Office of the President of the Federal Republic of Germany: International Architectural Competitions for the Capital Berlin* (Bonn: Birkhäuser Publishers, 1995) p. 123. In the light of the recent CDU political funding allegations this takes on greater resonance.
3 R. Jenkins, *Social Identity* (London: Routledge, 1996), p. 179.
4 For example, S. Hall and P. du Gay (eds), *Questions of Cultural Identity* (London: Sage, 1996). Within German literature the work of Barth is worthy of particular mention. F. Barth (ed.), *Ethnic Groups and Boundaries: the Social Organisation of Cultural Difference*, (London: George Allen and Unwin, 1969).
5 Jenkins, op. cit., p. 136.

6 M. Castells, *The Power of Identity* (Oxford: Blackwell, 1997), pp. 6–7.

7 Ibid., p. 7.

8 Ibid., p. 7.

9 A. Easthope, 'The Peculiar Temporality of the National Narrative', Paper delivered at *Time and Value Conference*, University of Lancaster, Institute for Cultural Research (10–13 April 1997) p. 6.

10 R. Samuel, *Theatres of Memory* (London: Verso, 1996) p. x.

11 D. Bouchet, 'Information Technology, the Social Bond and the City: Georg Simmel Updated: about the changing relationship between identity and the city', *Built Environment*, Vol. 24, Nos 2/3 (1998), pp. 104–33, p. 126.

12 Ibid., p. 126.

13 Ibid., p. 118.

14 S. Zukin, *The Cultures of Cities* (Cambridge, MA: Blackwell, 1995).

15 P. Cooke, *Back to the Future: Modernity and Locality* (London: Unwin Hyman, 1990) pp. 114–15.

16 R. Sennett, *The Conscience of the Eye* (New York: Norton, 1992) p. 42.

17 Ibid., p. 36.

18 K. Lynch, *The Image of the City* (Cambridge, MA, MIT Press, 1960).

19 M. Neuman, 'Planning, Governing, and the Image of the City', *Journal of Planning Education and Research*, Vol. 18, No. 1, (1998), pp. 61–71, p. 66.

20 Ibid., p. 66.

21 H. Lefebvre, *The Production of Space* (Oxford: Blackwell, 1991).

22 H. Liggett, 'City Sights/Sites of Memories and Dreams', Ch. 9 in H. Liggett, and D.C. Perry (eds) *Spatial Practices: Critical Explorations in Social/Spatial Theory* (London: Sage, 1995), pp. 257–8.

23 D. Harvey, *Justice, Nature and the Geography of Difference* (Oxford: Blackwell, 1996), p. 308.

24 Ibid., p. 309.

25 Ibid., p. 322.

26 C. Norberg-Schulz, *Genius Loci: towards a Phenomenology of Architecture* (London: Academy Editions, 1980), p. 5.

27 E.S. Casey, *Getting Back into Place: toward a Renewed Understanding of the Place World* (Indianapolis: Indiana University Press, 1993), p. xv, emphasis original.

28 Ibid., p. xvii.

29 C. Abel, *Architecture and Identity: towards a Global Eco-Culture* (Oxford: Architectural Press, 1997), p. 154, emphasis original.

30 Castells, op. cit., p. 8.

31 Easthope, op. cit., p. 1.

32 Jenkins, op. cit., p. 98.

33 J. Kramer, 'The Politics of Memory', *The New Yorker*, 14 August (1995), pp. 48–65, p. 48.

34 Easthope, op. cit., p. 3.

35 J. Habermas, *A Berlin Republic: Writings on Germany* (Cambridge: Polity Press, 1998).

36 P.U. Hohendahl, 'Introduction to J. Habermas', op. cit., pp. vii–xxiv.

37 A. Huyssen, 'Monument and Memory in a Postmodern Age', in J.E. Young (ed.) *The Art of Memory: Holocaust Memorials in History* (Munich: Prestel-Verlag, 1994), pp. 9–17.

38   Habermas, op. cit., p. 183.
39   Ibid., p. 25.
40   Ibid., p. 49.
41   Kramer, op. cit., p. 48.
42   Habermas, op. cit., p. 157.
43   Kramer, op. cit., p. 50.
44   Ibid., p. 57.
45   Ibid., p. 48.
46   M. Bodemann, 'Terrains of Violence, Terrains of Memory: German and Israeli Varieties'. Paper delivered at *Time and Value Conference*, University of Lancaster, Institute for Cultural Research (1997), 10–13 April.
47   R. Hodgkiss, 'The Bitter Tears of Fassbinder's Women', *Guardian*, 8 January (1998).
48   D. Morley and K. Robins, *Spaces of Identity: Global Media, Electronic Landscapes and Cultural Boundaries* (London: Routledge, 1995), pp. 95–6.
49   M. Bodemann (1996), *Jews, Germans, Memory: Reconstructions of Jewish Life in Germany* (Ann Arbor: University of Michigan Press, 1996), p. 211.
50   D. Morley and K. Robins, op. cit., p. 92.
51   H. Hone, quoted in I. Buruma, 'From Hirohito to Heimat', *New York: Review of Books*, 26 October (1989), p. 40.
52   E. Reitz, quoted in M. Hansen, 'Dossier on Heimat', *New German Critique*, 36 (1985), pp. 3–25, p. 9.
53   Habermas, op. cit., p. 51.
54   W.J.V. Neill, 'Memory, Collective Identity and Urban Design: the Future of Berlin's Palast der Republik', *Journal of Urban Design*, Vol. 2, No. 2 (1997), pp. 179–92.
55   The expression is borrowed from the animating concept in Daniel Libeskind's new Jewish museum in Berlin.
56   HMSO, *Parliament Buildings Stormont* (Belfast: undated).
57   P. Larmour, *Belfast: an Illustrated Architectural Guide* (Belfast: Friar's Bush Press, 1987), pp. 110–111.
58   J. Hendry and M. McEldowney, *Conservation in Belfast* (Belfast: The Queen's University, Department of Architecture and Planning, 1987).
59   HMSO, op. cit., p. 3.
60   D. Officer, 'In Search of Order, Permanence and Stability: Building Stormont, 1921–32', Ch. 8 in R. English and G. Walker (eds), *Unionism in Modern Ireland, New Perspectives on Politics and Culture* (London: Gill and Macmillan, 1996), p. 142.
61   Ibid., p. 137.
62   Pollock, quoted in J. Bardon, *Belfast: an Illustrated History* (Belfast: Blackstaff Press, 1982), p. 225.
63   B.J. Graham, 'Heritage Conservation and Revisionist Nationalism in Ireland', Ch. 8 in G.J. Ashworth and P.J. Larkham (eds), *Building a New Heritage: Tourism, Culture and Identity in the New Europe* (London: Routledge, 1994), p. 141.
64   Ibid., p. 143.
65   B. Faulkner, *Memoirs of a Statesman* (London: Weidenfeld and Nicolson, 1978), p. 202.

66 F. O'Connor, *In Search of a State: Catholics in Northern Ireland* (Belfast: Blackstaff Press, 1993).
67 Graham, op. cit., p. 145. Eamon de Valera was the first leader of the Irish Fianna Fáil party founded in 1926.

2

The Urban Planning Context in Berlin: a City Twice Unique

Hanns-Uve Schwedler

Over the last decade Berlin has come to be known as 'Europe's largest construction site', and as 'the construction site of German reunification'. There is no denying that since the Berlin Wall came down in 1989 the city has experienced dramatic economic, political and social changes, as well as a radical upheaval in urban planning and design for which there are few parallels. The urban development and restructuring processes in particular have demanded a great deal from Berlin's citizens, as construction projects are not just visible for all but are physically experienced and encountered on a daily basis. The rebuilding of urban spaces, daily adjustments to traffic circulation patterns, and the great volume of demolition and new construction all add up to influence what is known in German as a *Heimat* feeling, or a person's identification with a particular place. Thus it comes as no surprise in Berlin that all of the planning and development of the last decade has led – and continues to lead – to intensive and very controversial debates. This has to do with nothing less than the bringing together of two cities with a combined population of over 3 million, who were shaped by their extremely different urban development paradigms of the previous fifty years.[1] This also has to do with the conversion of the city into Germany's capital, a process that is not yet completed with the official move of the government and parliament from Bonn to Berlin in 1999. And this has to do with the economic repositioning of Berlin, not only regionally but globally speaking. This in itself is a considerable change for Berlin as such economic positioning played only a minor role in each of the two 'Front Cities' while they were representing their respective world powers. A primary question here is if it is possible for residents of this reunified city to identify emotionally with the new 'complete' city without letting go of their attachments to their old neighbourhoods (what in Berlin is known as the *Kiez*), and accompanying local structures and institutions.

Urban planning and development in two German states

Berlin's modern history is laden with powerful symbolic transitions, and the city is characterised more by fits of planning and upheaval than by organic growth, which distinguishes Berlin from many other European cities. Berlin first took on its present size in 1920 through the integration of seven towns and 59 rural communities, after which the city rapidly developed into a world city in the 'Golden Twenties'. The 'Great Berlin' urban design competition was carried out as early as 1910, in order to create, among other things, a plan for the restructuring of the downtown area. This plan was intended to help 'force a service-orientation of the downtown and an artistic or architectural emphasis to this area's central national standing with respect to research and culture as well as administration and politics'.[2] Berlin's two centres – one being its old downtown and the other the Kurfürstendamm which had been an expanding district since the 1890s – were to be connected through urban design measures. This plan was not to be realised, but history does have a way of repeating itself. The objectives of this historical plan, even if they are differently articulated today, are to be found again in the current Planwerk Innenstadt (Work Plan for the Inner City; *see* below and Chapter 4).

As the National Socialists seized power, a foundation was laid for the city's destruction: at first through Albert Speer's plan for the super-centre of *Germania*, and then through the bombing by the Allied Forces. Much of Berlin was reduced to areas of rubble by the end of the war, especially the downtown area, and in these devastated areas the two new states with their differing political systems went about setting up their respective metropolises. The GDR created a home for its national government in the eastern half of Berlin, while the FRG maintained its capital in the western half – even if this merely meant naming Berlin as the capital city in the FRG constitution. The building of the Berlin Wall in 1961 destroyed whatever illusions were left concerning the existence of *a single* city.

While it would be a great simplification to maintain that West Berlin's development could be explained by the Athens Charter and East Berlin's development by the Moscow Charter, we do find a corresponding polycentric spatial structure in the West and a monocentric structure in the East of Berlin.[3] The Athens Charter further relates to the ideas expressed below considering 'Berlin as a European City' – ideas that were decisive in discussions over the future of Berlin after 1990.

The following will concentrate on the urban development of the historical city centre (meaning that of downtown East Berlin) as it is really this area and its physical structures that were called into question after Berlin's reunification, and it is this area that has been the focus of the most heated debates.

Through a restructuring of the Alexanderplatz and the erection there of a 365-metre high TV tower, along with the development of the adjacent Marx-Engels-Forum and 'Palace of the Republic' with its parade grounds, the GDR fashioned a political and monumental centre for East Berlin very much in the spirit of the Moscow Charter. The Charter determined that: 'Political demonstrations, military parades and people's holiday festivals should take place on such representative public squares in the city centre. The most important, monumental structures should be constructed in the city centre.'[4] The most monumental of East Berlin's projects is the 'Palace of the Republic', built between 1973 and 1976, which today is a source of great controversy. The large building was home to the GDR People's Congress and also a significant cultural and leisure centre for city residents and tourists. The Palace has emerged as an important symbol for many East Berliners, embodying what they would like to preserve of their local history. Meanwhile, many others – especially nostalgic West Berliners – would like to rebuild the Hohenzollern City Palace that was torn down in 1950 to make way for the Palace of the Republic. At this point the discussion seems to be finding a more objective grounding today.[5]

The Leipziger Strasse that runs through the city centre also saw the demolition of streetscapes and buildings that remained after the war, and their replacement with large housing blocks in the spirit of socialist housing development. On the Fischerinsel (Fisher Island), the older structures were replaced with seven residential towers of between 18 and 21 storeys. These centrally located high-rises have also provoked a great deal of discussion due to their height (*see* below) and design that many find unsuitable for Berlin (*see* Chapter 5).

The famous Friedrichstrasse – that was largely destroyed during the war – remained a construction site well into the 1980s. At that time a change of mind was experienced by many planners and politicians in the GDR who became interested in a reconstruction of the historical city.[6] East Germany's leader, Honecker, envisioned redeveloping the Friedrichstrasse into the 'most attractive commercial street in the capital city', but this plan was only partially realised by 1989.[7] However, further development of this area after 1990 was able to build on what had been started, while using new resources.

Although some of the objectives and even end-results of urban development prior to 1990 are very similar to those after 1990 (for example, preserving residential areas in the downtown area and developing Friedrichstrasse as a valuable commercial street), it is still clear that the reunification of Berlin brought two very different city halves together, and with them their contrasting histories of development:

● The structures in the West were organised polycentrically, while in the East planning was monocentric with a considerable functional neglect of outlying city districts.

● The downtown area in the West around the Tiergarten was densely developed, while the East was characterised by large open areas in its central district between Alexanderplatz and Friedrichstadt.

● The Western centre around the Zoo district was characterised as having very little housing, while many tens of thousands lived around the East's Alexanderplatz.

● Institutions with the character of a capital city (for example, Federal buildings or embassies) had largely disappeared from West Berlin while East Berlin's centre was representative of the socialist capital city.[8]

The two part-cities did have at least one thing in common: numerous neglected open areas that had emerged along both sides of the dividing Berlin Wall. With the removal of the Wall came a shifting of the city's entire spatial structure, and unattractive vacant lots, such as the empty fields in East Berlin, suddenly found themselves in central locations, and quickly became desirable areas for development for investors and architects.

After reunification: Berlin as a construction site

The restructuring of Berlin after its reunification has been concentrated and is most visible in a few areas and large projects (Map 2.1). These have dominated expert discussions and often public conversation as well.

Potsdamer and Leipziger Platz as the busiest traffic intersections in Europe in the 1920s once connected the historical downtown area with the new developments in the West that along Potsdamer Strasse and Kurfürstendamm had grown to be important centres of their own.

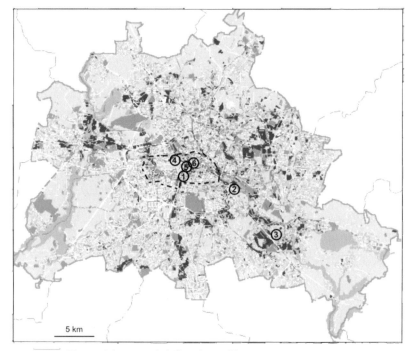

〃 ～ ～   Planwerk Innenstadt 1 Potsdamer Platz
○   Development area 2 Rummelsburger Bucht development zone
                     3 Johannisthal-Adlershof development zone
                     4 Spreebogen
                     5 Friedrichstrasse
                     6 Alexanderplatz

Main Source: Senatsverwaltung für Stadtentwicklung, Umweltschutz und Technologie 1994

Map 2.1 Major urban development projects in Berlin

Sitting directly adjacent to the Wall in 1989, Potsdamer and Leipziger Platz represented the largest vacant, buildable areas in Berlin's inner city. Today, the new developments by DaimlerChrysler, Sony and other large investors found here are symbolic for the 'New Berlin' and play an important role in the marketing of the city (*see* Chapter 11). However, in terms of their urban design these new projects are controversial.[9]

Other large *vacant and 'under-used' areas*, for example around Rummelsburger Bucht (bay) and Adlershof, have been redeveloped in recent years. The abandonment of the majority of such areas has not been due to their poor spatial location, but rather to the rapid decline of industrial and commercial production in Berlin in the 1990s.[10] Rummelsburger Bay is being developed into a mixed-use area and Adlershof into a centre for research, technology and media in which the natural sciences faculty of the Humboldt University is to be settled.

The *Pariser Platz* just east of the Brandenburger Tor (gate) is similar to Potsdamer Platz in that it is historically speaking one of Berlin's most important public squares. This gate and square were the main entrance to the historical centre, but their meaning was lost as they found themselves in the GDR's off-limits border zone. Pariser Platz is now regaining its status as banks, luxury hotels, cultural institutions and embassies are settling here once again. The Berlin approach of Critical Reconstruction (*see* below and Chapter 4) is finding support here in the interests of France, Great Britain and the USA, who are rebuilding their embassies around this historic square.[11]

A new administrative and governmental district is being developed around the *Spreebogen*, where the River Spree makes a bend around the Reichstag. Heated discussions concerning relationships between architecture and political symbols were provoked here by the renovation of the Reichstag following the designs of the British architect, Norman Foster. The Reichstag was erected in 1884 in what was then the German Empire, and was home to the House of Representatives during the Weimar Republic who were only able to muster a small amount of resistance to the rise of the National Socialists. The burning of the Reichstag in 1933 was the opening event for a wave of political persecution.[12] Could a building with such a historical burden be used as a home for the German Federal Parliament? And what would this mean for the architectural design?[13] Foster won approval for his concepts only after a considerable number of revisions, some of which were fundamental. While it was originally planned to cover the entire building with a glass roof, this idea gave way to the solution of the 'historical' glass dome. North-west of the Reichstag there is a building complex going up known as the 'Band des Bundes' (Federal ribbon), which is a row of three structures including the Chancellor's Offices and two other buildings that will span the River Spree with offices for federal politicians and parliamentarians.

The opening of the Friedrichstadtpassagen (department stores) in *Berlin-Mitte* along Friedrichstrasse was an important precondition for resurrection of this Eastern downtown area as a centre for high-class retailing and services. Close to Potsdamer Platz, the areas around Friedrichstrasse and Leipziger Strasse have generated the most activity on the part of private investors and developers. While these more recent investments have to a certain extent built upon developments that had already begun in GDR years, other urban development projects in East Berlin are still on hold. Some of the main questions to be resolved concern the future development of Alexanderplatz and Schlossplatz (the former Hohenzollern Palace) with its adjacent Palace of the Republic.

Actors and interests

A series of other large construction and development projects as well as urban redevelopment initiatives are worth mentioning here. These include Lehrter Bahnhof (railway station) just to the north of Potsdamer Platz; the Diplomatic District to the south of the Tiergarten, Berlin's large inner-city park; the new international airport being planned for Berlin-Brandenburg, and the renovation of large prefabricated social housing estates in which more than 700 000 people live.[14]

However, the examples briefly described above are enough to outline the range of actors and interests that have played a role in urban planning in Berlin over the last decade:

- national and international corporations, private investors and business associations;
- federal institutions;
- foreign governments;
- a broad range of experts, including architects, planners, and their professional associations;
- the urban population including citizen and neighbourhood initiatives.

Berlin politicians and planners have had to engage all of these actors and interests in long discussions regarding goals and objectives for the city's urban planning and development. These discussions were initially complicated by the fact that there was no formal, legal basis for planning following reunification at the beginning of the 1990s in Berlin. A land use plan based on West German legal standards was developed for West Berlin in 1988 that defined primary spatial planning criteria, but this plan was already irrelevant in 1990.[15] Meanwhile, a general development plan created in 1980 for East Berlin was at the very most only relevant in terms of provoking some thinking, and the GDR People's Congress had adopted substantial aspects of the FRG's legal codes regarding planning and construction months before Berlin's reunification.[16] West German law was in any case comprehensively applied after the official unification of former East Germany with the Federal Republic of Germany, but some specific planning instruments were still missing, such as the land use plan and the building plan (Flächennutzungsplan and Bebauungsplan).

As with urban restructuring in general during this challenging phase of Berlin's history, the development of new planning instruments and codes as called for by planning and building legal standards was further complicated by the fact that Berlin was governed throughout the 1990s by one coalition or another. While Berlin was governed by Social Democrats and Greens briefly at the time of the city's reunification, since then it has been ruled by Christian Democrats and Social Democrats. The two most important administrative departments concerning urban planning – 'Building, Housing and Traffic' and 'Urban Development and Environmental Protection' – have during this time been directed by ministers of differing political parties.[17] This 'party mathematics' was intended to ensure that the most important political (and therefore societal) interests, values and objectives would be taken into consideration in questions of urban planning. But quite often this only led to watered-down compromises, for example with the Planwerk Innenstadt (*see* Chapters 3 and 4) that was adopted by the Berlin Ministry in 1999, about which a critic expressed the following:

> The 'Planwerk' that has been adopted is a classic example of consensus democracy. The plan is without either teeth or authority, and it is implicitly acknowledged that critics will eventually reduce what is there to an absolute nothing ... One does not have to be a prophet to predict that this 'Planwerk' will find a quiet resting place in the overflowing archives of Berlin urban development plans.[18]

In addition to the above described 'dualism' regarding political and administrative responsibility for urban development, Berlin is at the same time a city and a federal state that is divided into 23 districts. Formally, the districts can be compared with cities in other states, but the districts have considerably less authority and fewer legal instruments at their disposal. Still, responsibilities for city and project planning along with the corresponding permitting processes are divided (and in some cases overlap) between the district and the Berlin ministries. This situation leads again and again to conflicts, that are due in some cases to political motivations and in others to the very different interests of the ministry and the districts, which differ among themselves according to their particular populations. The earlier presented list of actors involved in Berlin urban planning and development must therefore be complemented by those active at the district level, as these local actors often play key roles in discussions regarding individual development projects (*see* Chapter 5).

While a new legal planning framework was being created in the first half of the 1990s, vastly exaggerated forecasts concerning Berlin's further development were being made, which increased expectations in business circles. It seemed that the planning forecasters and commercial actors had a way of heating each other up, and so decision-makers were figuring on a yearly population growth of as many as 40 000 new residents.[19]   It was also predicted that the demand for office area would double in the next decade, and that a growth rate of at least 50 per cent could be expected in the demand for retail square footage.[20] Apparent factors behind these boom-forecasts were above all else the so-called 'catch-up' needs of East Berliners, but also the new capital city functions and the predicted role for Berlin as a 'gateway to Eastern Europe'. The demand expressed by investors and real estate companies in the early 1990s, especially in Mitte (central Berlin), was twice as high as the supply of possible projects estimated by planners.[21] And so land values and rents sky-rocketed.[22] Meanwhile, due to an escalating crisis in the city's own financial situation, Berlin was increasingly dependent on larger investors. High land costs and the financial power of such large investors and developers led repeatedly to conflicts (and compromises) concerning building densities and heights as well as building design. Such conflicts influenced discussions about the developing models of the 'European City' and 'Berlin Architecture'. Such questions were further debated in discussions involving the Planwerk Innenstadt and related method of Critical Reconstruction.

Urban development models and visions

'Berlin, the *European City*', is a significant expression that emerged in Berlin during the creation of Berlin's new comprehensive land use plan adopted in 1994. This phrase was expected to be of increasing importance in influencing further work on Berlin planning methods and models, whereby 'European cities' are characterised by their

- specifically European public qualities and separation of public and private spaces;

- mixtures of residential, commercial, service, and cultural activities and functions;
- special local identities that are manifested in historic physical structures, streetscapes and ground plans.[23]

This expression reflects ideas that were articulated in the 1980s during West Berlin's International Building Exhibition (IBA), 'accompanying a rebirth of the city neighbourhood and its defence with respect to the urban destruction of the 1960s and 1970s'.[24] As orientation for the more recent planning in Berlin, especially for the inner city, it has thus been possible to use the ideas of 'careful urban renewal' from the 1980s:

> The fundamental philosophy remains (until today) that of an emphasis on a respectful dealing with historical structures and patterns, the idea of a diverse and complex city, a process that encourages citizen participation, and a sensitivity toward Berlin architectural styles and their further development.[25]

This briefly mentioned *Critical Reconstruction* method helped provide some initial guidance to planners and investors during the early 1990s when planning instruments were not yet available (such as the earlier noted, legally prescribed land use and building plans). This method also offered a significant basis for judging the range of urban design competitions organised by the city authorities to give some direction to the variety of large development projects being carried out in Berlin.[26]

The Critical Reconstruction method argues not only for traditional street and building plans, but also for the restoration of historical streetscapes and building façades and heights as well as architectural styles and patterns and a return to block patterns (and the accompanying densification and in-fill of vacant lots).[27]

The city's application of these Berlin principles of urban reconstruction during the 1990s led to numerous conflicts with investors, with concerned experts and citizens, and also between differing city and district departments. While investors primarily wanted higher building densities to make individual projects more profitable, others were critical of increasing densities as they feared a loss of inner-city open and green spaces. The most heated debates took place between the city's urban development and transportation administration, and their respective political leadership. The call for rebuilding and narrowing some broad streets, especially those created by the GDR in the inner city, but also those developed during the 'auto-friendly' years of West Berlin, ran into great resistance from Berlin's Transportation Minister. But in addition to this, already existing conflicts flared up again over Planwerk Innenstadt between advocates of 'Critical Reconstruction' and critical planners and architects – especially in East Berlin.

Planwerk Innenstadt is discussed in some detail in other places (*see* Chapters 4 and 5), while here only some of the main goals and objectives will be presented (remembering that this plan contains much of the important guidance for future urban development in Berlin).[28] The Planwerk Innenstadt – as it was presented in its draft form to the public for the first time in 1996 – offered for the first time since the City's reunification:

> … a comprehensive concept for redeveloping both the historical inner city and the so-called 'City West' downtown. A primary objective was to encourage the development of the entire Berlin inner city in ways that would be attractive in urban design terms as well as being economically, ecologically, and socially sustainable … a stated goal of the Planwerk Innenstadt is to illustrate and encourage a city for the twenty-first century … guiding concepts are in such areas as mobility, density, sustainability, urbanity and identity. Related Planwerk Innenstadt discussions and refinements also offered a contribution to a mental reintegration of the formerly divided East and West Berlin populations, and to this end presented an outline of a formulation for a new, reintegrated city identity.[29]

And so the Planwerk Innenstadt pursued not only the goal of reuniting the two former city centres with urban design measures, but also the objective of bringing the people of the two city halves together again.

This second objective has apparently met with only limited success. There are for example very different opinions among politicians and planners regarding Planwerk's historically sensitive (as others state: nostalgic) picture (*see* Chapter 5).[30] The Planwerk Innenstadt is thus criticised for its assumptions regarding the necessity and desirability of a single centre for Berlin.[31] Critics here referred not only to the development of other European cities over the last fifty years (suburbanisation, loss of downtowns, and so on), but also to the argument that the creation of a single, new city centre would mean 'the rejection of a city of publicly lived and expressed social and political differences'.[32] Another form of critique – that seems to have more of a foundation – attacks the Planwerk Innenstadt and its applied method of Critical

Reconstruction not only for ignoring, but seeking to extinguish the urban development of the post-war decades in Berlin: urban development and an image of the city with which a substantial part of the local population identifies.

Undoubtedly, Planwerk Innenstadt created a strong model for redeveloping and densifying the inner city, and for seeking to maintain (or regain) housing in the downtown neighbourhoods. Further, Planwerk cannot be argued with for wanting to reduce further urban sprawl while encouraging sustainable urban development. But it has to be questioned just what Planwerk Innenstadt advocates hope to achieve when they respond to critics – who attempt to defend the GDR history of urban design and planning – with such comments as: 'The critique offered by ex-GDR intellectuals is a peculiar thing all on its own. There is no real reason to have to respond to or try to do justice to their arguments.'[33]

Such argument is however counter-productive to one of Planwerk's own fundamental goals – that of supporting 'mental reintegration' of the formerly divided populations. This is all the more true when one realises that after the adoption of the Planwerk Innenstadt by the Berlin Ministry in May 1999, it was not related to any legally binding instruments (such as the land use or building plans). Implementation of the Planwerk Innenstadt, according to the words of the Minister for Urban Development, will depend on 'judgement calls that must be respected by district planners'.[34] And so the Planwerk Innenstadt does indeed depend on a fairly broad consensus of all concerned parties for the achievement of its stated urban design objectives.

A new planning culture?

Berlin's reunification, and the accompanying euphoria as well as anxieties surrounding it, led at least to the beginnings of a new planning culture including broader public discussions concerning urban development issues.[35] Approaches developed in the 1980s through Berlin's International Building Exhibition also had a great influence here, such as the insight that precisely in times of transition, 'Politicians and administrators do not on their own have the capacity and know-how to answer all of the questions presented by urban development ...'.[36] With this in mind, the Berlin Minister responsible for the city's first comprehensive land use plan, organised in 1991 an advisory council known as the 'Stadtforum' (city forum), which brought together a wide spectrum of experts and facilitated public discussions around key issues. This minister wrote that 'the most important instrument in preparing the plan (1994 land use plan) was what we call the "city forum". Since 1991 the forum has provided the possibility of discussing basic issues and goals. The group consisted of 80 leading figures in the community.'[37] The forum has since met approximately 80 times, dealing with a wide range of urban planning issues.[38] Owing to its extroverted nature, the forum has also achieved a fair amount of media attention. Still, this group has remained a discursive instrument that provides politicians with advice and the public with information, but it is not an instrument of public participation. This deficiency regarding public involvement quickly brought forth criticism, and among other things led to the founding of the 'Stadtforum von unten' (city forum from below). Some of the main organisers of this critical forum were associated with the East German PDS political party, who focused attention on the lack of consideration given by the Stadtforum to experts from East Berlin.[39]

The Berlin urban development administration did at least respond to criticisms of inadequate public involvement by creating two further instruments concerning public information and participation:

> ... three areas dealing with public involvement have taken shape ... next to the Stadtforum which formulates and discusses future scenarios for the city ..., the StadtProjekte (CityProjects) as an event series concerns itself with more specific problem-based questions that emerge between the classical field of urban planning and other disciplines. Meanwhile, 'Planungswerkstätten' (Planning Workshops) involve relevant experts and take on and analyse concrete planning out in the field.[40]

Beyond this, a form of *Quartiersmanagement* has been developed to work with neighbourhoods characterised as being 'under-developed', seeking to upgrade these 'problem areas' both socially and spatially. A primary objective here is to increase public involvement and responsibility outside the formal and legally prescribed participation processes. A variety of Local Agenda 21 initiatives also work to increase participation.

It can be said that a range of innovative participatory instruments have been developed since Berlin's reunification, in particular in the area of public information services, and in spite of all the criticism, there are few large cities where there has been a greater amount of public discussion over questions of urban development. At the same time, it must be said that all this discussion has irritated some Berlin planners, and that some politicians have expressed a 'certain amount of ambivalence' towards such participatory instruments and methods. The Berlin Building Director (Senatsbaudirektor) has for example written about such questions with respect to Planwerk Innenstadt:

> When one reviews the large number of strategies that European metropolises used to direct comprehensive urban development efforts over the course of the twentieth century, then it can be seen that the created plans have only emerged out of the work of planners, and not as the result of democratic processes ... neither Scharoun's 'Collective Plan' nor the plan for the Kulturforum, nor the plan for the Märkische Viertel (urban quarter in West Berlin) ... and of course in no way were the plans for Stalinallee, Fischerkiez and Marzahn (in East Berlin) the results of complex, democratic decision-making processes ... this history is written into the record for all to read, especially those who have criticised the Planwerk Innenstadt for its weaknesses regarding participation.[41]

Such comments express not only ambivalence, but perhaps also reflect some of the wounds that were suffered during the (at times) very caustic arguments, especially those revolving around the Planwerk Innenstadt.

It could also be that behind such comments are realisations that urban planning is in any case only to be implemented through compromise, and that planning is a process carried out amid the tensions of a great range of differing interests. Hoffman-Axthelm, who as an urban planner played a significant role in developing the Planwerk Innenstadt, expresses such a view of planning as it revolves around compromises. He has written for example:

> Political decisions have to take into account the very real political context in which such a Planwerk Innenstadt is created ... the watchful eyes of competing governmental departments, political opponents, and reporters with their malicious glee ... Such departments are not even unified among themselves, but rather reflect all of the contradictions found in the real world. Positions are argued that are irreconcilable not only objectively speaking but also amongst varying professional positions ... It is clear that such processes demand numerous concessions from planners ...[42]

It remains doubtful in the end whether these concessions will lead to compromises that truly encourage a social and psychological reintegration of the formerly divided city. Even if it may not be politically correct still to be speaking of Berlin as a 'mentally divided city', the election results for the Berlin Parliament in October 1999 speak another truth. The PDS, as the successor party to the former East German state party, the SED, won about 4 per cent of the vote in West Berlin, but in East Berlin received about 40 per cent, and so is the strongest party in the Eastern districts, ahead of the Christian Democrats and Social Democrats who together govern the city. 'Berlin may be coming together more and more – but every election reveals once again where the dividing lines are. There is no doubt that this is currently one of the great political challenges ...'.[43] In the end, urban planning and development are perhaps the most important instruments available to city governments. Are planners up to these challenges? This will be seen more than anywhere else in further urban developments and projects in the old, new centre of Berlin.

Notes

1   In 1989 West Berlin had about two million and East Berlin about 1.2 million residents. The two city halves covered surface areas of about 480 km^2 and 403 km^2. Statistisches Landesamt Berlin, *Kleine Berlin Statistik* (Berlin: Kulturbuchverlag, 1999).
2   Quotation from: K. Trippel, 'Der Stadtumbau im historischen Zentrum Berlins. Planungspolitik in der Nachwendezeit', *HSP-papers*, 4/98, *Arbeitsschwerpunkt Hauptstadt Berlin, Freie Universität Berlin* (1998) p. 8.
3   *See* also H. Häussermann and R. Neef, *Stadtentwicklung in Ostdeutschland. Soziale und räumliche Tendenzen* (Opladen: Westdeutscher Verlag, 1996).
4   Quotation from: ibid. p. 79.
5   'An expert group is to be created – including urban planners and art historians – to provide some direction for the further development and to guide future activities of the Schlossplatz – time is passing and the asbestos removal process will be completed in mid-2001 – and so the question is pressing about what to do with the square. The German Chancellor Gerhard Schröder, Berlin's mayor Eberhard Diepgen, and his new Cultural Minister Christa Thoben can all envisage a new palace. The Urban Development Minister Peter Strieder pictures a collage of old and new structures – but the public uses of such a project remain a mystery ... The concept [of the PDS, which primarily represents voters in East Berlin; author's note] for a "Citizens' Forum" is based on the assumption that the Palace of the Republic will be renovated and reused after the asbestos removal – with new façades, roof terraces and a pedestrian bridge crossing the River Spree. The Palace should be an architectural ensemble with public spaces, squares, corridors, and courtyards, approximately on the site of the old Palace. The style and appearance need to be resolved in a public process.' (*Der Tagesspiegel*, 4 February 2000).
6   Also in this phase was the historically based reconstruction of the Nikolaiviertel – one of Berlin's oldest districts.

7 Quotation from: H. Bodenschatz, *Berlin. Auf der Suche nach dem verlorenen Zentrum* (Hamburg: Junius Verlag, 1995) p. 152.

8 Trippel, op. cit., p. 10 ff.

9 Ibid., p. 41 ff.

10 The number of manufacturing industries fell between 1992 and 1998 from 1397 to 950. At the same time, the number of workers employed in such industries decreased from 481 800 to 305 400 (Statistisches Landesamt Berlin, op. cit.).

11 But bitter diplomatic conflicts took shape concerning details such as the security or buffer-zone to be established between publicly accessible space and the American Embassy. *See: Der Tagesspiegel* (24 January 2000).

12 Similarly, the 'Pogromnacht' (trivialised in German as the Reichskristallnacht or 'crystal night') in 1938 symbolically introduced the Holocaust.

13 The awkward description ended up with – 'Plenarbereich (Parliament) im Reichstag' – reveals how difficult these questions are for the political decision-makers. On the one hand, this expression is intended to minimise connections between the historically burdened structure and the Federal German Parliament. On the other hand, decision-makers did not want to (or could not) take away this familiar name from the Berlin public.

14 M. Schümer-Strucksberg, 'The Berlin Strategy for Further Development of Large Housing Estates: Statement of Position', European Academy of the Urban Environment (ed.), *A Future for Large Housing Estates* (Berlin: published by EA.UE, 1998) pp. 91–7.

15 Feldmann v., 'Grundlagen des Planungs- und Baurechts in der BRD und Rechtsanforderungen an den Umweltschutz', Senatsverwaltung für Bau- und Wohnungswesen (ed.), *Kongreßbericht. Erste Stadtkonferenz Berlin. Planen, Bauen, Wohnen* (Berlin: Kulturbuch-Verlag, 1990) pp. 241–7.

16 K. Ganser, 'Instrumente von gestern für die Städte von morgen?' in K. Ganser, J. Hesse and C. Zöpel (eds), *Die Zukunft der Städte* (Baden-Baden: Verlagsgesellschaft, 1991) pp. 54–65.

17 At the end of 1999 both of these government departments were combined to form a 'Super Ministry' that is under the direction of a Social Democrat. It remains to be seen if the politically motivated conflicts concerning planning models will decrease or increase, as other urban planning interests may not continue to be adequately considered.

18 B. Schulz, 'Bau, schau, wem. Das neue Berlin: Die Stadt inszeniert sich selbst – und zieht Bilanz eines Jahrzehnts der architektonischen und urbanistischen Umgestaltung', *Der Tagesspiegel* (5 June 1999).

19 U. Pfeiffer, 'Berlin vor dem Boom?', *Bauwelt*, 36 (1990) p. 1840 ff. The reality looks in any case different as Berlin has a net loss of about 30 000 residents per year (M. Mönninger, 'Stadt im Leistungsvergleich', *Berliner Zeitung* (17 February 2000).

20 Senatsverwaltung für Stadtentwicklung, Umweltschutz und Technologie (ed.), *Flächennutzungsplan Berlin, FNP Erläuterungsbericht* (Berlin: published by Senatsverwaltung, 1994) p. 90 ff.

21 Ibid., p. 133.

22 A. Banghard, 'Berlin – Transformation einer Metropole', W. Süß (ed.), *Hauptstadt Berlin, Bd. 2 – Berlin im vereinten Deutschland* (Berlin: Berlin Verlag, 1995) pp. 441–61.

23 Trippel, op. cit. p. 34.

24 P. Strieder, 'Welche Stadt wollen wir? Das Planwerk als Wegweiser jenseits der Architekturmoden', *Stadtforum – Zukunft des Zentrums* (29 April 1998) p. 7 f.

25 H. Stimmann, 'Was nützt uns die Geschichte? Der historische Stadtgrundriß als Ressource für die Zukunft', *Stadtforum – Zukunft des Zentrums* (29 April 1998) p. 10 f.

26 *See* Ch. 4, n. 2 and 3.

27 The architectural design especially provoked a series of discussions regarding what came to be called 'Berlin Architecture'. This began with a number of expert talks during the Berliner Bauwoche (Berlin Building Week) in 1993. Debates over façades and building heights – more than anything else – formed the core of the discussions regarding new guidelines announced by the Berlin Building Ministry. Critics spoke of a 'Berlin stone fraction' (because of the demands for stone façades) and feared a visual loss of the old patterns of building plots due to forced monotony. *See*, D. Guratzsch, 'Auf der Suche nach der Neuen Berlinischen Architektur', *Die Welt* (14 July 1995).

28 Senatsverwaltung für Stadtentwicklung, Umweltschutz und Technologie, *Planwerk Innenstadt Berlin. Ergebnis, Prozess, Sektorale Planung und Werkstätten* (Berlin: Kulturbuchverlag, 1999).

29 Senatsverwaltung für Stadtentwicklung, Umweltschutz und Technologie, *Planwerk Innenstadt Berlin. Ein erster Entwurf* (Berlin: Kulturbuchverlag, 1997) p. 82.

30 K. Hartung, 'Berliner Ungleichzeitigkeiten', *Kommune*, 4 (1997) p. 6 f.

31 For example, M. Haerdter, 'Mythos Mitte', *Positionen*, 1 (1998) p. 17 ff.

32 For example, W. Kil, 'Würde, Idylle, Segregation. Wie ein "Planwerk" versucht, die Metropole zu bändigen', *Kommune*, 2 (1997) p. 13.

33 D. Hoffmann-Axthelm, 'Das Berliner Planwerk Innenstadt und seine Kritiker', *Kommune*, 12 (1997) pp. 6–11.

34 Quotation from: E. Schweitzer, 'Engere Strassen, mehr Häuser, weniger Tunnels', *Der Tagesspiegel* (18 April 1999).

35 While it is true that German legal codes concerning planning and building demand citizen participation processes, these guidelines are essentially limited to calling for making plans publicly available. Participatory processes that already inform and listen to citizens during the planning phases are relatively scarce and only organised for certain, limited building projects. *See*, for example: R. Schaefer and P. Dehne, *Aktuelles Planungshandbuch zur Stadt- und Dorferneuerung* (Augsburg: WEKA, 1994).

36 Hassemer was the Urban Development Minister during the first half of the 1990s, and he was quoted here in: H. Fassbinder, 'Stadtforum Berlin', *Harburger Berichte zur Stadtplanung*, Bd. 8 (Hamburg, 1997).

37 V. Hassemer, 'Strategic Planning and Development Programme of Berlin', in European Academy of the Urban Environment (ed.), *Strategies of Development for Central European Metropolises* (Berlin: published by EA.UE, 1993) pp. 19–22.

38 For example, Planwerk Innenstadt was the official Stadtforum topic three times.

39 S. Blau, *Das Instrument Stadtforum und die Demokratisierung der Planung*, Diplomarbeit (Master's Thesis) at the Geographische Institut der ETH Zürich (Zürich: unpublished manuscript, 1977) p. 41. The PDS is the successor party to the SED, which was the GDR state party.

40 P. Meuser, 'Wie demokratisch ist das Planwerk? Die Form der Stadt als soziale Angelegenheit', *Stadtforum – Zukunft des Zentrums* (29 April 1998) p. 34 f. *See* also: Senatsverwaltung für Stadtentwicklung, Umweltschutz und Technologie (1999), op. cit., p. 28 ff.

41 H. Stimmann, op. cit., p. 11.

42 D. Hoffmann-Axthelm, op. cit., p. 7.

43 *Der Tagesspiegel* (11 October 1999).

3

The Urban Planning Context in Belfast: a City Between War and Peace

William J.V. Neill

Since the violent outbreak of ethnic conflict in 1969 urban planning for Belfast has necessarily been concerned with the management of cultural diversity sometimes manifested in extreme forms of spatial segregation and the exclusion of the identity of 'the other'. In a short period of time planning strategy moved from its focus in the 1960s under reformist Unionism in providing the physical infrastructure and spatial structure for a modernised regional economy to one where planning strategy under British direct rule dovetailed with the political management of 'the troubles'.[1] In general terms government planning policy towards Belfast and the centre of the city in particular since the 1970s, can be periodised as follows:

a) Reactive policy of the 1970s: acceptance of cultural exclusion.
b) The tentative search for normality: encouragement of city centre recovery, 1980–84.
c) Transcending cultural difference: promotional planning 1985–94.
d) Vision planning 1995–present: the search for cultural inclusion.

Cultural exclusion: planning for extreme difference

The 1970s saw the start of a vigorous social house-building programme in Belfast which recognised the reality of people's desire for the security of residential segregation. So called 'peace walls' were erected (Map 3.2) at interface zones where cultural differences could sometimes meet each other, resulting in fatalities if not hampered by intervening bricks, mortar and fencing.

Between 1970 and 1975 an IRA bombing campaign destroyed around 300 establishments in Belfast city centre and over a quarter of

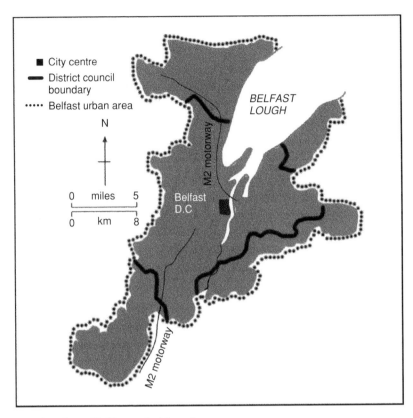

Map 3.1 City of Belfast and wider urban area

total retail floorspace.[2] Radical defensive security measures ensued, including the 'ring of steel' security cordon at entrances to the city centre, where pedestrians and entering vehicles were searched. The government's Review of Transportation Strategy in 1978 recommended the construction of a high-grade motorway link running to the north and west of the city centre and 'canyoned' through part of its length. This road, while achieving urban transportation objectives, also acted virtually as a moat, cutting off the city centre from the Catholic and Protestant housing areas of the Falls and Shankill. The spreading of riots emanating within these areas into the city was made extremely difficult, if not impossible, since the construction of the 'Westlink'. Where the road forms a flyover, or is at ground level, pedestrian access to the city centre is easier, but heavily fortified police bases

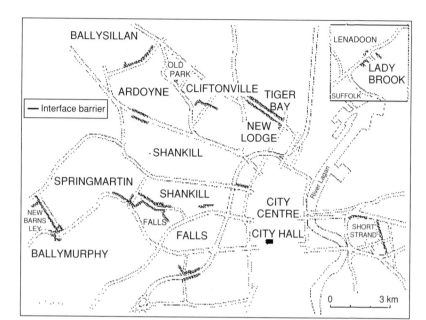

Map 3.2 Belfast's peacelines

guarded such entrance points, almost like bastions in medieval walled towns (Map 3.3).

Searching for normality

The seeds of future policy can be detected in a nine-point package 'to spell the rebirth of Belfast' announced by the Labour government's Secretary of State, Roy Mason, in 1978. This included the setting up of a working party to 'examine how sparkle can be brought back into city centre night life', the 'stepping up of schemes to spruce up the city and give it a brighter look' and the employment of consultants to explore the possibilities of government partnership with private developers to redevelop city centre sites. A key location was identified, occupying the site of the present Castlecourt downtown shopping centre. More government jobs were promised for the city centre and the report of a River Lagan Working Party was announced with 'extensive possibilities ... to beautify and enrich central Belfast'. The British government looked forward to the spread of 'oases' through the central area and 'the creation of a new Belfast of which all its citizens can be proud'.[3]

Map 3.3 Belfast city centre

Already in 1975 the Arts Council of Northern Ireland, assisted by a government grant, had bought for restoration the architecturally distinctive Grand Opera House which had been closed following falling audiences and bomb damage. Its reopening in 1980 was generally seen as symbolic of a return of some semblance of normality to downtown Belfast. The recovery of Belfast city centre in the early 1980s can be attributed to a number of factors, not least of which was a change in IRA strategy away from commercial bombing towards attacks on the security forces and other state personnel. This led to a relaxation of town centre security restrictions. Environmental improvements in Belfast were coming on-stream, including extensive pedestrianisation, which made a virtue out of a security necessity. City centre traders introduced late-night shopping one evening per week, and generous grant aid was made available by government for investment in the physical fabric of their businesses. In early 1985 the boast was that almost 140 new eating establishments had opened, mainly around the city centre, demonstrating that people were coming back to the city.[4] A government-sponsored seminar in October 1983 convened by Chris Patten, the new Conservative minister responsible for the environment, explored with retailers, the City Council and potential investors ways of orchestrating the emerging change in central Belfast's fortunes. The result was the Belfast Urban Area plan initiative, which got underway in 1985.[5]

Transcending cultural difference: a city of shoppers and spectacle

The mid-1980s to mid-1990s included the major initiative of the new Belfast Urban Area Plan itself, and in 1991 an upping of the ante by government in terms of promoting the cultural normality of Belfast with celebratory events and a new city centre local plan based almost exclusively on image. The signing of the Anglo-Irish Agreement in 1985 and the start of a new plan for Belfast in the same year was symbolic. The former represented an awareness by the British government that it was in for a long haul and that movement towards peace in Northern Ireland could only be achieved with the involvement of others. Crisis management had now been replaced by a concerted strategy in which the mobilisation of economic and physical development in both urban and rural areas had been identified as a key to resolving the problem. Improvement in the quality of life of people living in Northern Ireland was held as the precondition for greater equality, democracy, and achievement of a political settlement. This 'hands-on' approach to development was facilitated by the untrammelled powers held by central government, and was endorsed not only by the Irish government but also by the European Community through its Structural Funds, and by the United States of America, Canada and New Zealand through the creation of the International Fund for Ireland.

Belfast led the way. The attention of Chris Patten was drawn to the relationship between physical planning and economic development and, importantly, to the role that both could play in the management of the political process in Belfast and indeed Northern Ireland as a whole. The planning strategy in Belfast at this time was to directly incorporate physical planning into the overall process of political management of 'the troubles', using development in a proactive manner. A 'heart transplant' in 1985 was deemed necessary for Belfast city centre, an image which drew on urban renaissance experience in America and appealed to local business interests. This conjunction of political and private business interests allowed a mood of optimism to be quickly generated. Infrastructure investments and environmental improvements continued apace, giving the impression of considerable activity. The slogan 'Belfast is Buzzing' was coined at the same time as the new Belfast Urban Area plan as if to correlate the rate of change envisaged for Belfast with the lure of the millennium itself. Final adoption in December 1989 produced a 'designer' plan with state of the art graphics. A suite of positive images of newly built or planned developments was projected, counterpointed by anaemic-toned panoramas of the city of the past. This selective rendition of Belfast tapped into the pride of people about the industrial past of the city while indicating that the future would be brighter, and any reference to the sectarian divisions with which the city is riven was studiously avoided in both text and photographs.[6]

In the plan Belfast city centre was harnessed as a symbol for a normal Northern Ireland. The appearance in force, in publicly pump-primed developments, of the multiple retailers and their corporate logos came to symbolise normality. The new city centre shops were marshalled like icons to oppose the array of images painted on the gable walls of housing areas in the city, which portray divisive identity symbols of the past.

The iconographic battle in Belfast was such that commercial projects were used to dilute, if not entirely dissolve, the absolutism represented on the gable walls of the housing ghettos in the relativistic soup of the commodified space of the city centre. New shopping opportunities were combined with government-sponsored urban spectacle. Running throughout 1991, for example, was a Belfast festival of events, coordinated by a government-assembled 'Belfast 1991' board of directors and with administrative support provided by the Belfast Development Office, the promotional development arm of the Department of the Environment for the city. Sponsorship from government and private

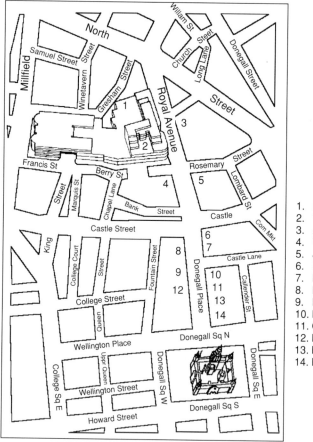

Key to Map

1. Debenhams
2. Virgin Records
3. Argos
4. Waterstones
5. Jaeger
6. McDonalds
7. Next
8. Habitat
9. Disney
10. Body Shop
11. C & A
12. Boots
13. Marks & Spencer
14. Principles

Map 3.4 The cultural neutrality of shopping on Belfast's main shopping thoroughfare

sources supported urban events intended, in the words of the Belfast 1991 chairman, to provide 'a glimpse of what the future might be all about' by projecting 'an image for the people' and injecting 'a new sense of community pride'. A secondary intention was to enhance Belfast's image abroad.[7] The highlight of the Belfast 1991 'celebrations' was the visit of the Tall Ships Race to Belfast in July. Commenting in a letter to the *Belfast Telegraph* in August on his interpretation of what was undoubtedly a popular cross-cultural urban spectacle, the Minister for the Environment, Richard Needham, pointed to the potential of civic identification in transcending 'cultural differences':

So what lessons can we draw from the tall ships carnival? What does it all mean to those on Short Strand, Springfield Road, Sandy Row or the Shankill [Catholic and Protestant inner city areas]. First, it means, we all belong to the same City, we can all share in the success of our City and be proud of our differing but complementing traditions and cultures ... Of course there was a ghost at the feast. The men of violence and their apologists have not gone away, but even they must now begin to realise how hopeless is their campaign, how useless their attempts to divide through violence and control through intimidation. The people of Belfast have given their answer to that in their tens and hundreds of thousands.[8]

Vision planning – the search for cultural inclusion

The announcement of a cease-fire by the IRA on 21 August 1994 unleashed a wave of optimism and a flurry of planning activity in Belfast. The planning 'gaze' for Belfast has subsequently been fixed in outlook on harmonious 'visions' for the future but while at least acknowledging the reality of conflict and the need for pluralist solutions has not, as yet, met issues of cultural diversity head on. Rather the communicative strategy has allowed a retreat to a hazy future vision which neglects the important ontological needs of both major ethnic stakeholders for 'belonging' in the city and for identification with it. With the establishment in 1999 of a new culturally inclusive power-sharing assembly and executive in Northern Ireland (unfortunately, in March 2000, in temporary suspension) the time may now be ripe to deal more directly with urban planning issues involving cultural pluralism. However, developments so far have been rather anaemic.

On 11 May 1995, Malcolm Moss, then Minister for the Environment in Northern Ireland, addressed a meeting of Belfast City Council, the first time a government minister had done so since the signing of the Anglo-Irish agreement a decade previously. In a seemingly thawing political atmosphere, the Minister appealed for civic leadership to formulate 'a strategic vision for Belfast which would provide the broad framework within which government departments, the City Council, major public bodies, the business and commercial sectors and the voluntary sector can work over the next 20 to 25 years'. The vision would seek to describe and define a way to move towards 'the sort of city which we could proudly hand over to future generations'.[9] A follow-up ministerial statement was just as vague, promising the establishment of a City Partnership Board to facilitate the creation of a Belfast Strategic Vision. 'Vision setting', this statement declared, required an act of faith:

> By stepping out into the future, say 20–25 years from now, envisaging what Belfast should look like, and working backwards from there, it can be possible to bridge the many differences and obstacles that currently hold back development.[10]

This exhortative retreat to the future in a city which has difficulty advancing from the symbolic landscapes of the past was reflected in an important government discussion document on the sub-regional context for Belfast's city vision published in January 1996. Articulating a vision for Belfast as 'a competitive, socially inclusive and sustainable city of the future',[11] the document recognising 'the prospect of a permanent end to violence, and the hope of a sustained period of normality'[12] broke from past planning documents by at least openly acknowledging the harsh physical and visual realities of sectarian division. The document, majestically entitled 'The Belfast City Region: towards and beyond the Millennium', is essentially concerned with options for managing the tension between accommodating development pressure in the wider Belfast commuting area over the next 25 years and preserving the built fabric of the core city. However, it located itself within a broader process 'which goes well beyond land-use planning'.[13] While drawing back from defining what this might mean at the level of the city or city region as a whole, the invoked language of inclusiveness, discussion, negotiation, compromise and consent expressed the philosophy underlying the reorganisation of inner city regeneration policy in Belfast in the previous year. Six partnership boards in areas of the greatest economic and social disadvantage were to draw up 'positive visions' for their local areas.[14]

A massive IRA bomb at Canary Wharf in London on 9 February 1996 in reaction to the fact that inclusive political talks on the future of Northern Ireland had failed to materialise for a while took the steam and euphoria out of micro and macro place visioning in Belfast. Against a background of hope from a reinstated IRA cease-fire, consultations presently continue on a vision for the city of Belfast and its regional context but in an atmosphere of pretence that a vision for the city can be detached, compartmentalised and negotiated without discussing issues surrounding cultural identity and its expression in the city.

That all political parties including the more extreme Sinn Fein and Democratic Unionist Party represented in Belfast City Council could agree in March 1997 on a joint city 'Vision Response' to government's thinking on the matter[15] is indicative of how conflict over the use of spatial practices in the constitution of identity in Belfast has been excluded from the planning discourse. The Democratic Unionist chair of Belfast City's planning committee could thus see no contradiction in launching Belfast's consensual 'Vision Response' one week and admonishing a Protestant demonstration the next for its decision not to march uninvited through a nationalist neighbourhood in the city.[16]

After the signing of the Good Friday Agreement in 1998 Belfast's place-visioning exercise was relaunched in June in the city's Waterfront Hall. However, a school choir and glitzy promotional videos could not hide the fact that the core issue of identity in this exercise continues to be avoided. It was reported that respondents to a questionnaire on how Belfast people felt about their city shied away from discussion on issues of identity with the disappointing and naïve conclusion drawn that 'it will be necessary for the vision to demonstrate that it goes beyond issues of cultural identity to the core shared values which emerged for a future Belfast'.[17] However, it seems more likely that a necessary 'bedding down' of the Good Friday Agreement will involve not 'going beyond' issues of identity but rather dealing with them. In a crucial overture to nationalists in efforts to operationalise the governmental institutions in what is also called 'the Belfast Agreement', David Trimble in November 1999, as Northern Ireland's First Minister, moved issues of cultural inclusion to centre stage 'in all areas of public life'. The implications for urban planning are such that some elements of his statement are worth recounting in full:

> The UUP (Ulster Unionist Party) is committed to the principles of inclusivity, equality, and mutual respect on which the institutions are to be based. It is our intention that these principles will extend in practice to all areas of public life, and be endorsed by society as a whole.
>
> The UUP sees a new opportunity for all our traditions in Northern Ireland to enter a new era of respect and tolerance of cultural differences and expression. For too long, much of the unrest in our community has been caused by a failure to accept the different expressions of cultural identity.
>
> Disagreements over language issues, parades and other events must be resolved if the stability and tolerance we all want to see are to be realised. These issues, in future, will be the means to promote mutual respect and tolerance rather than division and alienation.

The UUP is committed to securing equality and mutual respect for all elements of our diverse culture. The Agreement will help bring this about by providing a framework for a new political dispensation which recognises the full and equal legitimacy of our different identities and aspirations.[18]

It would now seem to be time in Belfast for planners to begin thinking about an enabling role in fostering a more inclusive cultural landscape with which both cultural traditions can identify and be proud.

Notes

1 W.J.V. Neill, 'Physical Planning and Image Enhancement: Recent Developments in Belfast', *International Journal of Urban and Regional Research*, Vol. 17, No. 4 (1993), pp. 595–609.

2 S. Brown, 'Central Belfast's Shopping Centre', *Estates Gazette*, 19 October (1985), pp. 256–8.

3 Northern Ireland Information Service, 'Nine Point Package to Spell the Rebirth of Belfast' (Belfast: 1978).

4 B. Simpson, 'Belfast – the Great Revival', *Belfast Telegraph*, 13 May (1985).

5 This plan, adopted in 1990, still sets the spatial framework for development in the Belfast Urban Area. It has some similarities to the German 'Flächennutzungsplan'. Such plan making in Northern Ireland takes place within a legal and administrative framework essentially based on the system in operation in England but with the crucial difference that since the early 1970s, under London direct rule, planning has been a central government rather than a local government function. The Town and Country Planning Service, located within a ministerially headed Department of the Environment for Northern Ireland, has overseen a statutory land use planning system where, as in the rest of the United Kingdom, all development requires planning permission. Decisions on development applications are made with reference to the relevant development plan and other 'material' considerations. In contrast to the German planning system, aesthetic control is generally not as stringent and Belfast has thus nothing similar to the guiding aesthetic of 'critical reconstruction' in the Berlin context. Local government districts in Northern Ireland, including Belfast City Council, have very limited powers and in relation to planning, housing and roads have simply been consulted by the agents of central government. With the formation of a Northern Ireland cross-community Executive Committee in late 1999 and the suspension of direct rule, physical planning responsibilities, previously under the umbrella of the Department of the Environment, were split between three new departments headed by locally elected politicians. This fracturing of planning functions between different political parties in some ways resembles the coalition politics and tensions within the Berlin Senat. This new arrangement is in temporary suspension.

6 Department of the Environment [NI] (1990), 'Belfast Urban Area Plan 2001' (Belfast: HMSO, 1990).

7 I. Oswald, quoted in M. Foy, 'Belfast 1991', *Belfast Telegraph*, 28 December (1991).

8 R. Needham, 'Gods Smile on Belfast', Letter to *Belfast Telegraph*, 8 August (1991).

9 M. Moss, Opening Remarks to a Meeting of Belfast City Council on 11 May (1995a).

10 M. Moss, 'A Strategic Vision for Belfast', June (Belfast: Department of the Environment (NI), 1995b).

11 Department of the Environment (NI), *The Belfast City Region: towards and Beyond the Millennium* (Belfast, 1996), p. 1.

12 Ibid., p. 3.

13 Ibid., p. 4.

14 R. McDonough, *A Partnership Approach to Regeneration: Some Guiding Principles* (Belfast, Department of the Environment (NI), 1995).

15 Belfast City Council, *Towards and beyond the Millennium: Vision Response* (Belfast: 1997).

16 M. Purdy, 'DUP in "Lundy" Jibe over Ormeau', *Belfast Telegraph*, 2 April (1997).

17 Belfast City Partnership Board, *What the People Said* (Belfast: 1998).

18 D. Trimble, Statement as reported in *Belfast Telegraph*, 16 November (1999).

Part II
Spatial Planning and Urban Design in Berlin and Belfast

4

A New Plan for Berlin's Inner City: Planwerk Innenstadt

Wolfgang Süchting and Patrick Weiss

Berlin's reunification is not only a political, administrative, social or societal challenge; this process must also be assisted by the creation of an overall urban structure that clearly serves to unite. Berlin, as we know, is different in many ways from other large German cities. Berlin not only suffered a great amount of destruction in the war – its long division into two separate cities led to two different societal structures with their different objectives and opportunities with respect to urban design and planning. The so-called 'wall in people's heads' still functions as a challenge for reunification in Berlin, as does the broad reluctance people express to incorporate the 'other' half of the city into their own daily routines. For the creation of a common identity, the city centre takes on a decisive importance as an area that connects and brings together citizens of the East and West halves of Berlin.

And so we can see that Berlin needs the inner city plan, Planwerk Innenstadt (Map. 4.1) as an integrated urban concept that encompasses the city centres that were divided for so many decades: Berlin-Mitte with its post-war development that dramatically built a centre over a mediaeval district, and the City-West (western city centre) that has emerged since the war as an independent downtown of its own. Planwerk Innenstadt[1] is designed to re-create and strengthen relationships between these two city centres, re-expose a common history and future, and assist the further development of these city centre identities.

Such challenges were not to be met with conventional planning processes, and the goal here was not to come up with rigid solutions, but to develop strategic concepts. Planwerk Innenstadt was based on intensive communication and interaction that involved the spectrum of the city's society.

Recent history

The challenges facing urban development have changed fundamentally since the opening of the Berlin Wall in 1989. German reunification and the Federal Parliament's decision to move the capital to Berlin have fundamentally altered Berlin's place in the larger scheme of things and hastened its transformation into a service-oriented metropolis.

Euphoric perspectives were common in Berlin in the early 1990s, such as the prediction of a rapidly increasing demand for residential and office space. These perspectives were based on the only partially realised dreams of 'blooming landscapes' in former East Germany, the failed bid for the 2000 Olympics, and expectations of a quick move by the Parliament and Administration from Bonn to Berlin. At the beginning of the 1990s planners forecast a demand for an additional 11 million square metres of office space in Berlin's inner city and along the S-Bahn-Ring (circular light-rail system). Of this demand 40 per cent was planned for independent office complexes such as Potsdamer Platz or Alexanderplatz. A demand was also forecast for an additional 1.7 million square metres of retail area – primarily in shopping malls – and 150 000 new residential units by the year 2010. With such goals in mind, the first land use plan for all of Berlin was adopted in 1994, expecting among other things an increase of 300 000 residents in the city and a rapid transformation from being a large industrial centre to a service-based metropolis. However, this expected future has until today been contradicted by a stagnating or decreasing population in the urban area, accompanied by a rapid outskirts sprawl that has led to the identification of a growing *Speckgürtel* (literally: fat belt) encircling Berlin. While a considerable volume of the new buildings sit vacant, further development plans and the already realised residential and office projects represent important elements in Berlin's transformation processes.

While formal planning instruments were scarce in the years around German reunification, experiences were accumulated with a diverse range of informal planning processes.[2] In 1992 a spatial development plan was created for the entire city, and urban design competitions[3] concerning particular development areas were quickly organised both regionally and internationally, and as invitational as well as open competitions. In only a few years a number of residential and commercial projects with city-wide significance were realised with a quality that was not imaginable in the previous four decades. It was possible to

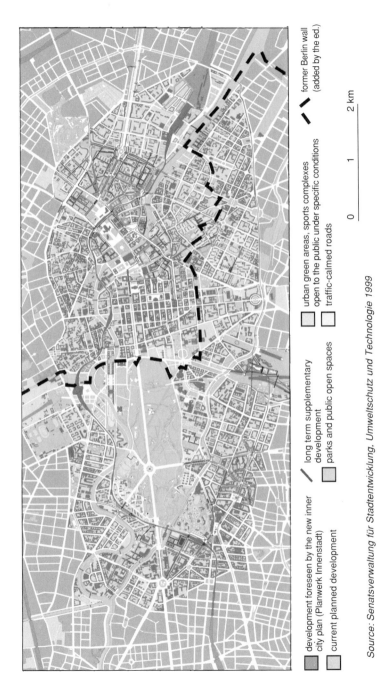

former Berlin wall
(added by the ed.)

urban green areas, sports complexes
open to the public under specific conditions

traffic-calmed roads

long term supplementary
development

parks and public open spaces

development foreseen by the new inner
city plan (Planwerk Innenstadt)

current planned development

0   1   2 km

Source: Senatsverwaltung für Stadtentwicklung, Umweltschutz und Technologie 1999

Map 4.1 Planwerk Innenstadt – a plan for the inner city

reach decisions on a wide range of urban design concepts in individual processes that were then adopted by city government. Among these projects – some of which are still under construction and others of which are completed – are the important developments of the new Potsdamer Platz, the government district around the Reichstag, the central areas of Friedrichstrasse and Hellersdorf, railway stations including Lehrter Bahnhof, Gesundbrunnen, Papestrasse, Spandau, Ostbahnhof and Nordbahnhof. Other examples include developments such as Wasserstadt Spandau, Rummelsburger Bucht, Karow, Eldenaer Strasse, Biesdorf Süd and inner-city densification projects such as at Lehrter Strasse and Heinrich Heine Strasse. Highly specialised jobs have also been created, for example through the new 'Science City' at Johannisthal/Adlershof[4] in south-east Berlin that is on the way to the planned Berlin-Brandenburg-International airport.

A number of urban renewal areas were identified and transferred to private or public trust developers, who were expected to be able to finance their own projects through future increases in land value. Meanwhile, the predicted land value increases have not occurred, and this has led to high vacancy rates accompanied by considerable protestations. Still, the construction cranes are in action and many people remain optimistic.

One of the great problems is structurally caused unemployment among industrial workers. Along with German reunification came a radical and extremely rapid de-industrialisation of Berlin, due to pre-existing unproductive industrial structures in both East and West Berlin and the changed position of Berlin in Europe. This led to a dramatic loss of industrial jobs that could not be made up through new service-sector employment. Of the 400 000 industrial jobs that existed in the city before 1990, only 150 000 remained by the mid-1990s.[5] The average unemployment rate has since hovered around 16 per cent for the entire city and has reached many times that in traditional blue-collar neighbourhoods. Voter turnout has dropped while disappointment has risen concerning the seemingly limited political alternatives.

While predictions for the end of the twentieth century of increased population and buying power have not been realised, it is such predictions that fuelled the construction of new suburban and urban shopping centres, and now vacancies in all building areas are not to be overlooked. Inner-city neighbourhoods with older building stock such as Wedding, Neukölln, or North Schöneberg, as well as post-war developments of social and mixed housing on both sides of the former Berlin Wall, have been dramatically transformed into problem areas by the exodus of middle-class residents. The greatest political hopes for a social form of urban development are now invested in Planwerk Innenstadt and the more recently implemented programme of Urban Quarter Management.[6]

Planwerk Innenstadt inspiration

While the context for urban development in Berlin is greatly determined by the migration to suburban and rural areas, planning needs to do much more to stabilise and upgrade the inner-city districts. This is the essential motivation for Planwerk Innenstadt which the Berlin Senat adopted on 18 May 1999 with the following objectives.

Planwerk Innenstadt objectives

A primary objective of this concept is to create an attractively urban inner city that reaches from Alexanderplatz to the City-West, and which offers an overarching structure with an interconnected network of attractive public spaces. A goal is thus to increase opportunities for living and working in this area as well as to offer support for culture and communication, and with this to maintain and expand on the preconditions for a cosmopolitan life in the inner city.

Berlin's identity should receive a focused expression here in the inner city, where it is possible for visitors to gather and for the urban society to present itself. In addition, residential conditions should be improved where there is existing infrastructure at already attractive locations. It is also a goal within the dense fabric of the inner city to improve the conditions for retail and culture, for hotels, restaurants and a variety of services.

There is consensus that inhospitable and monostructural areas exist in inner-city districts in both East and West: these are largely the result of auto-friendly, functionally segregating planning from the 1950s and 1960s. These areas have more to do with pure residential subdivisions than mixed inner-city neighbourhoods, and are now characterised by their grave losses of socially integrating populations as well as a loss of urbanity. Examples of this include areas around roads such as Lietzenburger Strasse and An der Urania, Leipziger Strasse with Spittelmarkt and Friedrichswerder, Grunerstrasse, Mühlendamm and Molkenmarkt neighbourhoods along with the developments on Karl-Marx-Allee and the Luisenstadt (inner) suburb.

The Planwerk does not offer a completely new design for the inner city, but proposes qualitative improvements through in-fill projects and added activities. This serves to strengthen the connective inner-city structures around the Tiergarten, in the City-West as well as the historical downtown, and it does this without any demolition of existing residential buildings. 'Critical Reconstruction' methods[7] are applied to expose traces of historical development patterns in the downtown area. Modern and post-war urban development projects are valued as they add layers to this historic base, and so altogether a significant inner-city structure is created for Berlin of public street spaces and squares. This redeveloped structure thus does not disown any phase of Berlin's development history.

Process

The refinement of Planwerk Innenstadt concepts and the corresponding public discussion has been underway since November 1996, with the objective of reaching the broadest possible consensus. This has taken place on various levels that relate to each other in terms of process and content: publicly organised discussions and presentations, expert planning workshops and consultant work on particular inner-city concepts.

Public discussions and presentations

The first level of general and fundamental questions concerning Planwerk Innenstadt is dealt with in the public Stadtforum.[8] Special Planwerk problems are also publicly discussed in city-project events, of which 12 have so far taken place. Themes to date have included: re-examining post-war urban design in East and West, analysis of public spaces and traffic in the inner city, new development types and residents, new inner-city building types and their feasibility, citizen participation in inner-city situations, public open and green places, urban society and the future of the inner city, and in addition a range of neighbourhood-specific events.

Another level of discussion includes presentations of concept refinements, that is, in the framework of the exhibition 'Stadtquartiere' (urban quarters) in the Märkisches Museum or a variety of exhibitions in the former State Council Building. These events have been held for the purpose of clarifying a number of essential questions and alternative solutions regarding inner-city themes. Reports and studies documenting Planwerk progress have been presented to various professional associations, which has helped to secure a broad base of support for the ongoing process.

Along with this, a number of other groups have organised their own Planwerk-related events. Lectures coordinated by the Chamber of Commerce and the Association of Berlin-Brandenburg Housing Developers have supported Planwerk's urban development strategy and argued for its implementation.

Focus areas and planning workshops

Specific Planwerk topics are also examined at another level, especially in planning workshops that serve to refine, revise and add detail. Here concepts are debated and alternative solutions are further developed together with representatives of city government, concerned city districts and residents, and property owners. This process has led to realistic local area concepts that enjoy a broad consensus regarding the further development of urban design concepts. Since early 1997 these planning workshops have been carried out on a regular basis with the involvement of independent consultants, leading to a constructive urban design process. Previously held discussions have led to many dozens of Planwerk changes, whereby misunderstandings have been cleared and concerns dealt with in the process of the dialogue.

The inner-city area

The Planwerk Innenstadt area with its 30 square kilometres covers about one-third of the land within the S-Bahn-Ring. This concerns the historical core which is described by the city walls of the seventeenth and eighteenth centuries, and also takes in the new centre of the West. Thus the downtown areas are included that Berlin people identify with in both the East and West. About 300 000 people live here and there are about the same number of jobs in this area. Although these numbers appear at first to be in balance, there are local areas that far from embody a cosmopolitan mix of uses or an inner-city character, but that are instead monostructurally developed as either locations for services or for housing. These districts are also characterised by their autobahn-like streetscapes and large vacant or open areas. They offer potential land area for new construction and in-fill – primarily on publicly owned lands – of about 170 hectares, or enough for about 23 000 residential units together with about two million square metres of total floor area for offices and retail. There is also a great potential here for an upgrading of public spaces.

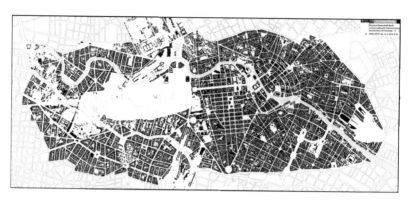

Map 4.2 Central Berlin around 1940

Map 4.3 Central Berlin around 1989

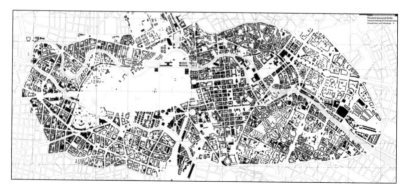

Map 4.4 Central Berlin around 2010

Sectoral planning

The small-scale densification and mix of uses proposed by the Planwerk point to a city of shorter transportation distances and improved connections. The Planwerk traffic concept proposes a so-called 'reduction model' for the inner city, whereby through traffic would be hindered by applying a variety of traffic controlling and speed-reducing measures. Single-person vehicle trips would be reduced to about 20 per cent of the total volume, to the advantage of public transport. This strategy would not limit mobility but it would substantially reduce environmental pollution.

With respect to traffic-caused noise pollution, local studies have shown that not only reductions in traffic flow can lead to improvements in the environmental quality, but that complementary new structures along the streets can produce such positive effects.[9]

The open space concept is based on a system of varying types of high quality public spaces. A strengthening is planned of clearly formulated and structurally defined public open spaces, such as urban squares, gardens and parks. Also dealt with here is a greening of streetscapes, and street landscaping or building setbacks that are of no clear use are to be redesigned.

The ability of existing social forms of infrastructure (schools, day-care and youth centres) to deal with additional residential construction has been studied. The results reveal that a considerable surplus in capacity exists for the near-term, due to substantial population decreases in mixed housing areas. Considering schools in the urban district of Mitte for example, the current need is found to be only two-thirds of the existing capacity, and this ratio is expected to decrease in ten years down to only a half. Questions of school closures will be unavoidable in the future. With this in mind, the Planwerk densification concept offers an ecological and sustainable approach to resource use.

The majority of buildable land in the inner city is located on easily accessible, exceptionally wide streets and easements. One of the main arguments for Planwerk is the relatively low cost involved in developing such land that is already publicly owned. Feasibility studies of a number of areas in the inner city showed that housing for middle-class groups could be built on such lots by private developers even without public subsidies. An objective here is a relatively small-scale division of ground lots that will encourage projects that are owner-managed and built. It is hoped that such small to middle-sized developers will live in their projects and put down roots in these neighbourhoods in such a way that middle-class, socially integrating households will again be attracted to reside in the inner city. It is also hoped that new building types will be constructed, and that the 'Stadthaus' (town house) will serve as a model for such new structures. This concept of smaller scale, diverse building types is sustainable in that it is flexible with respect to economic changes, and as such structures are, relatively speaking, less threatened than larger monolithic buildings by vacancies and vandalism.

Such a structure of building lots could also reclaim otherwise buried layers of historical development patterns in the older core of the city. Further, this would redevelop and strengthen the identity and character of the city centre with a lively variety of architecture, creating places for citizens to gather.

Conclusion

The conceptual phase of Planwerk Innenstadt is complete after working through an intensive three years. In this time a lively discourse was carried on between planners and citizens, politicians and administrators and representatives of various interest groups, leading to a broad consensus in many areas of planning for Berlin. These often controversial discussions also provided access to many in Berlin to the cultural resource of urban history and its identity-strengthening aspects. A result of this is a raised awareness of common roots and a greater consensus regarding the European City as a development model for Berlin.

Planwerk Innenstadt was adopted by the Berlin Senat on 18 May 1999 as an overall city planning framework and then recognised by the Berlin Parliament. In addition to its contributions to theoretical debates, this plan has taken on a practical and binding meaning for future planning in the centre of Berlin.

Notes

1 Senatsverwaltung für Stadtentwicklung, Umweltschutz und Technologie (ed.), *Planwerk Innenstadt Berlin – Ein erster Entwurf* (Berlin: Kulturbuchverlag, 1997); Senatsverwaltung für Stadtentwicklung, Umweltschutz und Technologie (ed.), *Planwerk – Next Generation: Internationale Hochschulprojekte zum Planwerk Innenstadt Berlin* (Berlin: Kulturbuchverlag, 1998); Senatsverwaltung für Stadtentwicklung, Umweltschutz und Technologie (ed.), *Planwerk Innenstadt: Machbarkeitsstudien für den instrumentellen Bereich* (Berlin: Kulturbuchverlag, 1998); Senatsverwaltung für Stadtentwicklung,

Umweltschutz und Technologie (ed.), *Planwerk Innenstadt Berlin: Ergebnis, Prozess, sektorale Planungen und Werkstätten* (Berlin: Kulturbuchverlag, 1998).

2 Legal planning instruments can be complemented with so-called informal planning. Official planning in Germany is particularly determined by the land use plan (Flächennutzungsplan) and building plan (Bebauungsplan). Informal processes such as urban design competitions are generally used to create a foundation for formal planning instruments such as building plans that are legally binding. Cities can also adopt informal planning instruments in ways that are at least partially binding.

3 Urban design competitions in Germany are organised according to official principles and guidelines. Through this process planners submit designs in response to given building programmes. An independent jury selects the best concepts through a documented and anonymous process. The authors of the winning entries are then involved in a search for appropriate designers that will carry out and refine the development plans.

4 The area is now characterised by its old industrial structures, vacant fields, and a former air strip. A new urban district is to be built here over the next two decades, covering about 465 hectares and including a landscaped park of 70 hectares in its centre. The Science City will involve technical and natural sciences research departments from the Humboldt University in Berlin, a media district and a technology park with commercial activities, as well as services and residential areas. Thirty thousand jobs and housing for 13 000 people are to be created here

5 Estimates by the Ministry for Urban Development, Environmental Protection and Technology. Statistically consistent data were not available for the period under consideration.

6 In early 1999 Berlin set up 15 different Urban Quarter Management demonstration projects, with the intention of exploring new paths in the field of social urban development. An objective here is to encourage many small projects and positive developments in a wide range of areas. Another goal is both to empower and manage, meaning to activate and coordinate the positive energies and resources that are to be found in every urban quarter. A foundation for this process is provided by the local knowledge of the citizens living and working in these quarters. This knowledge serves as a starting point for political action and for the development of projects and initiatives.

7 The modern urban design principles that shaped and radically changed post-war Berlin had distanced themselves from development concepts that were valid for centuries and rejected accepted design traditions of the European City. Streets, squares, parks, blocks and buildings were no longer seen as compositional urban building elements that worked together to create built environments. Increasing criticism of modern urban design principles and the resulting theoretical debates led to the development of the theory of Critical Reconstruction. This theory emerged in Berlin through the International Building Exhibition (1987) as a strategy for development in historical districts. Critical Reconstruction is a new interpretation of the European City model, with its specific places and their respective histories that relate to particular city development patterns, scale, composition and a mix of uses.

8   The Stadtforum (City Forum) – founded in April 1991 as an advisory
     council to the Ministry for Urban Development under Minister Volker
     Hassemer (CDU) – has taken on an important role with its publicly- oriented
     planning processes. Through public discussions the Stadtforum has dealt
     with fundamental questions and planning alternatives regarding Berlin's
     future. Particular details have been further discussed in the CityProjects
     (StadtProjekte) event series. The subject matter was expanded when
     Minister Peter Strieder (SPD) took over the Stadtforum in January 1996. In
     addition to questions regarding traditional urban planning, Stadtforum has
     been dealing with issues of society and culture, sustainability and globalisa-
     tion, and the changing nature of the urban population. The Stadtforum has
     already met 77 times.

9   Studies done by GRI traffic consultants regarding areas including
     Spittelmarkt, Fischerinsel, Luisenstadt and Lietzenburgerstrasse/An der
     Urania. The studies were commissioned by the Berlin Ministry for Urban
     Development, Environmental Protection and Technology.

5
Struggle for the Inner City – a Plan Becomes a Declaration of War

Simone Hain

In contrast to Belfast torn by an internal conflict, the city of Berlin with its Wall was generally speaking a victim of an international conflict, the Cold War. A 'hot' civil war conflict was fortunately not an experience the city had to undergo. But precisely for this reason the city should be prepared to learn from the Northern Ireland capital city. It is very unfortunate to see the disregard with which the city administration in effect provokes internal conflicts between East and West Berliners and in irresponsible fashion fuels the flames through its official urban planning.

Planwerk Innenstadt: commercial imperatives

What is at issue is Planwerk Innenstadt (inner city plan, see Map 4.1), as it is known, which during its preparatory phase was also described as a 'master plan'. This comprehensive plan which was drawn up in 1996 and covers the inner city urban districts of Berlin can be seen as a reaction to the sluggish demand for new office and commercial buildings which were erected in speculative fashion on formerly nationally owned land after the Wall came down. New gigantic structures along Friedrichstrasse and other central locations are still standing empty after many years. One reason for this is that the sophisticated inner city residential clientele for smart shopping malls and expensive restaurants still needs to become established. The inhabitants of Tiergarten, Central (Mitte) district and Kreuzberg, traditionally more working-class areas, do not take to being urban flâneurs or fit very well into the theatrical creation of a new urban way of life. Furthermore, the urban design structure does not communicate adequate metropolitan flair

69

and attractiveness to tourists. The current crisis in the commercial property market, which during a brief feverish boom grabbed all the available land for building, can better be resolved with the creation of high-class residential buildings for a clientele suitable to capital-city living. The new ideal in Planwerk Innenstadt of mixed use in the city centre – that is, living and working in the same area – can be seen as laid, as it were like a template, upon the large-scale lay-out of green spaces and roads comprising the open plan, post-war cityscape, where building land in public ownership can still be grabbed.

Planwerk: seeking legitimacy in uniting a divided city

In the glossy publicity brochures produced by the Berlin Senat (City and State government) there is a predilection to term the plan for the inner city a programme of reintegration for the two halves of the city after forty years of division. It is suggested that they really now ought to be reflecting upon their joint roots in history which have been buried during the post-war modern reconstruction phase. This past, ostensibly indivisible, is seen as a mutual source for east and west Berliners in creating an identity and crystallised in the ground plan of the city from the medieval to the early German Empire period particularly in the historical city centre: narrow streets, densely and multiple-owned and built neighbourhoods as well as the distinctive urban design styles of past ages. The image of the old city is supposed to arise again through the restoration of private ownership rights and by building over the modern city of roads and open spaces, breaking them up into small plots. Literally any middle-class inhabitant of the city will, as promised in the advertising, be able to repurchase these plots of land in public ownership, which will be offered for sale at 'political' prices, that is, considerably below the commercial value. Associated with this process is the hope that the inhabitants of Berlin will, after the dictatorships of the twentieth century, be able to return to their individual interests and bourgeois roots. At the same time, living in the city centre, as previously mentioned, will be encouraged and the flight from the city reversed. Motorised streams of traffic will literally be deprived of the precious ground beneath their wheels and clearly defined boundaries will be drawn between private and public land. Picturesque scenes will exist once more, in places where, it is claimed, rebuilding in the modern style left nothing but draughty, derelict or unused land and bare plots.

Planwerk: a declaration of war against the East

One glance at the first draft of the plan dated November 1996[1] reveals the Planwerk area processed in such depth as to show the detail of individual buildings stretching from the railway terminus station known as Zoologischer Garten in the western part of the city to the eastern terminus of Ostbahnhof in the district of Friedrichshain. Scattered between these locations are the major building projects currently in progress, in particular at the Potsdamer Platz site and in the Federal government quarters. However, the attack is concentrated on the built fabric of the eastern inner city. In the area once enclosed by the medieval defensive walls, desired new buildings will outweigh the current building stock. In this area the former plot boundaries have been incorporated into the plan with painstaking accuracy. This signal indicates that there are to be no mammoth projects extending over more than one block, no 'investor style refrigerator oblongs' all turned out of the same mould. On the contrary there are to be small stitches which gradually fill in the open spaces characteristic of the post-war city. Planwerk Innenstadt appears therefore to deny to global mega-actors their smooth capture of prominent sites, yet, conversely, it is at the same time a declaration of war against the other player, the public owner as major land-holding body. Prefabricated, large residential estates of the state socialist modern period will not be given a chance to find their own character. Wherever there is a too 'open' location, an open space which invites development, a Planwerk entry proposes immediately that the past be reinstated. Thus, using small-scale planning elements, it is possible to revision or replan the old royal urban district where, nowadays, the 2nd section of the Karl-Marx-Allee estate stands; or to bring back the bygone, demolished fishermen's hamlet on Fischerinsel (Fisherman's Island), where now five modern tower blocks house more people than the 'Old Berlin' picturesque neighbourhood. The new buildings scheduled in Planwerk Innenstadt are located amazingly close to these post-war buildings which are hardly more than 25 years old. They take over the play area, the sunbathing lawn and the garden of the old people's home. As well as light and sun, they are depriving these buildings of the characteristic quality of modern free-standing structures. The present building and land use arrangements are destabilised by means of a planning strategy which makes only too clear which way the wind is blowing: in the direction of a city with traditionally divided-up plots and thus a privatised ownership structure as far as land is concerned.

A colonisation by new settlers

Using this reconstruction plan for the inner city roughly in accordance with the pre-war street lay-out, approximately 30 hectares of publicly owned land will be privatised and set free for the use of 25 000 apartment buyers on top of a further two million square metres designated for commercial use. Right in the middle of large housing estates and mega-structures in post-war modern development, small-scale plot structures have been inserted. In this context, the language is one of providing 'enclosed private open space' and 'clearly defined residential complex sites' which are to be developed as 'sustainable urban quarters' with a promising future. 'Enclosed', 'clearly defined' and 'private' are value-laden concepts, which are being brought to bear in the debate in opposition to the fundamental socialised principle of the post-war city. Thus, the 30 square kilometres in the inner city of Berlin are seen as a continuous area which is to be colonised on land which is ready and waiting. However, the area is by no means depopulated as the references to 'urban wasteland' or 'deserted area' might imply. On the contrary, some 300 000 people live there, whose interests – with regard to well-planned green areas, sun and low rents – are now to be placed on the scales against the interests of 25 000 new settlers. In addition, there are the expectations of several million East Germans who believe that they have a right to find in the future some reminders of their former capital city. This means not only to continue using the Palast der Republik (Palace of the Republic),[2] but also to be able to trace in the former city centre the history of the state which was their starting point as they set out into the new and reunited republic.

The conflict

The whole Planwerk Innenstadt could all too easily be seen as merely a question of taste or of town planning theory. However, behind these plans – which are argued in aesthetic and seemingly neutral town planning policy terms – the drive to return to the density and street pattern of the past represents a resolution in favour of massive redistribution of public property or wealth and an interest in transforming the population structure in the district. Nothing less than this can be meant when reference is made in Planwerk to 'cost neutral' action in selling off land in order to allow shared history to find its voice once more in the old town part of Berlin's city centre. The Fischerinsel example, perhaps, makes a coming conflict concrete. In front of, alongside and behind the publicly owned, social apartments with their open spaces, owner-occupier units on small plots will be incorporated in new private dwellings. Each client will need to prove capital backing of at least several million marks in order to have an acceptable credit rating as builder. It is hard to believe that this competition for what is still publicly owned land can be conducted without serious conflict. In the first instance, an acute legal conflict arises. Who has the authority to control, or dispose of, collective property and determine the living environment of present inner-city dwellers? This is the question confronting at least one-third of Berlin's inhabitants since 29 November 1996 when the inner city plan was first presented to the public. What happens to the existing residents who are not able or willing to partake in selling off so-called 'modern wasteland areas' whilst the rest of the population feel Planwerk has invited them to be part of important 'colonising' projects in East Berlin's inner city.

Protest

Planwerk Innenstadt, which the city planning authorities describe as Berlin's route away from internal division, was a political issue of the first magnitude, even before its official presentation. As early as June 1996, when the first internal announcements were made, the town planning officers of the districts involved rejected unanimously any and every planning move by the Berlin Ministry of Urban Development which duplicated and ran counter to their own area development planning.[3] The issue here was to maintain local planning control in district hands. In the months to follow, as far as committed citizens were concerned, matters of controversy were, in particular, the question of defining communal property and rights to public space.[4] Immediately after the plan was announced, even Volker Hassemer, the former Minister for Urban Development, permitted himself to be quoted in the Süddeutsche Zeitung with a statement describing Planwerk Innenstadt as: '... taking possession of land like the lord of the manor'.[5] On the other hand, the proponents of the plan launched a propaganda campaign in which there were references to 'open-heart surgery'[6] and the need for political decisions which were long overdue. In view of a potential of 2.5 million square metres of gross floor area, they suggested it was a question of enforcing the 'distinctive worth of the solid citizen' and breaking the East Berlin hegemony comprised of grass-root, aggressively dogmatic know-alls, a protest, fed by the 'green' alternative culture scene, social-democratic lyricism on the side of the underdog and Ost-algie (nostalgia for the East). The tone of Dieter Hoffmann-Axthelm, chief town planner responsible for the Planwerk was that '… if you want land for building, you have to push this through at the political level'. In an unconsidered moment, when talking to journalists, he expanded his views pointing out that it is merely a question of stirring up the 'safari park'[7] in the east, because '… really, they cannot dig in there [in the city centre – author's note] forever'.[8]

Originally intended to be presented for a vote within five weeks, a two and a half year marathon of discussions was engendered, due to protests from citizens' action groups, professional bodies such as the Berlin Chamber of Architects and political parties. This took place within the structures of the official Stadtforum[9] (city forum) and in the 'alternative' Stadtforum von Unten (city forum from below), in universities and in community planning workshops. In the course of these discussions, a considerable number of experts from a wide variety of disciplines put forward well-founded criticisms of the whole procedure,[10] including the essential premises and objective. However, whereas articles supportive of the plan were placed in numerous publishing organs, dissenting views frequently disappeared from sight.

An example from personal experience of the suppression of dissent
To mention only one significant expert view, an extensive statement of opinion on Planwerk Innenstadt, arrived at after several meetings by the Regional Monuments Preservation Committee, was never published by the Ministry. It remained without any response whatsoever. As the deputy chairperson of this Committee, I would like to quote from the position paper in question, which for lack of interest within the city was finally documented in the members' magazine of the Architects' Association.[11] A Berlin Deputy Minister, annoyed by this move, was then heard to state that the committee's minute-taker had abused her position of trust as a member of the Monuments Preservation Committee. In the position statement, a development principle was urged to be applied, 'which takes into account the multifarious nature of the layers and achievements in town planning history, right up to the most recent past'. The following extract from the report is worth quoting in full:

> Within the scope of the proposed historical reconstruction, the currently existing ground plan position should be read as a historical document and very precisely analysed in the layers of which it is

comprised. In the course of this process, very particular importance should be attributed to the unique topography originating from the division of the city. In terms of fraught East–West polarity, expressed in townscape structure and semantics, the historical significance of Berlin – the international conflict between systems in the second half of the twentieth century – should be made perceptible for present-day tourists and future generations. The still transmissible characteristic feature of the contradictory 'double city', accessible in ground plan and design, is of vital commemorative value. Furthermore, particular attention should be paid to the contemporary cultural epoch of modern urban reconstruction after the Second World War. The present position of the relevant building stock should be carefully evaluated in an international comparison with other cities belonging to this historical period, such as Rotterdam, Coventry, Warsaw, Volgograd, Le Havre and Hiroshima. One of the most important characteristics of modern urban development with its 'open plan' style of building is the use which is made of the surrounding open space, which is integrated into architectural structures and is valid as an element within this structuring. Planwerk reveals, in this respect, current discredit and catastrophic lack of acceptance for art history and town planning history as seen in significant Berlin buildings and complexes dating from the 1950s and 60s. The eastern part of the city centre is, to a major degree, coloured by socialist town planning ideas. Here large-scale ensembles are preserved, structured in depth and on the basis of a different law of real estate. As part of town planning in a symbolic fashion, architectural items in their extensive structuring, worthy of a capital city, could, in every sense of the term, be considered authentic memorials of the art of urban planning and landscape design of that now concluded period: Karl-Marx-Allee, Alexanderplatz, Leninplatz, Nikolaiviertel, the huge 'Berlin's garden' forming the focal point of the central axis, as it is known ... It seems, furthermore, not very convincing to suggest that the consensus-forming objective of an 'urban regeneration or reconstruction through dialogue' ought to be or could be implemented in one and the same spot by using confrontational over-layering of different grammatical structures or styles. Rather, designed complexes of different architectural periods and decades should continue to exist alongside one another, with equal legitimacy; by means of further development in urban design they should be set effectively in relation to one another ....[12]

Press coverage

The above is extracted from professional argumentation by a committee, nominated personally by the Minister of Urban Development, consisting of members with impeccable professional qualifications – experts in monuments conservation, historians, architects, sociologists, investors and writers. In public debate contexts there has, on the other hand, been far less restraint in expression. Perhaps some of the following quotes from letters to the editor of the *Frankfurter Allgemeine Zeitung* will make clear what is at the root of the matter. When the FAZ, prompted by an essay dealing with the achievements and concepts of reconstruction in East Berlin after the war, wrote in a headline on 18 December 1995 that a gulf of fear is dividing Germany through its very centre, it was exclusively western Berlin readers who felt prompted to riposte in violent fashion. One writer fumed:

> Don't you agree that the GDR just let the country go to rack and ruin in a deplorable fashion, much worse than it was in Poland, Czechoslovakia, Bohemia and Hungary? ... Do you really believe new buildings in the GDR and in 'East Berlin' are worth preserving, not to mention whether one should have a sentimental affection for them? I believe it is a positive move that we are now actually clearing up this architectural trash and that in a few decades we will once again have a city which is worth looking at.

And another reader exclaims in amazement:

> Your view is completely topsy-turvy. What, on the contrary, do we see? With a few exceptions, everything laid to waste, the heart gone out of it, Bitterfeld in Berlin.[13] Below ground supply systems have had it, so have roads, house fronts, railways and tramlines, balconies are falling down along the whole length of some streets. That's how it is with these Communists, they spoil everything which already exists and leave behind a desert, as well as emptiness in people's minds![14]

East Berlin building achievements and their denigration

In the intervening period since the Wall came down, mutual bad feelings have become hardened into deep-rooted friction between East and West.[15] It was, therefore, not possible to provide impartial information to a wider public about the considerable and varied history of building in the eastern part of Berlin. This includes not only the controversial demolition of the remains of the Stadtschloss (City Palace), but also concurrent work to rebuild the National Opera House and the entire complex of cultural buildings known as the Forum Friedericianum; not only new residential building along Stalinallee[16] but also building new public parks, Alexanderplatz, the Nikolaiviertel (quarter) and the complex of buildings and square at Gendarmenmarkt.[17] It is still, even nowadays, possible to hear construction workers in East Berlin pubs recounting how adventurous and risky it was, rebuilding, for example, the Zeughaus or Arsenal building (Museum of German History), the Berlin Cathedral or the synagogue in Oranienburgerstrasse. They say they would not have believed it possible to put those crumbling ruins together again. They still talk of the great ballroom in the Palast der Republik, a miracle of modern building technology, and when it was extended for the first time to its full size how it was as complicated as rigging a four-master out on the ocean. However, due to the dominance of an opposing point of view, these anecdotes no longer have any social relevance. If the former nation (GDR) and its inhabitants are only perceived as a destructive force, naturally there cannot be any experts who might perhaps nowadays be brought in to collaborate on development or urban design projects. As expressed by Hans Stimmann, Berlin's Building Director:

> ... the entire professional position of architects was almost entirely abandoned, with a very few minor imperceptible exceptions, in the GDR and other Soviet Bloc countries. Along with the disappearance of the whole of the middle class, there is no longer anyone who understands what commissioning a building means. The concept of a 'builder' presupposes that a person is able to make some kind of cultural statement, to be able to consider in an informed way colours, shape, size of rooms, lighting, interior decoration and furnishing, and numerous other factors ... We have inherited a city of 1.3 million inhabitants and are governing it with the builders' sensitivity derived from the much-maligned West Berlin. (Because the) ... educated middle class with its highly refined eating habits, dress, consumption, etc. has gone. These things need to grow up again. The result is that, with the abolition of the architect as the bearer of design refinement in construction, a building design desert or vacuum arose. This must first of all be re-cultivated, ... People are much needed here to get the process moving again.[18]

The logical consequence of such a notion meant finally that emphatically not one single East Berlin architect or town planner was involved in Planwerk Innenstadt. On the contrary, there were two planning teams from the West. Thus it was obviously pre-programmed that there would be confrontations with Eastern Berlin experts in building, including those from the dissolved Construction Academy of the GDR and totally disregarded, 'non-person', architects. The controversy has risen to such a peak in temperature that it is now customary to refer to Berlin's 'nervous' climate. An attempt is made in Table 5.1 to summarise the position briefly. All the qualitative statements are either condensed or actual reproductions of arguments put forward in discussions about Planwerk.

Conclusion: the damage done

East Berlin experts and inhabitants as will now be apparent, together with a minority of west Berlin residents, became politically active over Planwerk Innenstadt in the interests of the city. This was not new. In the past they acted when the entire area surrounding and including Alexanderplatz was destined for the bulldozer and when the future of the Palast der Republik was being discussed. In reaction to Planwerk they drew up opposing plans, worked out residents' expert documents, compiled extensive analyses and pamphlets and directed hundreds of letters and submissions to the Minister of Urban Development. Every single one of these interventions was ignored. Open letters to Berlin newspapers were not published.[19] At the highest point of exhaustion amongst those involved,[20] Planwerk with amendments was passed by the governing Great Coalition (of Social Democrats and Christian Democrats) in June 1999. This single parliamentary decision, at the culmination of a debate which had been extremely emotionally involved, leaves behind it unprecedented damage in Berlin 'home affairs' policy. Despite a reduced scope, Planwerk drives forward a privatisation plan radically affecting, in the absence of actual demand, publicly owned land and properties.

This plan is based on a concept of history which sees the post-war historical period as abnormal, ahistorical and ultimately destructive. It thus in symbolic fashion, ignores forty years of an urban double existence – which was after all of major historical and international importance. Whenever reference is made to Berlin's identity, apart from the roots of the bourgeois city in the last century, it is always in terms of the former Western city at the forefront of the Cold War, with its former shop window function, which the city acquired in the con-

Table 5.1 Crucial West–East differences in perception and evaluation of the eastern inner city

	West	East
Perception	at last Berlin has its historical city centre again	this is what we rebuilt after the war
	some beautiful old buildings have survived the war, otherwise everything else has been smashed by those Communists	the buildings (Palast der Republik) belong to us
		memories of a living capital city
	very draughty derelict urban areas	cast out on to the scrapheap from public institutions and industry
	museums, theatres, 'in' places	public buildings returned to previous owners or knocked down
	beyond Alexanderplatz there is nothing but the Russian steppe ('Outer Mongolia')	the best locations have been given up/ fallen derelict
		theatres and places of entertainment not funded
		you just don't recognise where you are any more
		'investors building slabs'
		ruthlessness in town planning (Alexanderplatz)
		premises standing empty
		devastation in open spaces (no fountains or flowers)
		picture galleries and pubs, but no small food shops

Table 5.1 (continued)

	West	East
Activities	culture, investment, work, tourism, leisure, living, design	living, shopping, leisure, work, politics
Interests	economic, professional, political cultural	central to life, political, environmentally committed
Mutual conversation	we really have to talk in a controversial way to the 'east Berliners', because all their ideas are so old-fashioned	how on earth can we manage to understand and respect one another – for the sake of German unification
Advanced conflict positions	'Eastern safari park', they just can't stay there forever!	So long as nothing harms them, we don't exist as far as they're concerned
Sources of friction	the east is xenophobic and is forming a 'people's society'	the residents' association: 'We are all going to stay put' (they won't get us out) it's not worth wasting breath: the west is asocial, stupid and elitist
Escalating positions	contempt, scorn, passive aggression	contempt, hate, obstructiveness, boycott, reactive aggression

frontation between the two rival systems. Rather, it could well be the urban design and socio-spatial legacies of those decades which we now ought to recognise and through monuments conservation policy pass on to future generations as opposing symbols of the social systems they represented.

The theme of 'rebuilding the historical city centre with a view to a new centre' is a Berlin version of 'retrogressive urban planning'.[21] It forms a part of other international trends to deal with acute socio-spatial problems in city centre areas at the expense of the local residents' milieu. In Berlin, the euphemistic term for neo-liberal market strategies is 'acquiring land for building'. In more critical terminology it would be possible to refer rather to the politically sanctioned selling off of communal properties. This land lying vacant as roads and open spaces, is, however, in no sense of the term 'a no man's land'. On the contrary it has legitimate owners and users and those in possession are determinedly involved in the planning process.

Over a period of two and a half years, several hundred East Berlin residents and experts have taken part in this debate without any remuneration for their work, in contrast to the paid western agencies and consultancy offices. They are now learning that all their efforts to achieve consensus have been in vain, and on the contrary they have been publicly and noisily declared incapable of deciding their affairs themselves. It can be predicted that a process which was not conducted in good faith with democratic public participation and enlightened urban planning practices will now turn around into obstruction, depression or even violent altercations.

In the course of this 'open heart surgery', ostensibly in favour of 'mental reunification' as was claimed, what is at issue is ultimately a symbolic style of politics which is intended to demonstrate, expressed in numerous heated statements, who did actually win the Cold War, you or us? Instead of gradually breaking down 'the wall in people's minds', by means of confidence-building measures and patient work in conjunction with residents, a new 'social wall' is being put up, by attributing the status of residents of the city to the colonisers alone. All the remainder are 'those affected', and, according to an interview with Peter Strieder, Minister of Urban Development, their interests could not possibly influence future-oriented or sustainable urban planning.

But what sort of future is being envisaged here? Is it one in which the capital-loaded colonisers will have to protect themselves from the children of the deprived, using electronic surveillance camera systems? 'Gated communities' with enclosed private residential courts alongside the tower blocks on Fischerinsel? This struggle for social and spatial distribution was launched by a government planning document. It would be better if Berlin's political ruling classes had recollected in good time that modern town planning in the twentieth century was committed in its origins to a strategy of social redistribution, to easing social conflicts and to public provision of space. It is surely a priority to work against civil war and revolutions arising from pauperised and disenfranchised classes, by restraining or completely abandoning speculation over land and real estate.

Notes

1   *See* Ch. 4.
2   During the 1970s there was constructed on the site of the ruined Stadtschloss (formerly owned by the ruling Hohenzollern dynasty) a multifunctional public building called the Palast der Republik. This post-modern functionalist 'super box' was the location for – in addition to the parliament, the People's Chamber – numerous public entertainment institutions: theatres, art galleries, tenpin bowling gallery, post office, shops and discotheques, together with an absolutely remarkable gigantic room which could be adapted to many functions. This 'palace of the people and of culture' formed the focal point and the keystone of the newly laid out central representational axis of the GDR capital city, which was an element of town planning dating back to the 1950s; the palace became an extremely popular location for visitors from all over the Republic. The public areas of the building in the central entrance area were, as it were, the corso of the GDR, where people came to see and be seen. Closed up for almost ten years now because of asbestos risks, the Palace is the target of demolition wishes because of the claim that it is ugly. The entire West German political elite seems to be determined to confront openly East Germans and numerous experts, and against their expressed wishes for the Palace to be preserved, will try during the course of the next two years to remove the most significant GDR construction in favour of rebuilding the old Stadtschloss.
3   In its capacity as a Federal state of the FRG, Berlin is both a city and a state. Many tasks in building law which in other urban areas are the responsibility of the town council are in Berlin local authority or urban district (Bezirk) spheres of responsibility.
4   Leading vehicles for vehement protests – from a wide political spectrum ranging from the Green Party to the Christian Democrats – were the inner city area newspaper *Scheinschlag* and the *Tageszeitung*; later also the Berlin tenants' paper *Mieterecho*, and the NGBK, Berlin Association for Modern Art which held an exhibition entitled 'Randstadt Baustop' (Neue Gesellschaft für Bildende Kunst (ed.), *Dokumentation der Ausstellung und Aktionen vom 28.8.–11.10.98* (Berlin: published by the Neue Gesellschaft für Bildende Kunst, 1998) and the daily paper *Junge Welt* which ran a voluminous series of articles in 1996 by Hans G. Helms.

5 M. Heuwagen, 'Landnahme nach Gutsherrenart. Wegen massiver Kritik will Senator Peter Strieder das Planwerk Innenstadt öffentlich zur Diskussion stellen', *Süddeutsche Zeitung*, 12 December (1997).
6 K. Hartung, 'Der Hauptstadtplan. Operation am offenen Herzen', *Die Zeit*, no. 49, 29 November (1996).
7 *Der Spiegel*, no. 49, 2 December (1996).
8 This last remark by Hoffmann-Axthelm is witnessed by Barbara Jakubeit, Berlin's former Building Director, as an answer to her amazed question: 'But I always thought you were left-wing?'
9 *See*, Ch. 4, n. 8.
10 Specifically by Hans Adrian, Werner Durth, Georg Mörsch, Hartmut Häußermann amongst others.
11 *Der Architekt*, Vol. 12, December (1997) 721 et seq.
12 Ibid.
13 Bitterfeld, the area in Saxony-Anhalt dominated by the GDR chemical industry, became a symbol for neglect and deterioration of the physical environment.
14 *Frankfurter Allgemeine Zeitung*, December (1995).
15 Examples of friction have by now become tangible: in the absence of a more recent survey, I would point to that commissioned by *Süddeutsche Zeitung* in 1995, which was a representative cross-section sample poll. Whereas in 1990 51 per cent of the East German population accepted the Western German political system, five years later this figure had fallen to only 33 per cent. In 'West Germany' at the time the figure was 86 per cent, to give a comparison. Whereas one in three 'East Germans' stated that neither of the two systems was now able to persuade them, the percentage figure of those supporting the GDR system had doubled from an original 11 to now 22 per cent.
16 The former name of Karl-Marx-Allee.
17 An attempt to provide insights into the values and significance of the eastern city centre is given by the author in the following collection of essays: Institute for Regional Development and Structural Planning IRS (ed.): *Archäologie und Aneignung. Ideen, Pläne und Stadtfiguration. Aufsätze zur Ostberliner Stadtentwicklung nach 1945* (Erkner: published by IRS, 1996).
18 H. Stimmann, 'Discussion paper presented at the Trade Fair Constructa 92 in Hanover on 8 February 1992', Senatsverwaltung für Bau- und Wohnungswesen (ed.), *Pro Bauakademie. Argumente für eine Neugründung* (Berlin: by the Senatsverwaltung, 1992).
19 For example Bruno Flierl, Open letter to Peter Strieder with regard to Planwerk Innenstadt Berlin; joint expertise on Spittelmarkt by the Flierl–Kny–Krause group dated 16 February 1998. Open but unpublished letters were also written by the action groups and tenants' associations in Fischerinsel and Leipziger Strasse.
20 R. Lautenschläger, 'Vom Planwerk zum Restwerk', *Die Tageszeitung*, 2 June (1999).
21 This has been defined as a political response to the tremendous social restructuring processes which have occurred since the 1970s. In the first place, this reaction is aiming to regain for itself the city and the whole country. From the point of view of the rulers and the elites it is the home-less, the immigrants, the blacks, the trade unionists and the so-called

minorities who have taken away or stolen the cities and the country from them. And now it is their turn and time for them to reconquer the cities. *See*, N. Smith, *New Urban Frontier. Gentrification and the Revanchist City* (London: Routledge & Kegan Paul, 1996) and: StadtRat (ed.), *Umkämpfte Räume: Strategien in der Stadt* (Hamburg, Berlin, Göttingen: Libertäre Assoziation, 1998).

6

Victorian and Edwardian Belfast: Preserving the Architectural Legacy of the Inner City

C.E.B. Brett

Thirty years ago, Belfast was a predominantly Victorian and Edwardian city, with a very strong character of its own. During the nineteenth century, it had grown from a small Georgian market town to a great industrial city, manufacturing first cotton, then linen; after which it turned to engineering and shipbuilding. This brought an influx of workers from the countryside, especially after the Famine. Protestant workers settled largely in East Belfast and worked in the shipyard; Roman Catholic workers settled largely in West Belfast and worked in the linen mills. (That is of course an over-simplification, but largely true.) In 1800 the population stood at around 20 000; in 1831, 50 000; in 1861, 120 000; in 1891, when for the first time it outstripped Dublin, 250 000; by 1901, it had reached 350 000. It reached a peak of nearly 450 000 in 1951. Since then, the population of Belfast within the city boundary has declined sharply, possibly now to below 300 000, though the population of the urban area as a whole appears somewhat to have increased, depending where the boundary is drawn. However it is not only the population which has declined, but also the industrial base, and with it the visual character of the city, especially the inner city.

The architectural legacy

The heart of the Victorian city lay close to the quays and harbour of the dredged River Lagan. The Custom House and the Harbour Office, warehouses and banks, the memorial to Prince Albert, the old parish church and St George's church, all tended to cluster fairly close to the waterfront. But in the second half of the nineteenth century, the town's centre of gravity began to shift southward. And, at the turn of the century, it was to acquire a series of monumental buildings designed, I believe, whether consciously or unconsciously, to demonstrate and emphasise not only the new self-importance of Belfast, but also its independence from Dublin. These included: the Presbyterian Assemblies Building, with its spire modelled on that of St Giles' cathedral in Edinburgh, completed in 1905; St Anne's Church of Ireland cathedral, still lacking its spire almost a century later, started a few years earlier; the Technical College, modelled on the War Office in London, completed in 1907; and, grandest of all, the fine new City Hall, completed in 1905. It has occurred to me to compare this group of buildings with their near-contemporaries in Budapest – the Parliament House, completed in 1904; the Basilica of St Stephen, completed in 1905; the National Gallery and the reconstructed Matthiaskirche, both completed in 1896; the Fisherman's Bastion, completed in 1902 – all designed to emphasise the independence of Budapest from Vienna.

Fig. 6.1 The Albert Clock, long regarded as the centre of Belfast

The Georgian buildings of Belfast were, for the most part, built of locally made brick, since there was no good indigenous building stone close at hand; in the first half of the nineteenth century, as in England, rough brickwork or random rubblestone was often coated in stucco, and painted to resemble stone; but in the years of prosperity, during the second half of the century, imported stone was usually used for buildings of social significance. The standard of craftsmanship in Victorian and Edwardian Belfast was exceptionally high; sculpture, woodcarving, ornamentation of every kind was lavishly applied to new buildings. This tradition, unhappily, came to an abrupt end during the 1914–18 war, when many tradesmen were killed at the Somme or elsewhere on the Western front. It is only now beginning to revive.

The inter-war years

The inter-war years saw little change in the architectural fabric of Belfast, apart from the devolved Parliament housed on the outskirts of the city at Stormont, opened in 1933, and the Royal Courts of Justice not far from the Lagan, opened in 1934. A number of holes were punched in its fabric by the two major German bombing raids of 1941,

Fig. 6.2 Belfast City Hall completed in 1905, whose dome superseded the Albert Clock as the centre of Belfast

when more civilians were killed in a single night than in any other British city, except London. But in essence, the city I explored with a notebook between 1960 and 1965 was as it had been in 1914: a respectable handful of eighteenth-century, or later, Georgian buildings, and a street pattern largely laid out at that period; a great wealth of handsome and, often, ornate churches and public and commercial buildings in the inner city; a ring of mill and factory buildings with their tall, smoking, chimneys, interspersed with close-packed streets of workers' houses; and an outer ring of suburbs, churches, and merchants' mansions on the higher ground encircling the central saucer of Belfast.

Layout of the city

The layout of the city, and its street pattern, are not unimportant. The original, small, seventeenth-century settlement, at a strategically significant river crossing, was a very close-knit group of a few main streets, with numerous courtyards and alleyways linking one with another, within a polygon of ramparts long since swept away – though the security fences and barriers of the 1970s were to follow almost precisely the same lines. Outside these ramparts, the flat ground within its ring of hills was laid out in the late eighteenth and early nineteenth centuries, almost like the New Town of Edinburgh or an American town, in a rational series of interlocking grids, adapted, however, to pre-existing roads and streams. It was only later that building crept up the slopes, to the north, of the Antrim plateau, to the south, of the Malone ridge, and to the east, of the Castlereagh and Holywood hills. But generally, apart from the road leading up to the plateau through the Carnmoney Gap, building has never risen above the 150-metre contour line, above which water supplies have to be pumped, at serious extra cost, into new dwellings. In visual terms, this has had the delightful consequence that, until very recently, every part of the inner city enjoyed views of the surrounding hills, along the broad north–south axes of the main thoroughfares, or up Royal Avenue to the Cave Hill. The Georgian office of my own family firm stood close to the City Hall, in Chichester Street. Every time I stepped out of its front door, I used to pause on the top step to enjoy the vistas visible, on the one hand, to the Castlereagh Hills, on the other hand, to the low, symmetrical façade of Sir John Soane's Academical Institution of 1814, backed by the much higher slopes of Divis mountain. There were similar views up and down each of the parallel main streets of the inner city. Most unhappily, in the 1970s the planners permitted the new multi-storey Europa Hotel to be sited so as to block off the vista of the hills up Hamilton Street and Franklin Street. Instead of drawing a lesson from this, they have more recently allowed the BT Tower to block off views down Howard Street, Donegall Square South, and May Street. This is a shame, and a misfortune not to be repeated.

Change since the mid-1960s

In other respects, too, in the years since 1960 the city has changed almost out of recognition. In the mid-sixties, Northern Ireland entirely lacked apparatus for the listing and preservation of Georgian and later buildings: public opinion was startled and dismayed when, of all people, the Queen's University authorities demolished two particularly fine and well-loved Victorian buildings – the School for the Deaf and Dumb, of 1843, by the important local architect, Sir Charles Lanyon; and the Hall of Residence, known as Queen's Elms, by Thomas Jackson, of 1859, facing Lanyon's original University building. In each case, the replacement was an uncongenial slab of concrete in the contemporary international manner. Public outrage led to the formation, for the first time, of an active group of conservationists, the Ulster Architectural Heritage Society, of which I was one of the founders in 1967. And that, in turn, led to the passing of basic legislation for the listing and protection of the built heritage in 1973. Unfortunately, bringing in legislation is one thing, applying and enforcing it, quite another. There have been, I think, five principal causes for the very sharp decline since the 1960s in the visual character of Belfast. The first has been the greed of the property developers, and their resolute refusal to take into account aesthetic considerations, coupled with the failure both of architects and planners to stand up and be counted in favour of quality rather than crude profit. The second has been the inexorable process of inner-city decay. The third has been the equally inexorable growth in the demand for space by cars and lorries, including ever more enormous container lorries. The fourth, now much hoped to be drawing to a close, is 'The Troubles' – the long-drawn-out cycle of rioting, arson, shooting, and Semtex. The fifth has been the poor performance of the city's planners: how far this has been the cause, and how far the consequence, of the very low esteem in which planners are held in Northern Ireland, by politicians and public alike, is a matter of opinion.

Property developers and high-rise

The first cause means that the inner city has been irregularly sprinkled with inappropriate buildings, often high-rise, and far too often out of scale and sympathy with their neighbours. An early example was the loss of a very fine neo-classical warehouse block in Bedford Street, despite loud cries of protest, to make way for the 23-storey Windsor House, far too close to the City Hall and the heart of the city, both of which it overshadows. Other depressing examples of inner-city high-rise office blocks are Fanum House and Bedford House, neither of which has worn well. And the record of the public sector has been no more creditable. Churchill House, for example, was built on the site of a charming old warehouse called Banquet Buildings, and River House crudely overshadows the delightful National Bank next door. I do not know of anybody who now likes or admires any of these dreary intruders into what used to be a tightly knit streetscape. There still exists, I believe, planning permission for an enormous office block on the very central and important Ewarts' site; mercifully, it has not yet been built,

Fig. 6.3 Lanyon's Warehouse in Bedford Street built about 1855, demolished to make way for a 23-storey office block

and it is much to be hoped that it never will be. But now, a whole new generation of high-rise buildings is going up, many of them in the Laganside area, the most conspicuous being the new Hilton Hotel and British Telecom buildings: neither of them is a building with the slightest pretension to architectural merit or charm, and both completely overshadow not only the only recent public building of any merit in the inner city, the new Waterfront Hall, but also the Royal Courts of Justice, St George's Markets, and the not-long-rebuilt low-rise Markets area of social housing.

I do not assert that high-rise buildings are always and everywhere wrong. They are fine for Manhattan; they are wrong for an inner city packed with good examples of Victorian and Edwardian street architecture. We should have learned our lesson from Paris: once the Tour Montparnasse had gone up, the authorities realised what a ghastly mistake had been made, and resolved not to repeat it. Thenceforward, high-rise buildings were exiled over the horizon to the new quarter at La Défense, or to the outer suburbs. Belfast might quite easily have done the same; high-rise buildings would have done no great harm amongst the cranes, gantries, power-station chimneys and grain silos of the harbour. Unfortunately, apart from old buildings restored and the Waterfront Hall, many of the new buildings now going up in the Laganside area combine clumsy massing with inappropriate materials and shoddy detailing: they are designed to maximise lettable floor space and nothing else. I think this is acknowledged, and regretted, by the Laganside Corporation itself. It deserves great credit for the quality of its water management, its weir, its engineering works, and its riverside walkways; also, for its restoration of its own attractive dockside headquarters. But in general, though it has succeeded admirably in stimulating investment and development, it has not succeeded in stimulating high quality design or architecture.

Inner-city decay

The second cause, inner-city decay, is not unique to Belfast, but Belfast is by no means exempt from it. There are many seedy and run-down sections of the inner city; but in this regard, I think a serious effort to cope is being, and has been, made. The long-serving Minister for the Environment, Richard Needham, gave high priority, correctly in my view, to the regeneration of the inner city, in order to provide and enhance a neutral working environment for people both from the Protestant and the Roman Catholic residential areas. His success story was the building of the very large CastleCourt shopping centre at the very heart of the city. I was against it, because it involved the demolition of the excellent High Victorian Head Post Office of 1886; I do not at all care for the high-tech glass-and-steel style in which its replacement has been built; but at least its great bulk lies on its back, instead of sticking high up in the air; and it has certainly proved successful in bringing people, particularly those from West Belfast, back into the inner city. On this theme, my only reservation is that it may prove over-ambitious, with not unlimited resources, to seek to regenerate West Belfast, the Northside district, the Laganside scheduled area, and the city centre, all at the same time. But if it can be achieved, so much the better.

Traffic pressures

As in other western cities, the pressures of ever-increasing road traffic, and the demands for parking, have much influenced the face of the inner city. The four-lane Westlink, which cut a drastic swathe through the city, destroying many good buildings on its way, was effective when it was built, but lacks separation of levels at several busy crossroads, and is by now inadequate to meet the traffic demand. It is going to take a great deal of money, and much traffic disruption during the works, to remedy this. The new Lagan road and rail bridges, on the other hand, have been very successful; like the Lagan weir and its associated works, they are visually intrusive, but the engineering design is of a high standard, and must be accounted a success. But the biggest change has been the closure to most through-traffic – originally for security reasons – of the former main axis through the centre of the city of Donegall Place and Royal Avenue. The result does not amount to full pedestrianisation, but it has greatly eased the conflict between those on foot and those in vehicles, so marked in many other cities. The comparative success of traffic management in Belfast, at any rate in comparison with Dublin, has been achieved only at a high cost in townscape terms. There are unacceptably large areas of 'space left over', some colonised by travelling people with their caravans, others simply given over to random parking, others again mere weed-infested vacant lots. And, where in the past, main thoroughfares were invariably endowed with satisfying, dignified and coherent frontages, the new roads, such as the Dunbar Link, having been cut at an angle to the pre-existing street pattern, completely lack an appropriate sense of enclosure.

'The troubles'

The fourth cause of the deterioration in Belfast's visual character has, of course, been the thirty-year campaign of violence. Riots, petrol-bombs, fire-bombs and high explosive car-bombs (not to mention the ensuing dereliction and vandalism) have done much damage. Even now, there are to be seen, scattered about the city, the carcases of burned-out buildings, roofless buildings, blocked-up buildings and cleared bomb-sites. At some periods the campaign was aimed at 'economic targets'; at others, at publicly owned and official buildings; at others again, bombs were placed indiscriminately where they could inflict the greatest possible amount of damage over as wide an area as possible. And for every building actually destroyed, many others have suffered severe damage to slates, roof-timbers, chimneys, window-sashes, and so forth. The code of compensation for malicious injury to property, though not over-generous, has on the whole attained its object, and much of the major damage has been made good; but many historic details have been lost for ever. And the fabric of the inner city has suffered a lasting injury.

The planners

My fifth cause is the most awkward and controversial: the extent to which the planners and architects can be held responsible for the deterioration in the visual quality of Belfast. There are a few, but in my opinion only a very few, good recent buildings in Belfast. Does it follow that there are only a very few good architects? It may be so, but many architects will argue, forcefully, that they have no alternative – they must provide the developer client with what he asks for: and if what he wants is a shoddy box with a shiny tin roof, then that is what the architect must supply. I do not entirely accept that argument, but there is a sufficient element of truth in it to shift at least some of the responsibility back onto the clients. There is no doubt that some speculators and developers are, quite openly and unashamedly, complete philistines, in the business only for the profits. I suppose that there have always been capitalists like that.

But what is much more baffling is that large, wealthy, important corporations seem no longer to have any interest in quality of architectural design. I find it extraordinary that British Telecom, which has an outstandingly good track record for its support for the arts, should be responsible for a new office block which is as inappropriate to the site as it is mediocre. The same goes for the Hilton Hotel next door, with its silly-looking lop-sided hat. The same goes for the former Trustee Savings Bank, now First Trust, which acquired as its new headquarters a ready-made speculative venture quite devoid of aesthetic merit. The same goes for the Ulster Bank: for a hundred years, it provided Belfast, and Ireland, with many very fine bank buildings; now it has acquired yet another ready-made speculative venture, an appalling six-storey intrusion into the city's central square with the classical façade of the (listed) 1851 Methodist Church glued onto its front in the forlorn hope of pacifying the conservation lobby – a ludicrous example of façadism at its most spurious.

So then, what of the planners? Have they no responsibility for all these disasters? Of course they have. They should, and I believe could, have taken a much stronger line in restricting heights of buildings in the inner city; in encouraging better detailing, massing, materials; above all, in enforcing rather than compromising the rules applicable to listed historic buildings and conservation areas. (There are two declared Conservation Areas in the city centre, but they have proved, in practice, to be quite ineffectual: perhaps because there has never been a single Conservation Officer, qualified or unqualified, in Northern Ireland; and planners lack expertise in architectural history). The planners seek to excuse themselves by pleading that the quality of the architecture is not within their remit. They also plead, with some justification, shortages of staff and resources. But the sad truth is that, in Belfast, they have lost almost all their credibility. The Irish are not a disciplined race, like the Scots, the English, or the Germans, and they resent bitterly any interference in their liberty to do as they please with their own property. Moreover, a majority, perhaps a large majority, both of public and of politicians, would probably take the view that jobs, prosperity, and economic regeneration, should take a higher priority than aesthetic or environmental considerations.

The current failures of planning control in inner Belfast will not be rectified without considerable changes in the planning service and its leadership; without the increased resources recommended by a recent Parliamentary Committee; and without a greatly increased determination to attain a better balance between environmental and economic considerations, between quality and profitability. Let us hope the new Assembly and its Ministers are prepared to put political prejudices aside, and to address these matters.

Belfast – positive developments

I now turn from the negative to the positive. For there has also been a positive side to the development of Belfast over the past 35 years.

Housing

First and foremost has been the enormous improvement in the quality, and to a lesser extent quantity, of social housing. In 1971, when the Northern Ireland Housing Executive was set up, the public housing stock of Belfast was certainly the worst in the British Isles, and possibly amongst the worst in Western Europe, due to long years of neglect or – still worse – misguided replacement by unacceptable flats. Today, to quote a recent book by Richard Needham, former Minister, 'Northern Ireland has some of the best public housing in Europe.'[1] I had some hand in this transformation, for I served on the Board of the Executive from its inception in 1971 until 1984, for the last five years as its Chairman. During that span of time, the Executive built over 50 000 new houses throughout Northern Ireland, most of them excellent two-storey or three-storey houses rather than flats, built to high standards of space and layout. It gives me great pleasure that, quite contrary to my expectations, the wheel of fashion has failed, in this instance, to revolve. New houses are still being built by the Executive to almost exactly the same specifications, because they have continued to be exceedingly popular with users of both communities: in effect, just what their tenants wanted. Many of them have now been sold to their sitting tenants, and the initiative for housing new build has passed to the housing associations and to private developers. It also gives me great pleasure to record that both have taken note of the example set by the Executive, and that the standards of space and design in the private sector have been rising steadily to meet the wishes and aspirations evinced by public-sector tenants. The fact that the two communities largely prefer to live apart, in territories divided in many places by so-called 'peace lines', is very much to be regretted; the divisions will not begin to disappear until trust and confidence can be restored; but at least, bad housing is no longer a serious cause of unrest and violence.

Of course, most (though not all) of the public-sector estates are on the periphery of the inner city; but it has been satisfactory to see a return of housing demand in and near the city centre. This fairly recent development is perhaps still fairly fragile; it is unlikely that it could survive any resurgence of conflict; but it is an encouraging symptom of returning confidence. There have been some interesting new projects, mostly of flats or 'town houses', and some enterprising refurbishments. Some of the most exotic post-modernist projects have been waterside blocks within the Laganside Corporation's area.

The restoration of a number of terraced and other dwelling houses of historic interest has been successfully undertaken by the HEARTH housing association and its associated revolving fund, of both of which I am chairman. These include terraces of late Georgian houses in the Joy Street/Hamilton Street area, very much in the inner city; and a not dissimilar terrace forming a significant group with St Patrick's Roman Catholic church of 1877 next door, and St Patrick's School of 1828 next door again: this last was very recently well restored by the newly created Belfast Building Presentation Trust as its first venture. It would be highly desirable if more such groups of buildings could be similarly restored in a coordinated way, for there is a tendency to look at buildings individually rather than in their context, a shortcoming not unknown even amongst planners. HEARTH's most recent very ambitious scheme, supported by the Heritage Lottery Fund, involved the restoration, for social housing, of three very large bomb-damaged stucco terraced houses, and the construction of a replica of one completely destroyed: very much in context with the Old Museum building next door, of 1831 (the first museum to be built by public subscription in Ireland, now an Arts Centre). Unfortunately, on the opposite side of this once important street stands the roofless ruin of the very fine classical Christ Church of 1833 by William Farrell. It is greatly to be hoped that a suitable new use for it can be found before the building deteriorates further.

Important buildings

Over the past thirty years, a number of restoration schemes for important buildings have been carried out in different parts of the city. Amongst the most important early examples were the conversion of Elmwood Presbyterian church, of 1862, into a concert hall, by the University, which thereby made amends for earlier misdeeds; the very thorough restoration of Frank Matcham's greatly loved Grand Opera House of 1895 by the Arts Council of Northern Ireland; the splendidly florid and ornate Crown Liquor Saloon, of about 1885, by the National Trust; and the imposing Custom House of 1857, described as 'Belfast's finest public building and the peak of Sir Charles Lanyon's achievement', by the Customs and Excise service. The process is an ongoing

Fig. 6.4 Christ Church by William Farrell of 1833, burnt and vandalised, a victim of the Troubles, awaiting possible restoration

one, and has received a considerable boost during the past three years from the availability of National Lottery funding to provide part (but never all) of the capital cost of substantial projects. An interesting example, where extensive work by the Belfast City Council, with the aid of lottery funding, is now nearing completion, is at St George's Markets, of 1890, designed by the then City Surveyor, J.C. Bretland. A very lively market has survived successfully in this most attractive low-rise series of market halls, surrounded by brick walls punctuated by arches, pediments and knops. But unfortunately this building, like the neighbouring High Court building, and the two-storey residential district of the Markets next door, is completely overshadowed by the multi-storey Hilton Hotel and British Telecom headquarters just across the road. Two other schemes, which it is hoped to start soon, are for the restoration and stabilisation of the Albert Memorial clock, which used to be regarded as the centre of the city; and for the conversion to offices of the highly ornate late Victorian gasworks buildings.

There have also been some very creditable recent private ventures into conservation, usually with the assistance of Historic Buildings grants. One is the conversion into a restaurant of an attractive quay-side ship's chandlers, Tedford's, of 1855; another, the restoration, as a hotel, of a pair of important seed warehouses of 1868 very close to the Albert Clock. They had lain vacant for over twenty years, to the near-despair of conservationists, for they exemplify at its very best the rich ornamentation of which the local stonemasons – in this case, Thomas Fitzpatrick – were capable. Insofar as these buildings typify the best and most characteristic of the architectural legacy of Victorian Belfast, their retention and restoration is exceedingly welcome; but once again, these are buildings which have been singled out for restoration on an individual basis, rather than as part of a coherent group, and which suffer considerably from inappropriate and out-of-scale neighbours.

Contemporary architecture

As to contemporary architecture, there is little to please my eye in the inner city, with the exception of the Waterfront Hall by Victor Robinson opened in 1998. The interior is extremely fine, a most successful handling of spaces, masses, textures and colours. The front part of the exterior, in a clever combination of glass and stone, is also very fine; though I personally feel that the non-functional red-brick river frontage rather lets down the rest of the design, and I do not care for the fussy (and, again, non-functional) fins at the base of the dome. It is a great pity, as I have already remarked, that a contemporary building of so much architectural merit should be so brutally overshadowed by its unneighbourly neighbours. One other very recent modest, three-storey, white office building which I like very much is to be found at Prince's Dock: the offices of Stena Line, as sleek and elegant as a modern ferry, and not unlike one.

Conclusion

The architectural legacy of Belfast, today, is something of a plum pudding. There are many excellent ingredients; but the overall result is pretty indigestible.

It is not easy to see how this state of affairs is to be improved: but it is possible that new opportunities will open up if and when the new Assembly and Ministers take up their duties. One obvious step would be to give effect to the various changes recommended by the Northern Ireland Affairs Committee's Report on the Planning System of two years ago, which exposed many deficiencies. Another possibility, in the new spirit of cross-border cooperation, would be to look southward towards Dublin. Since 1973, it must be said that the legislation and structures for the conservation of the built environment in Northern Ireland have been far in advance of those in the South. It looks as if the balance is about to turn the other way, if the two Bills now before the Irish Parliament are passed. One lays down a completely new code for statutory listing and enforcement – with fines of up to a million pounds for those who accidentally-on-purpose nudge down historic buildings. The other refines planning procedures, and requires the appointment of architects and conservation officers. Is this not a field where it might prove advantageous to both parties to seek a closer rapprochement between the laws and structures for conservation in the two parts of Ireland?

Notes

1   R. Needham, *Battling for Peace* (Belfast: Blackstaff Press, 1998), p. 135.

7

Architectural Ambivalence: the Built Environment and Cultural Identity in Belfast

Malachy McEldowney, Ken Sterrett and Frank Gaffikin

The word 'ambivalence' has a particular appropriateness for Northern Ireland in that we consistently assume that our society, if we can refer to it collectively, can be defined in terms of two opposed and conflicting perspectives. Almost every aspect of our lives, including our politics, religious practices and culture can be read as Protestant unionist or Catholic nationalist. So when we speak of cultural identity in Northern Ireland, more often than not what we mean is ethnic identity. In Belfast, of course, we have some very obvious visible expressions of identity in the sectarian geography of working-class areas – although the terraced house architecture is almost universal, tribal markers such as flags, emblems and wall murals simultaneously celebrate and threaten.

'Ambivalence' is inherent in architecture and urban design – particularly in the eclectic, revivalist styles of the High Victorian and Edwardian eras when most of Belfast's urban design 'identity' was consciously established and promoted. It is also a feature of the current 'postmodern' era – indeed it has been argued[1] that complexity, ambiguity and, indeed, ambivalence are defining characteristics of contemporary approaches to design.

This chapter traces the relationships between identity and ambivalence in Belfast's built environment as it evolved from an era of economic self-confidence at the end of the nineteenth century to one of political uncertainty with the onset of 'The Troubles'. It then considers in detail two areas of current ambivalence as the city enters a period of relative stability, posing the questions whether, in urban design terms, it is now necessary to look forward rather than backwards, whether it is necessary to design for peace rather than for war.

Identity and the environment

There is now, however, a widespread hope that the current peace process will offer opportunities to promote the positive attributes of different identities while at the same time providing the conditions for the development of common aspirations. What role can architecture and the built environment of Belfast have in this; indeed what role has it played in the past? Before we review this and consider some of the key issues facing Belfast's future architectural identity, it is important to explore the relationship between the built environment and the sometimes rather nebulous concept of identity.

A number of commentators on planning practice have noted the re-emergence of aesthetics as a key concern in urban planning.[2] However what seems evident about this phenomenon is that it requires a redefinition of what we have traditionally regarded as aesthetics. Writing in 1989, and looking forward to the 1990s, Healy recognised a significant paradigm shift when she argued that planning needed to be concerned not only with functional concerns as they relate to the environment but also with 'what the environment looks like, what it feels like as we sense it, rather than as we rationalise it or moralise about it'.[3] To avoid reducing our responses to what she called a 'narrow subjectivism' which either concludes around the views of the most powerful or else defers to the views of 'experts', Healy suggested that we needed a more structured and informed debate which would 'separate out the expressive character of what things look like from the aesthetic'.

The *expressive* for Healy refers to the meanings, that is the 'social meanings' that people give to the built environment, while the *aesthetic* refers primarily to the 'internal integrity of the design' measured against what we might call traditional aesthetic principles which focus on form and composition. This dual approach to apprehending, appreciating and understanding the visual role of the built environment is gradually gaining recognition in debates about architecture and environmental design and in many ways reflects an increasing acceptance of popular culture as something of equal value to the more traditional elitist culture.[4] Indeed a number of commentators regard the disintegration of such cultural barriers as the defining characteristic of postmodern society. Lash and Urry for example, argue that in contrast to modern culture which promoted a high culture of distinctive aesthetic objects, postmodern culture denies 'the separation of the aesthetic from the social (and) in particular it disputes the contention that art is of a different order of life'.[5]

It is in the context of these debates about aesthetics and the meanings we give our environments that we need to consider the relationship between the built environment and social identity. Particularly important is Healy's point that the meanings we give our environment are constructed socially and therefore need to be comprehended within the context of social science-based understandings of 'community and class'. In seeking to develop this point we need to acknowledge that all societies are characterised by unequal power relations and conflict and this is manifest to varying degrees in the values and ideas of different social groups. Importantly therefore we need to dispense with the precept which continues to permeate environmental planning practice, that there is a definable public interest and it is the planner's role to identify and pursue it. The public sphere rather is characterised by social conflict which extends beyond material issues to include ideological conflict about values and meanings. Significantly therefore we need to recognise that the built environment is imbued with meaning through the same social processes and in this sense can be understood, as Savage and Warde[6] suggest, as an 'arena of contestation' where symbols play an important part in the ongoing struggles for cultural hegemony and social and political power. Moreover, and perhaps to challenge one aspect of Healy's argument, traditional aesthetic views which focus on the visual form and composition of buildings are not necessarily a separate concern from this and can reflect the pursuit of social distancing which in itself has political consequences.

Identity and evolution of the built environment in Belfast

As noted earlier, it is almost trite to say that in Northern Ireland social conflict appears to be ingrained in every aspect of life. Conflict and tension between the Protestant unionist community and the Catholic nationalist community seem to dominate every analysis. And yet when we re-examine our political history we can detect the interplay of a range of political forces which have both created our built environment and endowed it with meaning.

Although Belfast's history as a settlement can be traced back to the seventeenth century, its formative growth came in the second half of the nineteenth century when there was a significant expansion of both the linen industry and shipbuilding. During this period the population grew from 70 447 in 1841 to 349 180 in 1901, and this represented, as Weiner notes, the fastest growth rate of any city in the British Isles.[7] In turn, of course, there was a corresponding growth in working-class housing to accommodate the workers, and quite a phenomenal increase in both public and commercial buildings, particularly in the centre of the city. Brett[8] records, for example, that during the 63 years of Queen Victoria's reign 86 churches were built in Belfast, of which only 8 per cent were Catholic. This is despite the fact that by the end of the century Catholics represented around 34 per cent of the city's total population.[9]

The expansion of the major industries also brought the development of many purpose-built commercial buildings in the centre of Belfast. Banks, warehouses, insurance company offices, major new shops and department stores were developed to respond to the economic opportunities presented by Belfast's industrial revolution. The buildings, many of which now represent Belfast's architectural heritage, were exuberantly and expensively ornate and often quite ostentatious in a typical 'high Victorian' style. They celebrated and displayed a new culture of entrepreneurship, and a sense of the success that international trade within the British Empire could bring. Indeed many of the grand Victorian buildings which are now the key place markers in Belfast were decorated with sculptural references to royalty and empire. Public buildings followed the same stylistic path. The City Hall, completed in 1906 became Belfast's main monument to a developing political-economic culture which reflected an almost exclusive Protestant ownership of commerce and political power. Brett recognised this in his comments that the City Hall, the new Protestant Cathedral of St Anne's and the Presbyterian Assembly Buildings constituted 'the corporate expression of embattled Unionism, and of an effort (perhaps largely unconscious) to convert a brash and sprawling industrial centre into a politico-religious capital city'.[10]

It can be argued therefore that the architecture and townscape of central Belfast played an important part in a broader hegemonic mission. Arguably too, this mission was not exclusively designed to assert ascendancy over the Catholic population but also sought to offer a place at the cultural table for the Protestant working class. Significantly therefore the built environment of central Belfast was to serve not only a commercial purpose but also a political-cultural role. Functionally and symbolically it supported a renewed political order and sense of identity across Protestant class interests. Major 'public' events such as the visit of Queen Victoria, the opening of the City Hall and later the signing of the Ulster Covenant provided the fullest expression of this. Belfast city centre was not neutral space or even civic space, but neither was it simply the aesthetic manifestation of the skill of celebrated architects and sculptors.

Major changes to Belfast's built environment did not come until the late 1960s. The decline of the indigenous industrial base before and after the Second World War and the consequent rise in unemployment led to a series of regional planning initiatives which were designed to attract international mobile investment. At the centre of these initiatives was a restructuring plan for the physical environment of the Belfast region. The main proposals of the Matthew plan were a development stopline for Belfast and the establishment of a number of new towns and growth centres within the Belfast region. This was followed in turn by both a transportation plan for Belfast and the city's first development plan.

This overall restructuring of the Belfast environment was to have major consequences for working-class communities. The housing conditions for both working-class communities had been neglected by the city corporation whose interests, as Weiner[11] argued, were dominated by the Protestant middle classes, many of whom as land and property owners had a direct stake in maintaining the status quo. By 1960 Belfast 'was faced with a situation where 60 per cent of its dwellings were built before 1919 (and) a quarter of its houses were in need of redevelopment'. For the majority of Belfast's citizens social identity was equated with their immediate locality – what we might now call their urban village. Localities such as Sandy Row, the Pound and the Falls had been developed during the 'burgeoning' years of the late nineteenth century and which despite the often squalid conditions, nevertheless, provided a degree of stability and a sense of community identity for their residents.

The modernisation programme however required major physical changes which in turn necessitated considerable social upheaval. A new ring road through inner city Belfast and the need to decant labour to the new towns required a new language of persuasion. The place markers of traditional identities had to be devalued and new aspirations created. One of the key terms employed in this context was the word 'slum'. It abounded in all forms of literature, from official reports through propaganda sheets to the everyday reading material of Belfast's working classes. It was the expression of the time and in common translation it referred to inner city terraced housing and the way of life associated with it. What were previously rather patronisingly described as 'neat little palaces' in a 'city of villages' very quickly became 'slums' in need of demolition. The old way of life and the environments associated with it had to change. A new modern aesthetic was offered. It promised new bright houses in the growth centres or radically different housing forms *in situ*, all of which could provide the amenities that were lacking in the inner city. The architectural images presented to communities were important. In contrast to the rather worn-out terraced street environments, they displayed new residential areas shaped by geometric forms and clad in clean modern materials. Images of open space, trees and shrubbery offered the possibility of a new way of life.

The processes of modernisation collapsed in the early 1970s and this together with intensifying political violence across Northern Ireland and particularly in Belfast led to a more modest and sensitive reshaping of community environments. Already though, the processes of redevelopment and sectarian violence had led to a severe depopulation of the inner city. Interestingly, however, the period of transition from wholesale redevelopment to a more sensitive rehabilitation process was much shorter and more compressed than in other cities. As noted earlier, redevelopment or 'slum clearance' was not initiated until the late 1960s. However, within a decade this policy was reversed and this brought about an inversion in architectural imagery that saw the symbol of 'old as bad' being replaced by a new symbolism of the 'old as good' (*see* below).

Northern Ireland Housing Executive

Towards the late 1970s the Northern Ireland Housing Executive (NIHE), the new social housing body, started to pursue a new design agenda for Belfast's working-class areas – one which combined the concept of 'defensible space' with traditional vernacular form and detailing. For the architectural profession in Belfast this new agenda offered opportunities to engage with the broader revival of urban aesthetics. It encouraged the shaping of space to create variety and interest and it facilitated and supported the expression of unique architectural design solutions. However although this latest phase of housing architecture was generally quite well received by communities, particularly by those who had campaigned against high- and medium-rise flat solutions, there was nevertheless some scepticism about the underlying purpose of the designs. In the Protestant Shankill area for example, the community rejected the new urban aesthetic on the grounds that it did not reflect the old street pattern and they suspected that the NIHE was purposively lowering the density of the population for political purposes. Similarly in Catholic West Belfast there were widespread suspicions that the new layouts were designed to assist the security forces in containing and repressing political violence.[12]

The city centre

While social housing projects were reshaping the built environment of working-class communities during the 1970s and 80s, the city centre was suffering major assaults from the IRA bombing campaign. The commercial core of the city was regarded by the IRA as a 'legitimate economic target' in the war against 'the British forces of occupation'. However, the campaign was not confined to business premises but also targeted some of the key features of Belfast's architectural heritage such as the Grand Opera House and the Royal Courts of Justice. A major effect of all of this was a decline in the economy of the city centre and its virtual closure after 6.00 pm. Significantly too, the visual imagery of this decline including the 'ring of steel' (or security barriers) which surrounded the commercial core, armed military personnel on the streets, and an ever-increasing number of derelict properties,[13] was conveying a poor image to the 'outside world' as well as inculcating a culture of pessimism among the local population. Images of the city-centre environment did capture an aspect of Belfast's 'identity', but it was an identity of violence, fear and division.

Prompted primarily by business, professional and city council interests,[14] government launched a series of initiatives aimed at revitalising the city centre. The initiatives had a number of purposes including bolstering existing commercial ventures while attracting new investments. Perhaps as important though was an ideological offensive to secure a new imagery which would communicate an identity of relative normality, even an aspiring 'modernity'. The key to the success of this initiative would be to achieve the sort of investment which would be very visible and very transmittable. It was judged particularly important to attract the fashionable multiple retailers; that is those retailers that conspicuously populated the High Streets of other cities in Britain and elsewhere, but which had previously avoided the 'war-torn' environments of Belfast. The corporate logos of Next, Habitat, Gap and McDonalds could communicate not only a new investment confidence to the 'outside' but also the potential of 'modern' values to the 'inside'.[15] Significantly too, the traditional architectural environment of the centre was not regarded as an impediment to these imperatives. Although traditional vernacular forms were being promoted for social housing, the same 'sensitivities' did not prevail for the city centre. With assistance in some cases from an urban development grant regime, a wave of new corporate shopfronts and logos began to appear. The renaissance of the city centre was underway and it offered a 'neutral' non-sectarian commercial space for those who could afford it.

The pursuit of new investment and a confident modern identity for the city centre reached its zenith in 1987 with the opening of a major new shopping and office complex known as CastleCourt. Extending across a three-hectare site this prestigious development represented what the then government Minister Richard Needham regarded as 'the biggest single commercial investment in Belfast this century'. However underpinning the commercial investment 'risk' were a number of public subsidies including a £10 million grant and guaranteed tenants for the office space. Significantly though, this secured government a key role in the process of deciding an appropriate aesthetic for the development, particularly for the main elevation which fronted Royal Avenue. In view of the fact that the development process itself had required the demolition of a number of Victorian buildings along the Royal Avenue frontage, there was a strong lobby from conservation interests to recreate a Victorian façade. Indeed the initial designs for the site pursued this rationale and show the shopping centre clad in a neo-Victorian architecture. Government reaction to this, however, was negative. The new development was to play an important role in communicating Belfast's economic revival and its place in the modern world. This could not be achieved with an imagery of the past, albeit a reconstructed one. The aesthetic, it was argued, needed to communicate a confidence in the future, it needed to be bold and progressive and it needed to signify that Belfast had a role to play in the international modern world. A new design was created, and although there were some doubts about its originality, it featured an international high-tech style of glass and steel.

Reaction to this attempt to neutralise and modernise the city centre was, like much of what has been discussed above, 'ambivalent'. Some commentators[16] felt that Castlecourt was an example of Belfast 'exchanging a fine Victorian landscape for a building which will have all the charm of a tower-block laid on its side' while others[17] saw the whole city centre regeneration project as a fairly desperate attempt to apply 'lipstick to the gorilla'. Both were concerned about the loss of local identity in an attempt to transcend local conflict, although one was a conservationist viewpoint while the other was concerned about the superficial nature of modern 'reimaging' approaches to the marketing of Belfast and other 'problem' cities.

Marketing identity and the past: the heritage industry

The Europe in which Belfast must now compete is full of cities for whom 'looking backwards', in urban design terms, has been highly profitable – tourism is the world's most lucrative industry and 'heritage tourism' has been particularly profitable for cities. However, in the case of Belfast, urban conservation and heritage promotion have been dogged with self-doubt and ambivalence. It is interesting to consider this within the context of the recent backlash against 'the heritage industry' in other cities in the UK now prevalent in professional and academic comment.

In the UK, as in the rest of Europe, architectural conservation is extremely well-established – in England alone there are 9000 or more conservation areas, 600 000 or more listed buildings and a complex network of governmental, quasi-autonomous and voluntary organisations supporting a comprehensive 'heritage industry' which extends from parish-pump level to the upper echelons of political power. There are many justifications for this preoccupation – cultural, educational, aesthetic, functional and, most of all, economic – it is estimated that Britain earns some twenty billion pounds annually from tourism and that about three-quarters of foreign tourists are attracted mainly by 'heritage-related' factors. It also has widespread popular support – particularly where land and property values are bound up with perceived 'heritage' quality. Although much slower to respond to the conservation movement, Northern Ireland now has 50 conservation areas and 8500 listed buildings of which 6 and 1100 respectively are in Belfast. Compared with similar industrial cities like Liverpool (around 30 conservation areas) Leeds (30 plus) and Bradford (30 plus) this is still a fairly modest investment in a burgeoning industry.[18] Others, of course, may have over-designated.

Robert Hewison[19] was one of the first to articulate a sense of unease about the growing preoccupation with things past and its relevance to the question of 'identity'. He argued that although the past is the foundation of individual and collective identity there is a danger that 'through the filter of nostalgia we seek to change the past and through the conservative impulse we seek to change the present' – in other words a selective or bogus interpretation of the past may be detrimental to the present.

He documented and criticised the 'eighties phenomena of a growing "museum culture" ' where redundant industries sought to market their past for tourist income, a growing conservationism which sterilised modern architectural development, and a growing reliance on private patronage which stifled artistic innovation or challenge. In particular, he questioned the authenticity of the 'history' being told, he questioned the ownership of the 'heritage' being sold, and he expressed concern about the effect – both cultural and political – of such retrospective reactions to the challenges of modernity. All of these issues are particularly relevant to Belfast.

Journalist Neil Ascherson[20] has taken up the political theme, and suggests that conservation is closely associated with political conservatism – a point supported by the record of Mrs Thatcher's government, which expanded conservation legislative control in an era of massive reductions in other forms of planning intervention. David Harvey[21] acknowledges the importance of nostalgia as a reaction to crisis and a search for identity – 'it is indeed the case that preoccupation with identity, with personal and collective roots, has become more pervasive since the early 1990s because of widespread insecurity in labour markets'.

Architectural writer Martin Pawley[22] explains the reasons for the popularity of old environments as a return to fundamentalism which accepts the nineteenth-century revivalist conviction of the superiority of the past. He also suggests that architects espouse it as a safeguard against unpopularity since 'the thing a building must do to secure public affection is to have been standing a very long time'. Belfast, however, has not had the luxury of any certainty that buildings 'would be left standing for a very long time' so it is understandable that enthusiasm for conservation has been more circumspect. Another, related, reason for this has been the absence of the sort of collective identity referred to by Harvey, and, possibly, the decline of the city's middle-class Protestant population which would be expected to relate more to its Victorian/Edwardian heritage than the growing Catholic citizenry. A response from West Belfast (mainly Catholic) community groups to 1986 proposals[23] for additional conservation areas in Belfast criticised the absence of attention given to historical landmarks valued by the nationalist community (Clifton Street and Friar's Bush cemeteries and other places associated with the 1798 Rising). Some criticisms were also expressed by Protestant working-class communities about the omission of terraced housing areas from the conservation areas. This was responded to subsequently by the designation of McMaster Street in East Belfast in 1995, although nothing similar has been attempted in catholic West Belfast.

It would be a mistake, however, to over-stress the sectarian dimensions of community reaction to built environments – there were other, more deliberate reasons (*see* below) for the tardy implementation of conservation restrictions in the city centre. Indeed, pragmatic rather than dogmatic interpretations of the meaning of public buildings is well illustrated by the nationalist adoption of Belfast City Hall as the focus of 'their city', and by their acceptance of Stormont, at least for the time being, as a functional political forum. This should not be too surprising, of course, as newly empowered politicians in most Eastern European countries have been happy to preserve the monumental built environments of their previous masters and adapt them for their purposes (for example, Prague, Warsaw, St Petersburg and, of course, Berlin). This reflects an interesting combination of pragmatism and iconoclasm.

It also reflects the important point made earlier about 'expressive' and 'aesthetic' interpretations of meaning in the built environment – although some may argue that Belfast's city centre had developed over the years a symbolism which was inimical to some nationalist perceptions, there was nothing culturally 'pure' in the aesthetics of the buildings. Architectural styles have generally been borrowed from previous generations and from different cultures. Belfast, like most Victorian cities, has a wealth of imported architectural imagery. In stylistic terms, St George's Church façade is Greek, St Anne's Cathedral is Romanesque and both Marks and Spencer and Lambert Smith Hampton occupy Venetian palazzos; Belfast Castle is both Scottish and French, Stormont is an Italian Palladian villa and the City Hall refers to St Paul's in London and in turn to St Peter's in Rome.

Architectural ambivalence, or at least architectural multiculturalism, is as common in Belfast as any nineteenth-century city – but the reasons why it has been slow to preserve its particular version of architectural multiculturalism are fairly obvious – 'old' buildings, of whatever stylistic symbolism, referred backward in time, and Belfast's problem was that its people were seen to be morbidly preoccupied with looking backward in time. Buildings which referred *forward* were considered necessary – so the Belfast City Centre Conservation Area was not designated, as were most city centres in the UK, until after the subsidised development boom in 1998. Castlecourt, as indicated above, the Waterfront Hall and the new Laganside 'towers' of the Hilton Hotel and BT Headquarters have become the symbols of new 'neutral' Belfast.

There has been considerable 'over-compensation' in this approach – the loss of local identity (however perceived) may be an unnecessary price to pay for imposed normality. However, postmodernism in architecture now provides the opportunity to claim contextual justification. CastleCourt can be seen to 'celebrate the corner' in the manner of the the best Edwardian commercial buildings, Waterfront Hall to refer to the red-bricked terraces of East Belfast in its east elevation and the new BT Tower to relate to West Belfast by closing the long vista from Grosvenor Road through May Street. All of these are highly debatable, but they reflect a concern for local authentification which is in keeping with the times. They also reflect, perhaps, a new confidence that such buildings will survive – that their context will be peace rather than war. This prospect – and the ambivalence inherent in it – is the subject of the next section.

Architectural ambivalence: design for war or peace?

As Berlin and Belfast emerge from periods of conflict and division and look forward to periods of peace and reconciliation – of being like other 'normal' cities – it is both interesting and ironic that many 'normal' cities are now becoming increasingly concerned about threats to security and their effect on urban design. 'Design against crime' has become something of a universal architectural cliché and Belfast, for all the wrong reasons, has often been referred to as a prime example of a city with relevant experience of its necessity.

Some recent planning analysis[24] has identified many reasons for the decline of safety and security in city centres generally – suburbanisation, retail decentralisation and modernist urban planning policy leading to loss of centrality and 'sense of place' in city centres; these in turn have led to the privatisation of urban space, the loss of natural surveillance and, in particular, the decline of the 'public realm' in modern cities. This is increasing in European urban areas, although it has not yet reached the state of some American cities where the privatisation of urban space has been both a cause and a consequence of increasing crime and resultant 'defensible' urban designs.

Increased privatisation and the decline of the 'public realm' in modern cities are criticised by Richard Rogers[25] as the prime culprits in the transition from 'open-minded' to 'single-minded' urban areas – from multifunctional to monofunctional spaces and structures – which he regards as seriously detrimental to any sense of urban community and identity.

The disappearance of open-minded space is not simply a cause for regret: it can generate dire social consequences launching a spiral of decline. As the vibrancy of public spaces diminishes we lose the habit of participating in street life. The natural policing of streets that comes from the presence of people needs to be replaced by 'security' and the city becomes less hospitable and more alienating.

Alienation, of course, is a function of the perceiver as well as the perceived, and urban places affect different groups within society in different ways – women, the elderly, the disabled, children and ethnic minorities, for example, react to the city on the basis of different experiences and different priorities. Indeed it is evident[26] that the retail decentralisation which is helping to undermine city centres is itself partly a product of the increasing financial power of working women with a preference for safe, supervised shopping environments (particularly at night) over the more exciting, but sometimes dangerous, ambience of the traditional town centre.

Differential perceptions of urban character by different societal groupings are obviously relevant to any consideration of Belfast and Berlin, as indeed is the concept of alienation – the links between this and crime and terrorism are the subject of much academic and political debate. Belfast, in fact, features prominently in the chapter on the effects of urban terrorism on urban design in Pawley's ominously entitled 'Terminal Architecture'.[27] The 'Belfast effect', he argues, extends well beyond Belfast.

A consequence of the massive terrorist bombs in Baltic Exchange and Canary Wharf in London in 1993/4 and 1996 was the wholesale adoption by the financial services sector of 'business continuity services' to protect them from the loss of data storage and computing capacity which have been estimated to be much more valuable than the buildings containing them. These are effectively large storage 'terminals' in remote sites, where the 'back-up' office function can continue uninterrupted. The parent office in the City of London becomes less significant in functional terms – a 'shell' for the conduct of social and promotional activities. This contributes to Pawley's apocalyptic vision of an architectural future of remote but influential 'big sheds' and decorative but bogus city centre 'shells', a schizophrenic urban environment where form bears no relation to function and design is dominated by the requirements of the market, the security services and the heritage and tourist industries.

With regard to Belfast itself, he refers to Stollard's[28] identification of the key features of the city's 'defensible architecture' – anonymity rather than deliberate defiance (homely brickwork on police-station walls), reduction of horizontal (potential bomb-bearing) elements on building façades, use of sloping sills and slit windows on exposed elevations, separation of controlled access from architectural access (Central Station), blank and solid ground floor perimeters (BBC building – visually strong, British Telecom – visually bleak). He documents the shift in the use of materials – from pre-cast concrete structures (heavy and inflexible) to steel and aluminium frames (light and flexible), from brick and block to replaceable plasterboard panels, from widespread to very restricted use of external glazing. Pawley's concluding comments are journalistic exaggeration but offer food for thought on questions of image and identity:

> ... the results of these and a hundred allied measures is to create an architecture so styleless that it can scarcely be imagined ... its nondescript fortresses of serviced floors breathe freely only inside their armoured carapace ... like prisons, such places will certainly show people where they are and, by extension, who they are ... but they may not like what they find.

The agents of such town planning, he argues, are not town planners but the security services who vet all major applications – an argument which supports Anson's contention[29] that the 'establishment' is less concerned with architectural detail than with controlling the selection of architects and the policies of planners. In this sense, he argued, planning in Belfast in the 'seventies had more in common with Hausmann's Paris than with comparable cities in Britain. More journalistic exaggeration, perhaps, but it places Belfast in an interesting European tradition.

There is no doubt, however, that the effects of conflict on the urban environment in Belfast extended well beyond architecture – 'peaceline' walls between segregated communities, 'defensible space' in housing layouts, 'neutral territory' in a controlled city centre and ambivalent attitudes to conservation are also important issues.[30] Some of these have been discussed in the previous section, but one is particularly relevant here.

Peaceline walls have obvious resonance with the situation in Berlin and give rise to a particular kind of architectural ambivalence – should community segregation be institutionalised by the erection of permanent symbols of division, or should genuine community fears be ignored? Initial reluctance gave way to community pressure and temporary structures eventually became permanent. The then Chairman of the Northern Ireland Housing Executive[31] described the process and noted the historical immutability of the problem as follows:

> Whole terraces of houses were burned out and makeshift barriers were erected. A massive shift of population took place, accompanied by large-scale squatting and intimidation. A so-called 'peaceline', initially of corrugated iron, was hastily erected to separate warring factions. It was no accident that this barrier followed, to within a few inches, the demarcation line between the two communities noted almost a hundred years earlier.

Over the years, design variations of the peaceline walls – from single barrier to double barrier in structure and from functionally crude to disturbingly decorative in style – have symbolised an increasing acceptance of the segregation imperative in public housing areas, in defiance of the more optimistic trends in the wider political arena. Unlike Berlin, where the Wall appeared almost overnight and disappeared equally quickly, Belfast's walls, both metaphorical and physical, appear to be built to last. If walls are inimical to collective urban identity, then Belfast may still have some way to go.

In this section more has been said, perhaps, about war than about peace; in a historical sense this is inevitable, as Belfast has been the victim of 'low-grade war' for most of the past thirty years. There has also, however, been some consideration of current thinking on aspects of urban design in (peaceful) cities generally, and this suggests that many of the lessons learnt from our troubled experience may still have some general validity. Decentralisation, privatisation, architectural schizophrenia and the loss of public community space are universal problems and all have a bearing on the question of 'identity'. All mitigate against collective identity and the urban design that reflects it. Belfast has suffered from a particularly severe version of this malady but it would be a mistake to regard it as uniquely afflicted and it would be a serious mistake to institutionalise it in urban design terms. There may be much to learn from Berlin in this regard.

Conclusions

Ambivalence is, arguably, a function of both the Northern Ireland political psyche and of postmodern architectural expression. That it is a feature of contemporary Belfast's urban design identity is not surprising – it is a consequence of a certain loss of local confidence on the one hand, and an international stylistic trend on the other. The city's residential environments have sought the familiarity of the nostalgic vernacular while its city centre has sought the neutrality of consumerist modernity. In terms of identity it has looked backwards and forwards at the same time.

Neither, however, has been done with a great deal of conviction. Belfast's conservationist record is modest when compared with equivalent cities, and its espousal of innovative modern architecure has been equally lukewarm. It may have avoided the excesses of artificial heritage exploitation of other cities but it has also given the impression of having been slightly ashamed of its local character. The lack of a collective, shared identity has affected its built environment as well as its civic cohesion.

This has resulted in a perhaps necessary tendency to design for war as well as for peace. Defensive approaches to residential layouts, to city centre access, to façade protection and, particularly, to 'peace wall' construction project an uncomfortable image in an era of positive place marketing and promotion. Nevertheless, other cities have adopted defensive forms of architecture for other reasons so the differences are less significant than they appear to be at first sight. Decentralisation of retailing and the privatisation of public space are universal problems.

A common thread, it has been argued, in the evolution of Belfast's built environment this century has been the absence of perceived inclusivity. The Edwardian city was perceived to exclude Catholics, as some parts of the modern city are now perceived to exclude Protestants; the consumerist city of the 1980s was perceived to exclude the less well-off, while the terrorised city of the 1970s effectively excluded everyone. The lack of extensive open space in the centre is a long-standing problem, as is the continued over-reliance on private forms of transport. The combination of traditional attitudes to sectarian space and contemporary attitudes to privatised space have excluded citizens from full participation in the life of their city.

The great opportunity now, therefore, is to face the challenge of designing for inclusivity – to accept the logic of the new political accommodation and apply it to the built environment – to design for an 'open-minded' rather than a 'closed-minded' city. The Department of the Environment has recently encouraged inclusive approaches to strategic plan-making and to 'visioning' the city; Belfast City Council has recently 'opened up' the centre for pop concerts and entertainment events; Laganside Corporation has 'opened up' the riverside around

Waterfront Hall (although the preponderance of privatised development space is a concern); the political system, for so long ossified in
sectarian exclusivity, now shows signs of 'opening up' to the demands
of community integration. These are tentative signs but they are positive ones. The city's architecture should now begin to reflect local and
collective 'pride of place' in both its traditional and emerging town-
scapes. The age of ambivalence should now be over.

Notes

 1 C. Jencks, 'Post Modernism and Discontinuity', *Journal of Architectural Design*, Special Edition (1987).
 2 C. Boyer, 'The Return of Aesthetics to City Planning', *Society* (May/June 1988).
 3 P. Healy, 'Planning for the 1990's', Department of Town and Country Planning, – University of Newcastle upon Tyne, *Working Paper Series*, No. 7 (1989).
 4 R. Schusterman, *Pragmatist Aesthetics: Living Beauty, Rethinking Art* (London: Blackwell Press, 1992).
 5 S. Lash and J. Urry, *The End of Organised Capitalism* (London: Polity Press, 1993), p. 287.
 6 M. Savage and A. Warde, *Urban Sociology*, Capitalism and Modernity (London: Macmillan, 1993).
 7 R. Weiner, *The Rape and Plunder of the Shankill* (Belfast: Farset Co-operative Press, 1978).
 8 C.E.B. Brett, *Buildings of Belfast* (Belfast: Friar's Bush Press, 1985), p. 47.
 9 Ibid., p. 64.
10 Ibid., p. 65.
11 Weiner, op. cit., pp. 27–8.
12 T. Blackman, *Planning Belfast: a Case Study of Public Policy and Community Action* (Aldershot: Avebury, 1991).
13 Only two significant private sector investments were made over a 10-year period between 1972 and 1982. Belfast Chamber of Trade, Department of the Environment for Northern Ireland and Belfast City Council, *Report on the Belfast City Centre: the Way Forward Seminar* (1983).
14 Department of the Environment for Northern Ireland, *The Heart of the City Conference Report* (November 1980) and *Belfast City Centre – the Way Forward Seminar Report* (October 1983).
15 S. Mooney and F. Gaffikin, *Reshaping Space and Society: a Critical Review of the Belfast Urban Area Plan* (Belfast: Centre of the Unemployed, 1988).
16 M. Patton 'Looking Back in Anger', *Ulster Architect* (June 1985), pp. 2–5.
17 W.J.V. Neill, *Reimaging the Pariah City: Urban Development in Belfast and Detroit* (Aldershot: Avebury, 1995), pp. 50–76.
18 J. Hendry and J.M. McEldowney, *Conservation in Belfast*, Report to the Department of the Environment for Northern Ireland, Department of Architecture and Planning, Queen's University Belfast (1986) pp. 4–13.
19 R. Hewison, *The Heritage Industry* (London: Methuen, 1987) p. 47.
20 N. Ascherson, 'Why Heritage is Right-Wing', *The Observer* (8 November 1987).

21 D. Harvey, *The Condition of Postmodernity* (Oxford: Blackwell, 1990), pp. 62–98.
22 M. Pawley, *Terminal Architecture* (London: Reakteon Books, 1998) pp. 93–111.
23 J. Hendry and J.M. McEldowney, op. cit.
24 T. Oc and S. Tiesdall, *Safer City Centres* (London: Paul Chapman, 1998), pp. 1–20.
25 R. Rogers, *Cities for a Small Planet* (London: Faber, 1998), pp. 9–10.
26 A. Mandani-Pour, *Design of Urban Space* (Chichester, John Wiley and Sons, 1997), pp. 83–7.
27 M. Pawley, op. cit.
28 P. Stollard, 'The Architecture of No-Man's Land', *Architect's Journal*, No. 31, Vol. 180 (1984), pp. 24–39.
29 B. Anson, Response to 'Architecture of No-Man's Land', *Architect's Journal*, No. 37, Vol. 180 (1984), pp. 47–8.
30 J.M. McEldowney and J. Hendry, 'Protection and Neutrality in a Divided City', *Journal of European Spatial Research and Policy*, No. 1, Vol. 2 (1995), pp. 78–87.
31 C.E.B. Brett, 'Conservation amidst Conflict', *Icomos Information* (October/December 1986), pp. 15–20.

Part III
Cultural Diversity in Berlin and Belfast: Cultural Quarters within the City

8
Turkish Commercial and Business Activities in Berlin: a Case of Organic Urban Development and Contact

Renate Müller

The Turkish resident population of Berlin is the largest non-German population group in the city. In the course of the last three decades a complex Turkish infrastructure has developed in the urban area of Berlin, characterised not only by a vigorous cultural and group way of life, but also by many and varied commercial and economic activities on the part of Turkish self-employed persons or entrepreneurs.

The present chapter deals with the development of the Turkish economy in the Berlin urban area, characteristics of which are that during the last few years these commercial activities have become increasingly diversified, have grown in number and their physical distribution over the city area continues to enlarge.

Turkish entrepreneurs create through their economic activities a secure basis for their existence, not only for themselves and their families, but they also make an active contribution to creating a multicultural urban society. Their enterprises represent places for daily social intercourse and intercultural meeting and provide an example of spontaneous, organic, unplanned development processes in Berlin.

The Turkish resident population in Berlin

Out of the 444 000 non-Germans in Berlin, the Turkish population of approximately 137 000 persons represents roughly one-third of all the non-Germans in the city. There was an unabated flow of Turkish labour migrants until the end of the recruitment action in 1973;[1] in addition, family members joined the migrant workers; coupled with prospects of a more extended stay in the city – signs of which were already becoming evident by the early 1970s – all these factors contributed to continual increase in the Turkish ethnic minority population group. Many of these Turks in Berlin are already third generation and represent the largest Turkish community outside Turkey.

In comparison with other nationalities which have settled in Berlin, socio-spatial grouping within the resident Turkish population has developed in the most clear and visible manner.

The western urban districts of Kreuzberg, Neukölln, Wedding, Schöneberg and Tiergarten show the highest concentration areas (Map 8.1). Seventy-three per cent of Berlin's Turkish population live in these five districts. The Urban District of Kreuzberg, where the proportion of inhabitants of Turkish origin in some streets amounts to as much as 80 per cent of the total population, comprises with its 28 639 inhabitants the largest number of Turkish residents in absolute terms (18.4 per cent of Kreuzberg inhabitants), followed by Neukölln (27 025), Wedding

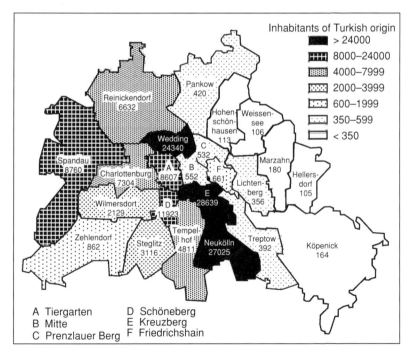

Map 8.1 Distribution of the Turkish population amongst the urban districts (Bezirke) of the city

(24 340) and Schöneberg (11 923). The Urban District of Hellersdorf in the eastern part of the city with 105 Turkish inhabitants (0.1 per cent) has the lowest number. Thus the former political division of the city is quite clearly reflected in the spatial distribution of the Turkish resident population in the urban area. Existing ethnic concentrations in the western part of the city are obviously very persistent, since up to the present time Turkish residents have rarely moved from western to eastern urban districts.

From the end of the 1960s onwards, Turkish labour migrants moved increasingly into urban redevelopment and potential redevelopment areas designated by the Berlin city and regional government in inner-city pre-war housing areas (zones in transition). In these areas Turkish families were able to obtain inexpensive housing quickly and without complications, because a major part of the German population had left the areas prior to the proposed demolition of the dwellings. Generally speaking, landlords granted foreign families short-term leases on small, ill-equipped apartments in dilapidated buildings due for demolition. Rental agreements were concluded at short notice; it was also possible to have more people than permissible in an apartment (overcrowding), with the result that primarily large Turkish families with children settled in these areas. By means of ethnic networks it was possible for related families, friends and acquaintances to find accommodation in neighbourhoods of close proximity.

This process of physical concentration in the Turkish resident population in western inner-city pre-war housing was accompanied in many instances by structural transformation, of which the principal characteristic features were:

- gradual decrease of other population groups, in particular German;
- decrease in German businessmen, industry and craft practitioners, compared with Turkish counterparts; and
- Turkish provision of culture, sport and entertainment facilities.[2]

In these residential areas in the course of the last thirty years, ethnic structures have become established which have kept these parts of the city attractive for new immigrants. At the present time they can provide many and varied economic, social, cultural and political infrastructure services for the Turkish population, and also for non-Turkish Berlin inhabitants.

The development of Turkish commercial life in Berlin

The Berlin-Turkish economy initially came into being at the end of the 1960s to supply Turkish immigrants' needs in the population concentration areas. In the 1970s economic niches in trade fields were occu-

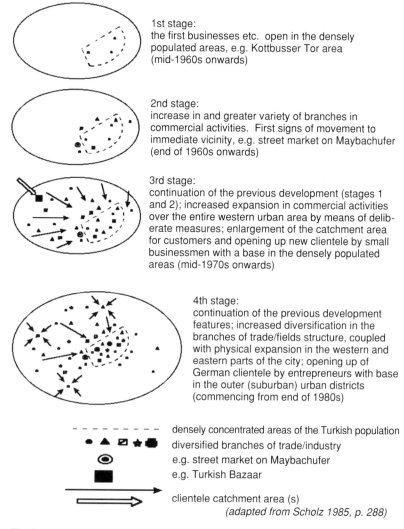

1st stage:
the first businesses etc. open in the densely populated areas, e.g. Kottbusser Tor area (mid-1960s onwards)

2nd stage:
increase in and greater variety of branches in commercial activities. First signs of movement to immediate vicinity, e.g. street market on Maybachufer (end of 1960s onwards)

3rd stage:
continuation of the previous development (stages 1 and 2); increased expansion in commercial activities over the entire western urban area by means of deliberate measures; enlargement of the catchment area for customers and opening up new clientele by small businessmen with a base in the densely populated areas (mid-1970s onwards)

4th stage:
continuation of the previous development features; increased diversification in the branches of trade/fields structure, coupled with physical expansion in the western and eastern parts of the city; opening up of German clientele by entrepreneurs with base in the outer (suburban) urban districts (commencing from end of 1980s)

- - - - - - - - - densely concentrated areas of the Turkish population
● ▲ ▨ ★ ▆ diversified branches of trade/industry
◉ e.g. street market on Maybachufer
▆ e.g. Turkish Bazaar

⟹ clientele catchment area (s)
(adapted from Scholz 1985, p. 288)

Fig. 8.1 Model for physical expansion of Turkish commercial activities in Berlin

pied which had formerly been dominated by Germans, and nowadays Berlin economic life is supplemented with a rich and varied supply of goods and services. In the past several years Turkish commercial life in Berlin has shown a high level of dynamic development, after having first reflected the various stages in the establishment of the Turkish resident population of Berlin.

First stage

As early as the first phase of immigration (1964–73), when Turkish labour migrants came to Berlin, Turkish businesses sprang up in the areas where the Turkish population was most prominently represented as far as numbers are concerned (Kreuzberg, Neukölln, Wedding). The chance of going into business on one's own account was available to Turkish entrepreneurs, in particular in those locations where a German had ceased trading and a niche existed in provision of goods or services. The opportunity arose in the first instance with the aim of providing for the specific needs of the Turkish immigrant population, particularly in food products. In the course of continued Turkish immigration, a wide variety of businesses was founded in the niche economy area, for example food shops, tailoring and mending shops, bakeries, shoe repairers (cobblers) and so on (first stage, niche economy, Fig. 8.1). These businesses were frequently more than a mere source of income; they formed part of a network, a social safety and security system which could protect relatives and acquaintances who did not have good residence entitlement rights from the danger of being expelled or deported from Germany.

Second stage

Together with the increase in the Turkish population, as family members followed wage-earners to Germany in the second immigration phase (1973–84), demand grew not only in a quantitative sense; in addition, the requirement for not previously supplied goods and services specifically designed for Turkish consumption characteristics expanded (2nd stage: supplementary economy, Fig. 8.1). Turkish entrepreneurs set up businesses in quite large numbers[3] which supplemented the previous goods and services provision (for example sweets and fancy bakery shops, butchers, clothing and fabric shops, household goods, video and pre-recorded tape cassettes, import–export businesses, travel agencies, translation agencies, general medical group practices, banks and so on). This development of a more differentiated business spectrum was also supported on the part of the German population, because certain Turkish products had become an integral part of German customers' demands. During this phase the movement of Turkish businesses into the immediate vicinity of the concentration areas began, areas in which the Turkish resident population gradually began to rise as a result of contact diffusion.

Parallel to this development a decline in German small businesses and craft trades in these areas began to become apparent. In particular Turkish entrepreneurs became active to an increasing extent in the fields which, due to staff, time and cost intensity, had become less attractive for German traders. Comparative advantages for Turkish businessmen, arising for example through division of labour within families and lower wages, favoured taking over businesses which were formerly in German hands. The result of this was that Turkish businesses were increasingly catering for the demands of the resident German population as well; both from the point of view of range of goods and from their display they sought to cater to this clientele.[4]

A demonstrative example for purposive expansion of Turkish commercial activities beyond the areas of population density is the street market on Maybachufer in Neukölln, which is held regularly on Tuesdays and Fridays.[5] Once the biggest open market in Berlin, it was threatened with closure at the beginning of the 1960s. As Turkish families moved into the area, the first Turkish market traders began to work there. Since this time there has been a noticeable steady and continuing rise of Turkish market dealers. The development of this open market is characterised by a structural change in demand and by a qualitative and quantitative extension of provision supplied by the market through the Turkish inhabitants.

Third stage

Alongside the continuation of the previously identified development elements (Stages 1 and 2), since the mid-1970s Turkish entrepreneurs have been shifting their business locations away from their principal residential areas into the adjacent and also into outer urban districts, with the aim of opening up new customer bases. This was prompted by the intention to reach Turkish people who were living outside the concentration areas. However, there was also evident an increase in the number of Turkish businesses aiming by means of their supply provision to attract German customers as well. This enlargement of local amenity provision took place in the main through street markets, kiosks and snack bars. A purposive move within this spatial expansion process was the opening of a Turkish Bazaar in 1980, at Bülowstrasse in a disused railway station in the Urban District of Schöneberg (3rd stage, Fig. 8.1). With Turkish provision of craft goods, antiques, jewellery and leather goods, it was intended to become an attraction for the city. Instead of the anticipated Berlin visitors from other parts of the city and tourists, however, the market attracted primarily Turkish customers. After reunification, the underground line returned to regular use and the bazaar closed at the beginning of the 1990s.

Fourth stage

At the time the Berlin Wall came down, new commercial areas became open for Turkish entrepreneurs in the eastern part of the city. Since this time Turkish traders have increasingly moved their commercial activities to the urban districts in the eastern half of Berlin as well. They were the first to supply the resident population of these districts at street markets and in abandoned shops.

For the outer western urban districts it has been shown that stable commercial existence opportunities for Turkish businessmen are also present in urban districts in which the Turkish population is in a clear minority. Small Turkish businessmen in these districts have by now a steady German clientele to call upon.

In addition to increasing spatial expansion and numerical increase in businesses, the branch structure of the Turkish economic activity continued to diversify during the 1990s (fourth stage, Fig. 8.1). In 1997, the Turkish 'Yellow Pages' (Is Rehberi), which has appeared annually since 1996, listed as many as 124 different branches of trade. This development responds on the one hand to the needs of the Turkish population which is becoming more socially differentiated, and on the other hand reveals increasing orientation towards the local German population. Thus for example in the gastronomy field, in addition to snack bars and Turkish cafés where only Turkish people get together, there have arisen high-class restaurants with good cuisine; in the motor trade, car showrooms, specialist car parts businesses and qualified car repair businesses were set up, whereas in the 1970s there were only small vehicle repair workshops.

Distribution of Turkish commercial activities

Turkish entrepreneurs with their businesses are represented to varying degrees in all 23 Berlin urban districts. The distribution pattern of

Turkish commercial activities parallels the distribution of the Turkish resident population in the urban districts. Admittedly, there are no official figures for the total number of Turkish businesses, but according to the Association of German-Turkish Employers in Berlin-Brandenburg, there are approximately 5000 Turkish self-employed persons in Berlin. In 1997, Is Rehberi listed in all 3548 Turkish companies, 3235 in the western part and 313 in the eastern part of the city (Fig. 8.2).

In addition to the intensive fields of activity in the typical residential areas for Turkish immigrants in the urban districts of Kreuzberg, Neukölln and Wedding, new points of main emphasis of activity are arising in the inner city urban districts in the eastern part of the city. In the urban districts of Prenzlauer Berg, Mitte and Friedrichshain, Turkish commercial activities are numerically particularly great, in comparison with the number of Turkish inhabitants. It may be assumed that these businesses are operated by Turkish entrepreneurs from the adjacent western concentration density areas who are tailoring their provision of goods and services towards non-Turkish groups of the population. Currently Turkish gastronomy businesses maintain a strong position in the eastern part of Berlin: at 55 per cent they represent more than half of Turkish commercial activities (in the western part the figure is 23 per cent). Similarly to the situation in the 1970s in the western part of Berlin, using market niches, Turkish small businessmen have attempted rapidly to compensate to some extent for the lack of local traders, by means of their local amenity provision businesses: 'In this way they brought life back to the streets and thus contributed to regeneration of urban areas which were at risk.'[6]

Motives for setting up in business

Surveys of Turkish businessmen in Berlin revealed that these businesses represented for many entrepreneurs an important symbol of independence. This self-actualisation in working for oneself was always a powerful impulse to found one's own business, even for the many Turkish entrepreneurs of the first immigrant generation. Many now see their self-employed status in Berlin as an alternative to their own business in Turkey. Changed intentions with regard to staying or returning home have over the course of time led to them abandoning their original goal of setting up a business in their own country. A lack of betterment opportunity, dissatisfaction with their income level and pressure in the

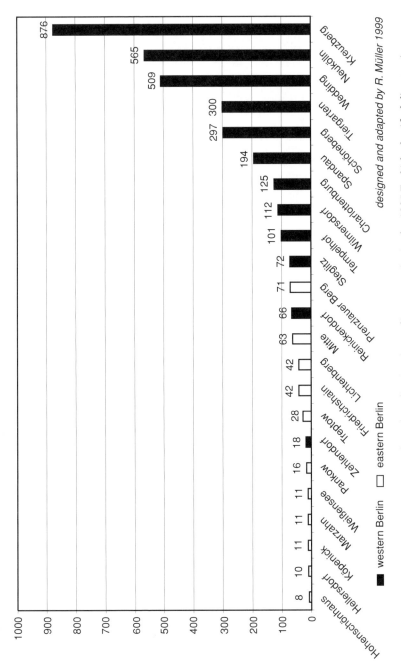

Fig. 8.2 Turkish economic activities in Berlin urban districts (according to entries in the 1997 Turkish classified directory)

labour market, which has only been revealed in Berlin in its full sever-ity since the Wall came down:[7] all these have effected, precisely in Turkish young people, an increased focus on becoming self-employed. At the time of reunification, Berlin experienced quite a boom in new businesses: since 1991 annually 1400 firms with Turkish owners have been registered – although annually about 1000 are also de-registered

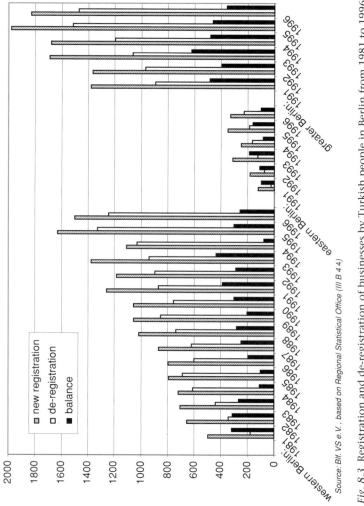

Fig. 8.3 Registration and de-registration of businesses by Turkish people in Berlin from 1981 to 1996

(Fig. 8.3). Despite frequent failure, becoming self-employed is chosen as a way to combat job loss.[8]

Integration aspects of Turkish commercial activities

If integration of the Turkish population into the urban economy of Berlin is considered, the description given above means it is possible to identify a development involving entirely positive opportunities to participate in the economic life of Berlin. The numerical growth of Turkish economic activities can be assessed as an indication that such opportunities for economic participation do exist and are being used. In addition, the differentiated range of provision of goods and services supplied by Turkish businessmen reveals numerous intertwining relationships with the domestic economy and is also directed – to some extent additionally – towards German clienteles.

Turkish entrepreneurs with their base in the concentration areas (Kreuzberg, Neukölln and Wedding) appreciate, of course, physical proximity to their homes, familiarity with the neighbourhood, proximity to their circles of acquaintances and the pronounced presence of the Turkish population as significant locational factors in setting up businesses; however, the ethnic origin of their customers does not relate exclusively to the Turkish community which has settled in these locations. In the field of local amenity provision, orientation towards German customers cannot be discounted, even in the areas of the city which are primarily inhabited by Turkish immigrants. The overwhelming Turkish clientele of numerous businesses is in many cases attributable to their specific provision of services. Dealings for example in the cosmetic or insurance fields depend to a high degree on an 'advance issue' of confidence on the part of the customer. This is positively reinforced by shared ethnic origins and common language.

Deliberate attention to German clientele can be identified in Turkish businessmen who set up businesses in Berlin urban districts where they provide services which, despite demand, are not made available by German traders. One example of this could be the Turkish garment alteration and repair shops which can frequently be found in the outer Berlin urban districts.

Turkish–German commercial relationships are however not only furthered by means of the clientele. Many Turkish small businessmen can call upon intensive contacts with German business partners and work in conjunction with German outside supply companies. Advertising strategies are now being targeted towards being represented in addition in German media vehicles, for example, in the Berlin 'Yellow Pages'; Turkish companies are encouraged to appeal to German customers.

Conclusions

It is hard nowadays to imagine the greater Berlin cityscape without Turkish businessmen. This is particularly pronounced in the fields of gastronomy and food or grocery shops. Those parts of the city where inhabitants are primarily of Turkish origin seem unusual, with their mixture of many and varied businesses, at first glance to a German eye. Greengrocers, bakeries, snack bars and other commercial enterprises create stimulating impressions; most of all, people have come to appreciate their culinary specialities. Outside the inner city, an increasing number of Turkish businesses in a variety of fields are now to be found in Berlin urban districts. Turkish businessmen are in this way making an active contribution to a multicultural urban society. Their places of business represent crucial interfaces of everyday intercourse and encounter between different walks of life. Equally, they are, through the medium of their entrepreneurial initiative, pursuing the individual goal of creating employment which ensures a secure existence for themselves and for their family.

Notes

1   Recruitment of foreign labour immigrants to the Federal Republic of Germany (West Germany) occurred on the basis of bilateral agreements which the FRG concluded in 1955 with Italy, in 1960 with Greece and Spain, in 1961 with Turkey, in 1964 with Portugal, in 1965 with Tunisia and Morocco, in 1968 with Yugoslavia. From these eight countries, the Federal Office of Employment (Employment Agency) using official recruitment commissions, placed in all 2.39 million workers who migrated to Germany between 1955 and the end of the recruitment drive in 1973.
2   F. Scholz, 'Räumliche Ausbreitung türkischer Wirtschaftsaktivitäten in Berlin', B. Hofmeister *et al.* (eds), *Berlin. Beiträge zur Geographie eines Großstadtraumes. Festschrift zum 45. Deutschen Geographentag in Berlin* (Berlin: Reimer, 1985) pp. 275ff.
3   Approximately 2000 Turkish businesses existed in 1983. E. Seidel-Pielen, *Aufgespießt – Wie der Döner über die Deutschen kam* (Hamburg: Rotbuch Verlag, 1996) p. 50.
4   Scholz , op. cit., p. 289.
5   U.B. Spies, 'Der Türkenmarkt am Maybachufer (Kreuzberg/Neukölln)', *Occasional Paper Geographie: Türkische Wirtschaftsaktivitäten in Berlin*, H. 3 (Berlin: Freie Universität Berlin/Institut für Geographische Wissenschaften/

ZELF, 1998). F. Scholz (ed.), 'Türkische Bevölkerung in Kreuzberg. Gewerbe – Handel – Wohnen. Kreuzberg-Projekt Sommersemester 1996, Institut für Geographische *Occasional Paper Geographie,* H. 8 (Berlin: Freie Universität Berlin/Institut für Geographische Wissenschaften/ZELF, 1996).

6   A. Ersöz, 'Türkische Ökonomie nach der Wende in Berlin', R. Amann and B. von Neumann-Cosel (eds), *Berlin. Eine Stadt im Zeichen der Migration* (Darmstadt: Verlag für wissenschaftliche Publikationen, 1997) p. 115.

7   Major industrial businesses have either relocated or closed down.

8   Ersöz, op. cit.

9
Contacts and Conflicts over Worship and Burial in the Kreuzberg District of Berlin

Peter Heine

After the two major Christian confessions, Islam represents the third largest religious grouping in Germany. Estimates suggest that there are approximately three million Moslems living in the country, about three hundred thousand of whom are German citizens. About three-quarters of the resident Moslem population are from Turkey, the next largest groups are from Bosnia and northern Africa. However, by now there is virtually no area in the Moslem world from which people have not come to live in Germany.[1] In particular it is the major conurbations along the Rhine Valley, in the southern part of Germany and in Berlin where Moslem immigrants have settled. In Berlin itself, the districts of Wedding, Neukölln and Kreuzberg[2] are home to the majority of the Moslem population. Various estimates have taken as their base figure about three hundred thousand members of the Moslem faith in Berlin.[3] According to assumptions by leaders of the Moslem congregations and the author's own observations, it can be stated that about one-third are practising Moslems. The overwhelming proportion of Moslems carry out their religious duties only sporadically, if at all. However, ritual observance carries with it the potential for cultural conflict manifest in a spatial form.

Ritual observances: prayer and mosques

Primarily for practical considerations, the need arose for immigrants to organise themselves in some way as Moslems. In this context, assembling a form of congregation is in the first instance not necessarily required for reasons of dogma. In his relationship to God a Moslem does not require any human mediating institution or human authority. There is therefore no priesthood in Islam. The believer stands in direct communication to God. In addition Islamic dogma is so straight-forward that it does not require any particular explanations. On the other hand there are, however, requirements to form a congregation for ritual reasons. On Friday afternoons Moslems are enjoined to come together to pray as a congregation. This requirement has physical implications, which can lead to conflict.

Mosque clubs

The prescribed ritual cleanliness required for compulsory prayers can be practised more easily in the community of Moslems. The Friday prayer meeting needs a mosque or a prayer room which in fact need only fulfil a number of ritually prescribed conditions. However, the prayer area must be clean and needs to be regularly maintained. In the Islamic world costs arising out of the maintenance of mosques are derived from 'pious foundations' or through state funds. Of course, in the German situation neither of these is available. Since it was unlikely that an individual Moslem would be in a position to bear the costs and risks of maintaining a mosque, Moslems in Germany organised them-selves by means of registered associations. In a short space of time these associations applied to be recognised as charitable or non-profit organisations, which makes a number of privileges and tax concessions possible. The community structure of the local Islamic congregations was therefore dependent on the regulations in German club and associ-ation laws. This meant a certain amount of organisational regulations for the Moslem communities, who thus had to adapt themselves to organisational given facts in the Federal Republic. At the same time prerequisites in the Federal law led to certain conflicts within the Islamic community in Germany. If a Moslem congregation establishes itself in Germany according to the law on associations, it must among other things elect a committee, decide on the amount of membership fees and specify the purpose of the association. In numerous cases this led to disagreement, the reasons being not so much dogmatic as matters of personal prestige, political affiliation and practical matters concerning the organisation of the specific association in question.

Religious heterogeneity and mosque clubs

These 'mosque clubs' were set up in particular according to national and/or ethnic differences, including, for example, some Arabian or Bosnian mosques. The overwhelming majority of 'mosque clubs' were associations affiliated to the Sunni sect; the number of Shiite-influenced mosques is, by contrast, very small. The most recent figures for Berlin make this clear: out of 74 Berlin mosques, 58 belong to the various Turkish affiliations. Of this global figure, only four can be indisputably identified as Shiite mosques.[4] The freedom of faith and religion in Germany which is guaranteed by the Federal Basic Law has played a part in facilitating Moslem cultural heterogeneity. Since the early part of the 1970s, some mosque communities have come into being, founded by religious and/or political organisations and parties which, due to state control, would have no chance of operating in the country of origin. This process led to the Turkish Prime Minister's Office for Religious Affairs being prompted to set up in Germany organisations to rival those which would be outlawed in Turkey.[5] In particular at the end of the 1970s, this effort to stop the fragmentation process was very successful. Very quickly imams sent from Turkey were able to set up their own mosques or to drive away oppositional associations from existing mosques, taking over leases on premises as they expired, but primarily carrying out a straightforward campaign of religious propaganda against opposition groups. These 'officially recognised' Islamic-religious organisations are gathered together in a group known as DITIB.[6] Half the mosques involved are located in the Neukölln district. Another organisation, called the Islamic Federation, which adopts a critical stance towards secularist Turkish ideology associated with the name of Kemal Atatürk, also reveals geographic concentration, this time in Kreuzberg. The Association of Islamic Cultural Centres (VIKZ) is, however, widely distributed with its mosques in numerous districts in the western part of Berlin.[7] Political changes in Turkey since the end of the 1980s have meant that tensions between the official Turkish Islam in Germany and these independent groups have declined. At the present time there is a 'distanced friendly co-existence' or perhaps better expressed as a sort of rivalry as it were between fellow workers.

Mosques: design for permanence

Whereas most of the Moslems who came to Germany as migrant workers or asylum seekers in quite large numbers, starting from the middle of the 1960s, were assuming that they would return to their native country in a few years' time, for about the last ten years they have come to realise that they have settled permanently in the Federal Republic.[8] This realisation of their situation had a number of consequences, including those in the religious sphere. Initially it must be clearly stated that for Moslems it is not just a matter of course that they can live permanently in a country outside the Islamic world. This is because they assume that they would not be able to practise their faith as precisely in a non-Islamic society as in their country of origin. Staying, particularly permanently, in a religiously alien world needs special justification which can be achieved quite adequately by reason of economic factors. However, it must be ensured that Moslems are able to practise their faith without state hindrance.[9] Once they became aware that their stay was to be permanent, there was a change in the attitude of Moslems and their organisations with regard to the German public and vice versa. Up until the mid-1980s, Moslems had been carrying out their religious duties virtually unnoticed by the German public. Mosques could hardly be identified as such: they were in disused garages, empty factory buildings or away from the road in back courtyards. Frequently, all that attracted the notice of the German neighbourhood was that at certain times the number of available car parking spaces was considerably reduced. The fact that this phenomenon occurred principally on Fridays or on Moslem holy days was not perceived. Moslems were obviously not concerned to identify the particular character of a building or its function to the outside world. Official German institutions were also little interested in the facts of Islamic life. Evidence for this attitude may be shown by the fact that, after an academic survey in the mid-1970s of the mosques and prayer rooms which existed in Berlin, there were no official or semi-official studies of this question, and at the Institute for Asian and African Studies at the Humboldt University of Berlin it was not until 1998 that a similar study was carried out and the results published with support from the Berlin Government Commissioner for Foreigners.[10]

In the last decade this situation has undergone a marked change. Moslem organisations in a number of German towns and cities were successful in initiating the construction or setting up of mosques which because of their architectural styles were recognisable as such. In this context, they are always what are known as 'Friday mosques', that is, those sacred buildings in which Moslem inhabitants of a municipality are able to comply with their religious duty of communal Friday prayers. If these structures are built by Turkish organisations they are in the neo-Osman style with one or more minarets. There have regularly been protests by German residents against the building of such mosques. Berlin, too, has not been free of conflicts on these grounds. Since the mid-1980s the Turkish Consulate-General and DITIB have been trying to erect a central mosque in Berlin. Numerous requests to the relevant local authority institutions were either processed with many delays or turned down immediately. At least, this was the impression received by the Moslem organisations.[11]

Ritual observance: burial and cemeteries

A second problem confronting the Moslem population in Germany and in Berlin is the question of burial of the dead. In this instance the differing Islamic traditions and the prescriptions of Islamic law are in direct conflict with German regulations in cemetery management. A deceased Moslem is to be buried if at all possible within 24 hours of the time of death. The body is to be placed in the earth wrapped in a grave cloth, but not in a coffin; it is to be laid to rest in such a way that the head points towards Mecca. For many years it has been the practice of German cemetery operators to bury the body in the coffin with no particular attention being given to the geographical alignment of the rows of graves. Such differences in burial traditions have led, amongst other things, to the fact that the oldest Moslem ritual site in existence in Germany is a cemetery, the Mohammedan Cemetery, as it is known, on Columbia Damm immediately adjacent to Berlin's Tempelhof Airport. This cemetery on Columbia Damm has received over many years the bodies of Moslems who died whilst in the city. In this way it has become a remarkable document of, and testimony to, Islamic life in Berlin, and in particular bears witness to the various groups of immigrants who in the course of time have lived and worked in the metropolis of Berlin. In view of the number of foreign workers coming to Germany, it was quite evident that the cemetery would not be suitable for long-term use. Over the course of time, and with the increasing age of the Moslem population, the problem of Moslem burials has become more and more pressing. One of the solutions was for major funeral undertaking companies to arrange for immediate transport of the deceased to the country of origin which still happens, in many cases, at the present time. However, by now there have been changes in this practice as well, due to the fact that increasingly large numbers of Moslems have hardly any relatively young family members in their country of origin who would be able to tend the grave and carry out the regular prescribed rituals. The number of demands by Moslems for grave sites in German cemeteries has therefore risen considerably.

If Moslem deceased are to be buried in this country, one of the problems is that in German municipal cemeteries the rights to a grave site can only be acquired for a specified period of time of between 15 and 20 years. After this time the grave site can be reused.[12] In accordance with the feelings of the majority of Moslems resident in Germany, this practice constitutes disturbance of the peace of the dead in their graves. They are accustomed to thinking that by the tradition of their country of origin the graves will remain in place for eternity. In accordance with Islamic belief, the dead remain in their graves and await resurrection on Judgement Day. In this context it is not a factor that opinions amongst Islamic legal experts may differ: the Moslems who live here are of the opinion described. A variety of Islamic organisations do make attempts to secure special grave sites for Moslems in German cemeteries. Even when these are successful, up to the present time no solutions have been found to the question of the duration of the peace of the dead. Other organisations are anticipating setting up private Moslem cemeteries where the problem would not arise. They have also by now come to realise that, with the number of plots required and in view of the number of elderly people in the Moslem population living in Germany, they would quickly reach the limit of their capacities.[13] The question of how to deal with this problem continues to be unresolved, in the Berlin situation as elsewhere.

Notes

1. P. Heine, 'Verbreitungsgebiet der islamischen Religion: Zahlen und Information in der Gegenwart', W. Ende and U. Steinbach (eds), *Der Islam in der Gegenwart* (München: Beck, 1996) p. 48.
2. Map 8.1.
3. A. Kapphan, 'Zuwanderung und Stadtkultur. Die Verteilung ausländischer Bevölkerung in Berlin', R. Amann and B. von Neumann-Cosel (eds), *Eine Stadt im Zeichen der Migration* (Darmstadt: Verlag für wissenschaftliche Publikationen, 1997) pp. 36–41.
4. Cp. the address list (register) of mosques in Berlin; G. Jonker and A. Kapphan (eds), *Moscheen und islamisches Leben in Berlin* (Berlin: published by Ausländerbeauftragte des Senats von Berlin, 1999) pp. 73–5.
5. W. Schiffauer, 'Der Weg zum Gottesstaat. Die fundamentalistischen Gemeinden türkischer Arbeitsmigranten in der Bundesrepublik', *Historische Anthropologie*, I (1993) pp. 468–84.
6. DITIB = Diyanet Isleri Türk Islam Birligi (Türkisch-Islamische Union der Anstalt für Religion – Turkish-Islamic Union of the Office for Religion).
7. J. Eisenberg and E. Meister, 'Wohnumfeld und soziale Schichtung', Jonker and Kapphan (eds), op. cit., p. 28.
8. Author's interview with Ismail Birol, Managing Director of the Islamic Academy Islah in Cologne in December 1998.
9. Hagemann, Ludwig and A.T. Khoury, *Dürfen Muslime auf Dauer in einem nicht-islamischen Land leben? Zu einer Dimension der Integration muslimischer Mitbürger in eine nicht-islamische Gesellschaftsordnung* (Altenberge: Oros, 1997).

10 Jonker, Kapphan (eds), op. cit.
11 R. Przybyla, 'Projekte und Perspektiven einer Zentralmoschee', Jonker and Kapphan (eds): op. cit., pp. 59–65.
12 G. Kokkelink, 'Islamische Bestattung auf kommunalen Friedhöfen', G. Höpp and G. Jonker (eds), in fremder Erde. Zur Geschichte und Gegenwart der islamischen Bestattung In Deutschland, *Arbeitshefte Zentrum Moderner Orient*, Vol. 11 (Berlin: Das Arabische Buch, 1996) pp. 63–82.
13 Y. Karakasoglu, 'Die Bestattung von Muslimen in der Bundesrepublik Deutschland aus der Sicht türkisch-islamischer Organisationen', Höpp and Jonker (eds), op. cit., pp. 83–106.

10
Remaking the City: the Role of Culture in Belfast

Frank Gaffikin, Michael Morrissey and Ken Sterrett

This chapter explores the diverse contribution of culture in regenerating a city like Belfast, badly divided both in social and sectarian terms. Beginning with a brief historical account of Belfast's industrial development, it identifies the sequence of planning initiatives in more recent decades in order to reshape the city in a more post-industrial period. It notes the emphasis accorded the city centre as an assumed neutral space capable of accommodating new growth in the service sector, and the relationship between this revitalisation and the prospects of the city's most deprived communities. At this point, the chapter considers the potential of the cultural industries in the city as a whole, and in particular in those communities, such as West Belfast, most scarred by economic restructuring and political violence. There is a problem here. The very term 'cultural industries' is ill-defined. Clearly, this sector is significant and growing. But, at the most generous interpretation, it can include every barman and waiter working at the interface between tourism and the cultural sector. However, whatever the problem with precision in this regard, the chapter considers the capacity of Belfast to deploy the sector as a contribution to regeneration (especially through the notion of a 'cultural corridor') while coping with deep social and sectarian division. Outlining the difference between ethnic, neutral, transcendent and shared cultural space, it examines the possibility of a city whose international appeal could rest with a more multicultural future, where diversity is prized as a social and economic asset.

Belfast: historical development

A century ago, Belfast was the industrial heartland of Ireland. Its rapid advance had given it a global status as a production site. In shipbuilding, for instance, the technical and design skills won international plaudits, and its business boomed.[1] A commentary of the time proclaimed:

> We mark the eminent status of Belfast in the modern world, her high commercial and industrial distinction, her wealth and influence, her constant growth, and the meritorious character of her municipal institutions ... we are bound to admit that very few cities of the present age owe more to the splendid public spirit of their residents.[2]

An economic base centred on shipbuilding, engineering and linen also accommodated a ropeworks, which by 1900 was the largest in the world, and a printing industry that in the same year employed 1400 men.[3] This vibrant growth had seen the old Georgian town remade into a buoyant Victorian and Edwardian city, and the population rise from under 20 000 at the start of the nineteenth century to nearly five times that in mid-century and to almost 350 000 by 1901. This was an urban growth rate unsurpassed by any other urban centre in the British Isles.[4] The nineteenth century and early twentieth century also witnessed the cramming of large families into mazes of terraced housing, where squalor, poverty and disease were common. Sectarian conflict persistently divided Belfast's working-class communities and this only briefly and very partially abated in the 1930s depression years. Though in 1960, the city's shipbuilding employed close to 20 000, deindustrialisation saw a loss of 14 000 manufacturing jobs in the urban area between 1961 and 1968. By the end of the decade, the shipyard employed around half of what it had at the start, attempts at stalling the job drain in traditional sectors like linen were failing, and the outcome was severe unemployment in Belfast, particularly acute in predominantly Catholic districts. By the 1970s, with its significant public sector dependence for jobs and income, Belfast's future as an industrial city seemed doomed.

However, the death of cities, frequently predicted, has rarely translated into reality. Cities contain significant human resources and communication infrastructures that can regain their competitive advantage. Belfast remains an important regional centre. With 18 per cent of the region's population, it has 30 per cent of the region's firms and 21 per cent of its retailing. Downtown has been restored. Laganside has helped turn the city to the river. Flagship schemes like the new Concert Hall are re-imaging the place. Major infrastructure such as the cross-harbour bridges has been invested. And all of these changes can help Belfast in its formidable challenge to recast itself in an age of a more service and knowledge-based economy.

Belfast at the crossroads: the need for a multicultural city

Nevertheless, Belfast stands at an important crossroads. It cannot recreate the glories of its industrial past. For one thing, the spatial constraints of a nineteenth-century city cannot accommodate the needs of twenty-first-century manufacturing. For another, it lost the productivity advantages of its traditional industries like shipbuilding and aircraft manufacture while unable to compete on price with the low-cost, low value-added production of developing economies. Moreover, fiscal stresses on central government ensure that there is no long-term public expenditure solution to urban problems. The city must therefore lift its trajectory and find a niche of competitive advantage in the global economy. Successful cities are competing on traded services, on the one hand, the new technologies of IT and communication and, on the other, the exploitation of cultural resources to find new products, new services and new means to attract tourism, the world's fastest growing industry.

This is not an easy path. For a start, the process is not symmetrical. Failing to take this path may guarantee failure, but seizing such opportunities does not guarantee success. The more cities compete with theatres, cultural activities, design, smart pubs and restaurants, the sharper will be the diminishing returns for what can be substantial investment in physical refurbishment and human resources. Nevertheless, Belfast has to look at culture as a source of regeneration and attempt to define its specific role among the many European cities with significant cultural attractions.

There is a second sense in which Belfast is at a crossroads. For thirty years, the city has been the site of the most intense expression of the Northern Ireland conflict. Over 40 per cent of those killed in Northern Ireland's Troubles died in Belfast, a rate of almost five deaths for every 1000 residents over the period. As a result, the city is a mosaic of ethnic territories. The North and West of the city have a majority of Catholics, the South and East a majority of Protestants. Within each segment, there are micro territories, frequently divided by 'peace' walls where people still hide behind their tribal ramparts and contested spaces that remain a perennial source of friction. In every sense, Belfast, like Berlin, is a divided city.

Culture in Northern Ireland is inseparable from identity, religion and politics. The republican challenge to the Northern Ireland state has been cultural as well as political, ideological and military. Belfast is the site of competing cultures and this competition extends to the use made of civic facilities and direct rivalry over the funding of different cultural events. As Northern Ireland drags itself slowly, painfully and with great difficulty towards peace, there is a crucial imperative to find the tolerance for a multicultural city. Belfast must thus look to a post-industrial future in which its rival cultures can find synergy rather than conflict in their differences.

Economic and physical modernisation in Belfast

As early as the 1960s, government reports in Northern Ireland implicitly acknowledged the inadequacy of the current forms of state intervention to achieve economic modernisation.[5] The Matthew Report specifically recommended industrial dispersal from the Belfast Urban Area to Greater Belfast and beyond to new 'key' and 'growth' centres.[6] To encourage this demagnetisation and requisite labour mobility, a stop line on Belfast's further expansion was proposed, together with new town developments. Matthew also emphasised the urgency of a concerted attack on dereliction to enhance Belfast's image. These reports culminated in the 1969 Belfast Urban Plan. The cumulative consequence of a much delayed housing programme[7] was comprehensive redevelopment for many traditional Belfast working-class communities. Apart from new build housing, land in the inner city was to be designated for major elevated motorways and new commercial/industrial development. Sections of the inner urban population were to be encouraged to 'decant' to the suburbs and new towns, the locations for anticipated multinational investment. There was scant evidence that the consultants were enthusiastic about Skeffington concepts of the need for public participation in planning.[8]

The implementation of Belfast's redevelopment coincided with the onset of the political crisis, which complicated the process by contributing to population shifts and urban blight.[9] By the early 1970s, the oil crisis and related recession dislodged predictions for investment and consumption patterns, car ownership and use, and economic growth. Fiscal retrenchment also impacted on the Plan's spending implications. Community protest,[10] violent conflict and starker economic times induced reconsideration of some key proposals of the 1969 Plan. Most obviously, this resulted by 1978 in a scaled-down version of the elevated motorway proposals.[11] Nevertheless, this extensive reshaping of space marked a departure for a region where the tradition of planning was weak.[12] The main legislation, the 1944 Planning (Interim Development) Act, had not created an experience of strategic land use planning, and proliferation of local government in a small region had not helped to coordinate Belfast's development in its regional context.[13]

The 1970s witnessed the continued relative shift to services for the Belfast urban economy. Manufacturing accounted for a third of employment in 1971, but just under a quarter of a decade later, government-sponsored industry had become very significant, growing from just over a fifth of manufacturing employment in the early 1960s to nearly a half by the early 1970s. But, the global economy of the 1980s rendered attraction of mobile capital to depressed regions like Northern Ireland more problematic. Local economic development agencies put less faith in the prospect of new inward investment restoring the manufacturing base to its former status. Since 1973 jobs in externally owned plants dropped by 53 per cent (over 46 000), and the number of plants by 41 per cent. Such plants accounted for over 50 per cent of local manufacturing jobs in 1973, but only 39 per cent in 1990.[14]

Post-industrial Belfast: planning in the 1980s

Within this shift to services, the main focus has been on resuscitating the central business district with retailing and office expansion, and extending its catchment by opening the city to the river by means of the waterfront Laganside scheme. The general rationale has been that 'improvements to the central area and the Lagan will play a major role in the regeneration and attraction of investment to the urban area as a whole'.[15] This reasoning was not without merit. At least nine supporting arguments can be cited:

- In each recent decade, regional investment has been mainly generated from one clear source. Up to the 1950s, it was still from indigenous industry; in the 1960s, it was from multinational capital, while in the 1970s, it was from boosted public spending. The 1980s saw an upsurge in private consumer spending,[16] and it was natural that planners should seek to accommodate this apparently buoyant sector.
- Manufacturing collapse in the 1970s led some observers to proclaim the inevitability of post-industrialism. Accordingly, a development package based on services seemed opportune.

- Emphasis on such service sector activities in turn was held to offer urban centres a new purpose, since many of these services remain labour intensive and, unlike new manufacturing, they still require to be located in large settlements of population.
- Focusing much of the regeneration effort in the concentrated space of the urban core lends it a high visibility. Arguably, similar investment spread more widely across the city would have a diluted impact on citizen morale and business confidence.
- Downtown Belfast suffered the ravages of the 1970s intensive bombing campaign, which destroyed property, and deterred custom and investment. Its rehabilitation in the 1980s could be considered proper recompense.
- The new employment generated in these downtown developments could be said to offer labour market opportunities in a neutral and safe location to some of the unemployed deterred by the 'chill factor' from seeking jobs elsewhere in the city. The former Minister, responsible for the current statutory Belfast Urban Area Plan published in 1989, emphasised this point. In justification of public investment in a mega shopping mall, known as CastleCourt, and in Laganside, he noted:[17] 'it will actually be spent so people currently in the ghettoes can find jobs in the city centre and enjoy a quality of life and an opportunity of choice which they don't have now'.
- By the 1980s, there was a trend to out-of-town shopping complexes. Without intervention to revitalise the urban core, there could have arisen a 'doughnut' effect, with further suburbanisation of people and activity and greater urban desolation.
- Belfast is a compact city. Thus, its downtown is more accessible to many of its neighbourhoods than its counterpart in many similarly sized cities.
- Since the new Belfast Urban Area Plan anticipated that 'most of the future growth in employment will take place in the service sector',[18] Belfast city centre, accounting for approximately a quarter of the urban economy's employment, was thought to be well placed to enhance its role as a regional centre.

Boosting Belfast in the 1990s

In recent years, a series of spectacular events have been held, dedicated to the city's international promotion, such as the Tall Ships Race, attracting 350 000 people, Hot Air Balloons attracting 250 000 people, and an international powerboat racing event on the Lagan, attracting 150 000. These were designed to raise local morale and to draw positive international attention.[19] But, cities can be 'sold' in different ways. In official promotional material for Belfast, for instance, emphasis is given to 'low labour cost, positive work ethic', and 'excellent labour rela-tions'.[20] Recently, great significance is reposed in the development role of public–private partnerships in the city.[21] Overall, the drive is to image Belfast as largely about its city centre, which is then projected as a normal and neutral space, free from the imprint of sectarianism: As expressed by one commentator, 'a post-modernist consumerist kaleido-scope of images floats uncomfortably on top of the brutalism of terrorist-proof buildings and the symbolism of the past. It is a condition of visual schizophrenia.'[22] The fragility of this projection in a city still torn by entrenched social and sectarian rivalries suggests that the city's full regeneration is dependent on its deep divisions being redressed.[23]

Social and sectarian division

Presently, Belfast is a city of just under 300 000. Between 1971 and 1991, it lost a third of its population. During this period, its population share of the wider Urban Area (BUA) fell from 70 to 59 per cent. But, the big decline happened in the inner city, where residents decreased by over half. Much of this pattern is familiar in industrial cities in Britain like Liverpool and Glasgow. What is distinctive about Belfast is the way this change has also been tracked by deepening segregation during a period of massive public housing redevelopment and inten-sive violent conflict. It has become a more 'Catholic' city. Thus, whereas Catholics made up a third of the city population in the early 1970s, they now constitute over two-fifths. Meanwhile, there has been increasing residential segregation, based on both religion and class. This can be seen starkly in the division of the city between the two sides of its main river, the Lagan. Whereas the core city to the west of the Lagan is 55 per cent Catholic, to the east it is only 12 per cent. (In the late 1960s, six in ten of public-sector households in the urban area lived in streets that were segregated. A decade later, it was nine in ten households.) The city faces a challenge to ensure that these dividing lines do not become battle-lines. Neighbourhoods working against the odds cannot afford to be at odds with each other.

In the 1980s, Belfast's share of the region's population fell by just over 3 per cent. Its share of regional employment fell by nearly

4 per cent. The city centre was experiencing a revival. The city was also reopened to its river by a prestigious waterfront development. But, the job gains of these major investments have so far mostly benefited commuters over city residents.[24]

Economic and social malaise remains rooted in the North and West of the city, which for most of this decade have accounted for nearly eight in ten of total inner city unemployment. If anything, this underestimates the problem because substantial numbers of men in these areas have dropped out of the labour market altogether. Of the fifty most deprived wards in Northern Ireland, six are in North Belfast and eight are in West Belfast.

Urban deprivation involves spatial concentration of poverty as part of a markedly uneven distribution of poverty across the city, a feature described by Byrne as 'socio-spatial segregation'.[25] In this sense, the urban poor are often not merely socially excluded but also spatially contained in enclosures, which inhibit physical as well as economic access to wider city opportunities. In these areas people not only suffer from particular problems such as poor health, low income, and educational underachievement. Rather, they are caught in a dynamic of the reproduction of poverty, whereby the interplay of these factors creates a social exclusion, marked by its severity and durability.

Moreover, they have borne the brunt of the violence. Large barriers of brick and metal which form 'peace walls' to protect each side of the community from the other, scar the landscape and bear grim witness to the bitter sectarian animosities. Yet, despite, or maybe because of, these relentless assaults on the decencies of life, people in these areas have shown remarkable resilience and resourcefulness. And their ingenuity finds no better expression than in the vitality of their culture.

A tale of two cities: downtown versus neighbourhoods?

As intimated in a previous section the 1980s saw a prevalent trend for declining cities in the UK to adopt US models of urban regeneration, which focus pre-eminently on Downtown. Reservations have arisen about several features of such models.[26] These include unequal public–private partnerships[27] and the largely physical development emphasis;[28] the tendency to produce highly segmented cities, most acutely between the gleaming towers of glass Downtown and the dereliction faced by 'the urban underclass'; the significance accorded image investment – place-marketing, geared to conveying the city's conformity to cosmopolitan traits, while simultaneously identifying its distinctiveness for tourists and investors; and the sidelining of contentious urban issues.[29] Upbeat proclamations that Belfast's 'got the buzz' or that Glasgow is 'miles better', meant to mobilise citizenry in common identity, may underplay the extent to which cities are sites of contest as well as of consensus.

Government relocation of jobs to new city centre offices has helped reinforce demand for core retail activity. The expanded presence of UK multiples in Belfast city centre, attracted by reduced security risk, relatively low occupancy costs, and sound trading figures, has in turn been linked to significant rental growth, which itself has encouraged property developers to boost investment and construction. The rush of prestigious developments following CastleCourt, suggests a speculative element to this boom. Building has begun on malls before anchor tenants have been committed. Such speculative schemes can help increase competition for land, and thus inflate land costs for other much needed social consumption such as housing, play and open space or health facilities. Once built, they may require that key tenants are given incentives to come and stay. But, from another viewpoint, such prestigious developments signal not just an economic revival but also a political recovery of a city subjected to years of deliberate destruction. As one Northern Ireland Minister expressed this 'normalisation':

You cannot be anything but impressed by the new skyline of Belfast city centre as shops and offices rise to herald a new era of prosperity. On the cultural and entertainment side, too, there is an encouraging spirit of enterprise.[30]

This is echoed by leading local planners in their promotion of the 're-birth' of Belfast in professional journals: '... the physical evidence of achievement in Belfast stares you in the face. Witness the commercial confidence and new prosperity in the city centre ... The city is being re-built. For citizen and businessman what this signifies is a new spirit of hope and confidence in the future.'[31] This pride demonstrates the distinctive symbolic importance attached to development in Belfast's centre. There, in physical form in the region's lead city, is evidence of ultimate government triumph over a sustained paramilitary campaign, designed to deny the normality and reformability of the region as a political entity. But, insofar as development comes to be equated with building, and all development comes to be seen as virtuous, building

can occur with primary concern for rental yield and image enhancement, with only secondary concern for its impact on social need, open
space, aesthetics and ecology.

Meanwhile, Belfast's neediest communities did not attain a propor-
tionate share of the benefits from the physical-led regeneration in
terms of jobs and income. Government recognition that this 'regeneration gap' demanded more focused intervention led especially in the
1990s to specific compensatory urban programmes, targeted at the
most deprived communities, particularly in North and West Belfast. At
the same time, in both the depressed local communities and the city as
a whole, a new awareness emerged about the potential of sectors such
as tourism and the Arts to draw in outside investment. Throughout the
city, but particularly in West Belfast, local cultural societies have been
flourishing. Increasingly, they are seeking to translate this energy into
an economic dividend that can provide local jobs and income. At the
same time, the city as a whole is recognising that its need for a
diversified economic base could include a cultural sector.

The role of arts and culture in Belfast's regeneration

Against a formidable background of decline and division, government
and local communities are exploring the way that *cultural industries* can
contribute to the restoration of the city, and in particular to the
prospects of its most battered communities. A recent study[32] has
assessed the economic significance of the Arts for the region as a
whole. Amongst the good news, it noted that:

- the sector accounts for 8330–9000 jobs, both direct and indirect
  (somewhere around $1\frac{1}{2}$ per cent of total regional employment);
- there has been a notable recent boost to artistic talent (evidenced
  by such honours as the Nobel Prize for Literature bestowed on
  Seamus Heaney);
- the voluntary sector component to the Arts is strong relative to
  Britain;
- the market has increased in the last five years, pointing to more positive developments in N. Ireland compared to those in Britain;
- there is good scope for expansion of local demand, which peace and
  stability will further promote;
- and that recent moves by the local Arts Council and different
  strands of government to think more strategically about the sector
  represents an improvement, which can be developed further with

proper policy coordination (particularly between the departments of economic development and of education).

However, it also recorded that:

- the sector is smaller relative to other metro regions in Britain such as Greater Glasgow;
- a much lower share of the adult public attend Arts events than in Britain;
- problems within the sector which impede its progress include: a narrow production base; skills deficits; low market volume; poor marketing and promotion capacity; lower public sector resourcing than the UK average; and a limited venue infrastructure, even allowing for a new Waterfront Concert Hall in Belfast.

It also found that relative to Britain, the patrons of museums, concerts and theatre come disproportionately from the wealthier social classes with arts funding involving a redistribution of income from poorer to richer persons. The Northern Ireland Arts Council is now recognising this, and suggesting ways for improvement, such as stronger links being formed between the arts and deprived communities; greater awareness and wider promotion of the arts in the media; encouraging the provision and use of a broader range of venues; and expanding the provision, promotion and awareness of the arts in education.

This under-use of the traditional Arts by the most deprived populations contrasts with the vibrant condition of local community arts in the worst-off areas of Belfast. A recent review showed that:[33]

- the city's Community Arts was very vibrant relative to other UK regions;
- its range and quality are impressive;
- its very diversity, however, within the current funding regime and limited budgets, promoted internal competition;
- this rivalry was not conducive to collaboration and coordination;
- while community-based arts in the most disadvantaged areas impact significantly on the quality of life, social cohesion, and training and job opportunities, they suffer from weak management;
- it is not helped by the fact that funders themselves do not operate a coherent strategic approach to the sector.

Currently being examined are the policy and institutional implications of the report's suggestions for developing a sector that provides:

- diversity;
- good channels for public participation;
- clarity of objectives, which allow for flexible response to demand and opportunity;
- sustainable viability;
- voluntary underpinning to help protect community ownership, and
- proper accountability in terms of efficiency and effectiveness.

At a local level, a contribution to a new multicultural city would be a *community arts corridor* linking North and West Belfast to the city centre. Recent successes in the operation of community radio and the organisation of comprehensive community festivals in the Shankill, Catholic West Belfast, and North Belfast bear testimony to significant cultural talent and interest. There has been a renaissance of the Irish language and Gaelic culture in part of this area over the past two decades, typified by the creation of primary schools and a secondary school where teaching is through the medium of the Irish language. Scope for broadening the cultural ambit to include music, film and video production also exists.

There are six clear gains to developing a Community Arts/Cultural Corridor in North and West Belfast. It would:

- *tap creativity* in the area, helping to bond civic culture, and promote cultural pluralism, which are key to a tolerant politics, and thus greater social stability. If Belfast is to become a pluralist city, its citizens must be prepared to engage with and embrace more than one culture. The ghettoisation of particular cultural forms will not contribute to overall city regeneration. Without a greater sense of common ownership and stakeholding in the city by the two sides of the community, there will not be the civic pride necessary to market the city to its full potential for tourism and investment;
- contribute to the city's *'liveability'* which is important for the quality of life of existing citizens; and which could be a factor in attracting inward investors concerned about lifestyle opportunities for their imported management;
- provide direct and indirect *jobs* in technical and artistic contracts, and in the purchasing of goods and services;

- attract *visitors and tourists*, and particularly function as a magnet for 'business tourists';
- stimulate *land values* and thus the local property tax base for the area; and
- enhance *morale and confidence* in the many communities in North and West Belfast, battered by a quarter of a century of violence and hardship.

In the longer term, a flagship multi-purpose Performing Arts Centre is needed in the city. Some insist that it should be located in the city centre as a neutral location to give expression to diverse and pluralist cultural forms. We argue that it should be located in North and West Belfast, which badly needs more landmark civic buildings, which attract people from other parts of the city.

More ambitiously, a more fully fledged *Cultural Corridor* could be established. Such a Cultural Quarter has to embody the right mix and critical mass to ensure an animated ambience and distinctive character attractive to a range of interests and ages. Following experience elsewhere,[34] this includes a network of galleries; artist studios; fashion and furniture design outlets; alternative book shops; literature and language facilities; specialist retailing; music warehouses; theatres; craft and jewellery stalls; print and photography facilities; diverse ethnic restaurants, and so forth. But beyond the particular composition, certain features seem critical to success:

- *capacity for exchange of services and ideas:* for instance, the availability of expertise and provision in multi-media and film technology could support artists and designers; the centralisation of props, costumes, script/video archives could be beneficial for different users;
- *major flagships, which act as magnets for the whole area:* for instance, an attraction like an interactive Children's Museum brings parents, children, schools, and so on;
- *flexible use of amenity and space:* for instance, a quality public square could also offer opportunities for open-air performances; studios could operate as exhibition space, and small conference facilities; rooms above shops and lofts in warehouses could offer attractive accommodation for a socially mixed resident population;
- *an environment with visual and security appeal:* for instance, one that is pedestrian-friendly; offering access for elderly and disabled; with good street furniture and public art; and surrounded by a 'greening' of trees, plants and flowers;

- *respect for historical roots:* for instance, identifying landmark sites, artefacts and buildings which capture the distinctive and memorable in past social life in the area;
- *a business support service:* for instance, a set of advice and help services, which recognise the need for regular information bulletins within the area; promotion and marketing of the area; legal and accountancy advice; and customised training for 'cultural entrepreneurs';
- *a partnership management board for the entire complex:* comprising representation from funders, users, owners, and local community, and
- *a broad financial base of funding subsidy:* for instance, Northern Ireland Tourist Board; City Council; Arts Council; Making Belfast Work; Community Relations Council; International Fund for Ireland; European Investment Bank; European Peace and Reconciliation Fund, the Northern Ireland Film Council, and such like, together with consideration of any helpful tax, rental and property tax concessions.

The issue of location is problematic. It could link to the City Centre from the Old Museum up to and including the site around Conway Mill. The limit here is that it may seem to be associated with one community. Another version is to stretch it from Laganside, the Design Centre, taking in the organic development of cafés and crafted furniture shops around St Anne's Cathedral, through to what may be the vacated Campus in York Street and out to Northside.

Another suggestion is to see how the courthouse and jail on the Crumlin Road (soon to be vacated) could be remodelled for cultural/artistic purposes. There would be two clear advantages to this siting. The road embraces both communities on either side of it and also contains empty space for the provision of new cultural facilities. Yet another alternative is to site it along 'neutral space' adjacent to the possible new Campus at Springvale. There it could be linked to the University's Art and Design, Multi-Media and student facilities.

Whichever approach is adopted, the process requires active discussion with language and cultural groups in North and West Belfast to identify needs and decide strategies. The purpose should be to ensure a result that is more than a series of separate and isolated developments. Funding could be graduated to reward those projects prepared to collaborate with others. But importantly, it has to be appreciated that converting cultural talent into commercial opportunity requires systematic forms of enterprise learning through appropriate channels for business training.

Cultural industries: problems of definition

Such issues throw up the wider question of the role of Arts and Culture in renewing industrial cities. As smoke-stacks surrender to the gleaming towers of modern offices in revamped city centres and riversides, where does this sector fit into the scenario of urban economies built more upon services? The first obstacle to clear thinking on this is the *problematic definition* of the sector. If the Culture industry is to move beyond its esoteric image as 'frills and thrills' to a more centre-stage position in the overall economy, we have to be able to designate its range. Clearly, it embodies the visual and performing arts from music to dance to theatre, to film and photography, to literature, painting and sculpture, and so on. And, we know that these can be found as much in festivals as in museums. But, what else may be included? Increasingly, some are throwing in libraries, parks, zoos, and botanical gardens, and also 'supplier' areas like publishing. Beyond all this, the interface between the Cultural industries and the Leisure industries, and between both and the general 'Hospitality' sector remain ill-defined and poorly measured.

The underlying factor that drives the increasing economic significance of Arts and Culture is the relationship between economic development and the changing composition of demand. As societies become wealthier, the satisfaction of material need is supposed to leave ever greater scope for the satisfaction of aesthetic and cultural pursuits. In a world determined largely by the concrete and practical, people are thought to welcome that which graces and decorates the otherwise grey routines of life. Moreover, as those in work operate under greater stress, the premium on quality relaxation and cultural enrichment is said to increase. But, all this raises further critical questions. Can you consume culture just as you consume a car? What about the *equity* dimension, in relation to those whose material well-being is not adequately met? Would they welcome public resources being devoted to an abstract piece of public art over that money being spent to enhance medical care?

Culture and the economy: key dimensions

In grappling with these difficult questions, there are *six* distinct dimensions of this relationship between Culture and the Economy that may reward further detailed consideration.

First, the *implications of the global market:* we are told that we are now all subject to the process of globalisation, a single market world increasingly subject to the standardised and homogenised, in which the emblem of a McDonalds signals development and sophistication, and in which culture is neutered to a point where all human drama can be depicted through the bland lens of American or Australian soap-opera. Clearly, this is not the case. Multiculturalism thrives. And, even if we fail to engage with it for its intrinsic value of human enrichment, we have to learn to appreciate and respect diverse cultures as the key to doing business world-wide. In this sense, it has been said that 'the greatest distance between peoples is not space, but culture'.

We can see this on the European doorstep where people who share space in Kosovo divide to the point of death over culture and identity. So, even as we are told that the new global economy order erodes national sovereignty and diminishes cultural distinctiveness, we are seeing the re-emergence of exclusive cultural expression. The challenge we face here – and we know this only too well in Belfast – is to elevate the civic over the ethnic, but in a way which affirms difference in language and cultural form.

Second, even if we don't buy into all the analysis of post-modernism, we know that old-style economic and urban planning no longer offers the path to utopia. We don't live in a world subject to certitude and ready prediction. It is a much more messy and chaotic place than that. Thus, nobody has a ready-made blueprint for how to remake cities enduring industrial decline. There is even legitimate argument over whether we should set our sights on moving to *The Advanced Industrial City* or *The Post-Industrial City*. For instance, some say that we need still to produce tradeable goods, but that this can be done at comparative advantage to the developing world if we concentrate on high-value niches based on cutting-edge technologies. They insist that if we in cities throw all our economic eggs into the one basket of services, that we will become a basket-case economy.

But, what is really needed is the *Creative City*, in which networks of innovation and fresh-thinking are nurtured through multi-agency and cross-sectoral partnerships. Out of this will derive a distinctive agenda for regeneration appropriate to the particular histories and current needs of particular places. And in this process, Arts and Culture have a special role, because their whole 'ethos' is built around creative imagination. In a way, a vibrant cultural base to a city can act as a leaven that generates many other kinds of productive activity.

Third, in an information age based on micro-chip and digital technologies, there is the likelihood of a proliferation of audio and visual output. The prospect of multi-channel television alone promises an *overload* of material and images to digest. Several risks loom. For instance, it offers heaven for the couch-potato resigned to passivity. But, it stands to turn culture into *spectacle* rather than *activity*. Furthermore, insofar as it may lead to a 'more equals less' phenomenon, an increased diet of pap may corrode the critical faculty to discern and discriminate. In such a scenario, the *technical* world of machines and gadgets will dull the *creative* world of social interaction.

But, such reservations should not reduce us to a new Luddism. With appropriate adaptability, multi-media, which brings together the capacities of text, broadcasting, computers, and other forms of telecommunication, could be a servant to local Arts in terms of community video, community cable channels, computer graphics, animation, and so on. And surely, the world of Arts and Culture that can accommodate the surreal, can readily accommodate the new worlds of virtual reality. So, the challenge here is to adapt the high-tech products of the new economy for an interactive and creative expression. These can be used at community level in ways which promote confidence, celebrate cultural pluralism, and which in turn can produce marketable outputs with their own economic dividend.

Fourth, we speak much these days of sustainable development, forms of development which are particularly sensitive in their use of non-renewable resources. Well, certain aspects of culture are like that. They are non-renewable. For instance, if we package our heritage into an endless round of theme parks, we may start to deform the meaning of architecture and place. Selling history and past culture purely as commodities risks debasing and destroying the very assets you wish to exploit, the distinctive tapestry of former ways of living which makes particular places unique. Some cynics characterise industrial England as a 'vast floating museum' of quaint tourist attractions, designed to depict in aspic bygone days of industrial community life.

And indeed, if we venture down to some of the riverside developments around our cities, we can see a sanitised version of the real textured maritime tradition, a version that leaves little signature of the hardship and struggle of those who devoted their working lives to building its former wealth. We need here to safeguard standards of conservation so that the cultural rendition we get from rehabilitated industrial architecture speaks to us in a more rounded historical narrative.

Fifth, in the field of urban regeneration, we strive hard these days to see planning in an integrated way, to connect the social with the economic, and both with the built environment. Again, Arts and Culture can help bring vision and shape to these links. For instance, many environmental improvement schemes are meant to improve residents' quality of life while enhancing business investment confidence. Such schemes could benefit from a greater role being given to aesthetics and design. This includes the more imaginative use of public art – gateways, sculpture, murals, banners, street furniture and so on. But, it has to offer quality in conception, material, and production, and participation by the community being 'served'.

Too often, in Belfast what passes for community murals for example, are ill-conceived, tatty, carried out with materials that are not resistant to the vagaries of our climate, and which can end up in truth as scars on the community landscape, which depress rather than exalt. That is not to insist that we stick with a grand notion of Art as that which is capable of universal and durable appreciation by the well-initiated. Rather, it is to draw the simple lesson that good Community Art, *like all good Art*, does not come cheap. And, this leads to the sixth point:

Much in Art and Culture can benefit from public subsidy. But, it is also true that public subsidy carries with it a public accountability. This is not simply down to the current robust economic climate, in which perhaps we have learned 'the price of everything and the value of nothing'. It is simply that when social spending as a whole is subject to rigorous prioritisation, funding for Arts is going to come under greater scrutiny. Yet, an appropriate accountancy is not easy to specify. Do we justify subsidy in terms of *size* or *type* of audience? Can we ensure that subsidy does not infringe *artistic freedom*? Do we fund mostly that which seems likely to *bind* best various civic interests? If so, will this not demote an important role of cultural expression, to challenge through the contentious and controversial?

Of course, good Art both soothes and stirs the human spirit. It offers no simple calculus for any of this. In that sense, we have to go *beyond the economic* dimension. We have to look more at the 'social wealth' created. To put it crudely, if Man is *Nature*, humankind is *Nature plus Culture*. It is culture that marks us as social beings. We used to speak of 'the *cultured* person', as an elitist reference. One index of how seriously we take the role of culture in social life is when that reference has a purchase on the popular imagination, when being *cultured* is considered a prized attribute by all.

Conclusion: the challenge of culture in a divided city

While acknowledging the contribution that cultural activities can bring to the new urban economies and to the quality of urban living, the thorny issue of how diverse cultural expression operates in a conflict-ridden city needs to be addressed. In Belfast, the republican community was first off the mark in its recognition of the Gramscian links between culture and politics. The legitimation of an Irish space in what was professed to be a British city demanded visible signs and symbols of an Irish identity. Thus, the apparent cultural autonomy of places like West Belfast is linked to the aspiration of separatism from the British state. As such, it is seen to challenge the loyalist identity in the city with its allegiance to the union with Britain. Loyalist communities now vie with their republican counterparts in expressions of their fidelities, through wall murals, flags and emblems and other cultural forms. The intensity of the conflict for the last three decades has seen the most troubled parts of the city carved into mutually antagonistic 'turfs', where those who do not share an affinity with the cultural/political orthodoxy in particular neighbourhoods can feel under severe pressure, if not intimidation. Such heightened senses of territoriality have, at times, inhibited efficient and equitable allocation of social resources such as housing. For instance, a particular community may suffer from poor or overcrowded housing. But, it is difficult to infringe on the space of an adjoining community of the opposite persuasion, even where land and housing supply is more available, since such a move is seen as a threatening incursion. Thus, the growth of cultural activities on both sides of the Belfast community has been successful *within* each community in terms of offering a channel for creative expression and a common bond amongst local residents. But, by the same token, it has been a source of some division and tension *between* the two protagonist sides.

To offset the segregation of these 'ethnic spaces', government has tried to emphasise common accessibility to the 'neutral spaces' of the Downtown and Waterfront. But, simplistic assumptions that the entire city centre is open to all are not borne out by research. For instance, a study[35] of young people living at the interface between the two sides of the community suggests that some young Protestants regard the prestigious shopping mall, known as CastleCourt, as largely a preserve for young Catholics.

Of course, it is possible to designate certain areas and events that could be regarded as 'transcendent spaces', that operate above the conflict and draw audiences from the two traditions in the city. In particular, major stage shows in the new large concert hall and music festivals that attract big international entertainers like Garth Brooks or U2 win attendance from throughout the city. Indeed, in an apparent effort to erase the image of the local Parliament Building from being regarded as the site of a partisan government, a recent concert by Elton John was held there.

A different ambition would be to create alongside the 'ethnic', 'neutral' and 'transcendent' spaces, genuinely 'shared spaces' that express a common belonging to the city. At this stage, it remains a challenge to find cultural forms that can cover this ground. For instance, an attempt to create a St Patrick's Day Festival for the whole population, tapping into the talents of all the local cultural societies across the city, did not succeed. The Protestant community argued that St Patrick had been appropriated by the Catholic community as an Irish icon, in a way that did not respect their British identity. Similarly, there was an appeal in 1999 for Catholics to join Protestants in displaying the symbol of the poppy, deployed in the annual commemoration of those who died in the Second World War. But, this appeared to be greeted by Catholics with the view that the symbol was associated with the British Legion, and therefore alien to their Irish affiliation. Meanwhile, Sinn Fein as the political wing of the IRA, now functions as the second largest party in the City Council. It maintains that the ambience and appearance of the City Hall is mostly loyalist, and that such a prominent civic building should evoke a common belonging by all citizens. Such disputes mark the persistence of the basic fault line in the city between Catholic nationalists and Protestant unionists. Yet, there is a minority third tradition in Belfast, which has never been animated by these kinds of ancestral and tribal contests. Much of this 'third' section is liberal and labour in politics, but has lowered its voice amid the polarisation in the city in the past thirty years. Another section of it is a population, mostly young and disaffected with all politics and into alternative lifestyles and music. Besides this 'third' group, there is a small population of ethnic origin, mostly Chinese and Asian. More positive recognition of such differentiation, and related cultural nuances, could see in time the creation of a more multicultural city, wherein 'shared space' represented the coming together of these separate idioms for a rich diversity appreciated by all in the city.

Notes

1   M. Moss, and J. Hume, *Shipbuilders to the World: 125 Years of Harland and Wolff 1869–1986* (Belfast: Appletree Press, 1986).
2   H. Crawford, *Industries of the North 100 Years ago: Industrial and Commercial Life in the North of Ireland 1981–91* (Belfast: Friars Bush Press, 1986, p. 35).

3 B. Collins, 'The Edwardian City' in J. Beckett *et al* (eds) *Belfast: the Making of the City* (Belfast: Appletree Press, 1988).
4 B. Walker and H. Dixon, *No Mean City: Belfast 1880–1914* (Belfast: Friars Bush Press, 1983).
5 Hall Report, *Report of the Joint Working Party on the Economy of Northern Ireland*, Cmnd. 446 (Belfast: HMSO, 1962); Wilson Report, *Economic Development in Northern Ireland*, Cmnd. 479 (Belfast: HMSO, 1965).
6 Matthew Report, *Belfast Regional Survey and Plan: Recommendations and Conclusions* (Belfast: HMSO, 1963).
7 Planning Advisory Board, *Housing in Northern Ireland: Interim Report of the Planning Advisory Board*, Cmnd. 224 (Belfast: HMSO, 1944).
8 Skeffington Report, *People and Planning: Report of the Committee on Public Participation in Planning* (London: HMSO, 1969).
9 J. Darby and G. Morris, 'Intimidation in Housing', *Community Forum* 111, No. 2 (1973) 7–11.
10 R. Wiener, *The Rape and Plunder of the Shankill* (Belfast: Farset Cooperative Press, 1980).
11 Lavery Report, *Belfast Urban Area Plan: Review of Transportation Strategy* (Belfast: HMSO, 1978).
12 P. Buckland, *A History of Northern Ireland* (Dublin: Gill and Macmillan, 1981).
13 D. Birrell and A. Murie, *Policy and Government in Northern Ireland: Lessons of Devolution* (Dublin: Gill and Macmillan, 1980).
14 D. Hamilton, 'Foreign Direct Investment and Industrial Development in Northern Ireland' in P. Teague (ed.), *The Economy of Northern Ireland: Perspectives for Structural Change* (London: Lawrence and Wishart, 1993).
15 Ibid., p. 17.
16 Coopers and Lybrand Deloitte, *The Northern Ireland Economy: Review and Prospects*, January (Belfast: 1990).
17 R. Wilson, 'Putting the Gloss on Belfast', *New Society*, 13 May (1988).
18 Ibid., p. 17.
19 B. Rodwell, *Elevating Belfast*, Omnibus, Autumn (Belfast: Northern Ireland Information Office, 1993).
20 Belfast Development Office, *Belfast? Belfast!: Communications* (Belfast: DOE (NI), undated, p. 2).
21 Press Release, *New City Centre Forum Launched* (Belfast: Northern Ireland Information Service, 15 October 1992).
22 W.J.V. Neill, 'Anywhere and Nowhere: Reimaging Belfast', in D. Smyth, (ed.), *Whose City? The shaping of Belfast:* a two-day seminar organised by Community Technical Aid, Fortnight Educational Trust and Royal Town Planning Institute (conference proceedings, Fortnight Educational Trust, June, 1992, p. 9).
23 W.J.V. Neill, 'The New Plan for Belfast: a Model for the Future or Dancing on a Volcano', Pleanail, Journal of the Irish Planning Institute, No. 7 (1987) 45–55.
24 Based on data supplied by DOE (NI) Statistics Branch and analysis for DOE (NI) by Andreas Cebulla, NIERC.
25 D. Byrne, op. cit. (1989).
26 B. Frieden and L. Sagalyn, *Downtown Inc. How America Rebuilds Cities* (Cambridge, MA: MIT Press, 1989).

27   G. Squires (ed.), *Unequal Partnerships: the Political Economy of Urban Redevelopment in Postwar America* (New Brunswick: Rutgers University Press, 1989).

28   T. Barnekov, R. Boyle and D. Rich, *Privatism and Urban Policy in Britain and the United States* (New York: Oxford University Press, 1989).

29   M. Davies, *City of Quartz: Excavating the Future in Los Angeles* (London: Vintage, 1990).

30   Quoted in R. Wilson, 'Putting the Gloss on Belfast', *New Society*, 13 May (1988).

31   B. Morrison, 'Making Belfast Work', *The Planner*, December (1990), 32.

32   J. Myerscough, *The Arts and the Northern Ireland Economy* (Belfast: N.I. Economic Council, 1996).

33   Comedia, '*Within Reach: a Strategy for Community-based Arts Activities in Belfast*, Belfast City Council, (Belfast: 1995).

34   For instance, the concept of Temple Bar in Dublin as elaborated in Temple Bar Properties, *Development Programme for Temple Bar* (Dublin: 1992); and Temple Bar Properties, *Temple Bar Shopping, and Temple Bar Living* (Dublin: undated).

35   Community Relations Council, *Interface Project* (Belfast 1998).

Part IV
Promoting the City in Berlin and Belfast

11
The Variety of Identities – Experiences from Berlin

Bernhard Schneider

My first reaction to the use of the term 'identity' in the working title for this publication was: 'No, not again!' Nowhere do people talk so much about identity as in Berlin and nowhere does this talk do so much to blind people to the present and the future of their city. Nonsense has been propagated in the name of Berlin's 'identity' not just since the great European and German revolutions of 1989 but as early as the planning discussions of the 1970s and 1980s. As so much creativity and innovation in the areas of planning and architecture has been frustrated over these years through appeals to 'identity', I am moved to cite again a decisive sentence from an article by Leon Wieseltier that has the provocative title: 'Against Identity: against the Identity Fuss'. 'The question, "What is your identity?" really asks "Who are you like?" In other words, identity is a euphemism for conformity.'[1]

The pressure to conform, the disciplining of deviations and the general idea of a unified, homogenous culture are what paralyse the cultural potential of Berlin and hinder it from fully taking advantage of the once-in-a-century chance that has come the city's way.

Berlin's second chance

A century has just ended in which destruction, injustice and misfortune not only impacted Berlin: such forces were also unleashed from within Berlin on Europe and the world. Now Berlin has a very rare opportunity to make a new beginning, and the city has recognised this situation. While in recent years Berlin has done much to take advantage of the new situation, this is often more clearly seen by outside observers than people in the city who are directly affected by the ongoing processes related to Berlin's transition and new start.

Berlin's economic strength has rapidly declined since German reunification, and the economy continues to weaken. Berlin's Minister for Economics has interestingly compared Berlin to a falling aeroplane whose navigators are intending to bring the plane yet lower from where they hope to transition into a controlled flight and eventually to regain altitude. While the city is still in a steep dive, the engine has already been overhauled. Economic structural changes that other regions have been labouring over for decades must be mastered in Berlin in a few short years. The city has some significant resources that could be drawn on during this painful and rapid process: its cultural potential and capacities. For Berlin this is not simply a question of choosing between two competing camps, but rather we see a variety of positions, often conflicting. Culture is not the great unifying factor of all perspectives, nor is it simply a duality of two camps such as those of East and West. Culture is essentially about difference and diversity, about identity and 'not identity'. Culture involves the ability to distinguish between and to create difference – and the strength to tolerate what is different and strange as well as the ability to cope with change.

Deviations

Consider any part of Berlin's cultural history, and it can be seen that insofar as Berlin's culture is acknowledged as having more than a regional significance, its importance and its identity are found in its deviations. The English language reveals significant relationships between difference and identity, for example in the expression 'making a difference'. The question concerning cultural identity is thus not, 'Who are you like?' but rather, 'In what ways are you different?'

Berlin was settled after the catastrophe of the Thirty Years' War by Huguenots, Jews, Bohemians, Austrians, Poles and Swabians – all of whom represented considerable deviations from the population of the surrounding countryside in Brandenburg. Further, the settlements and architecture of the 1920s, the ideas of the Dadaists, and the designs of Mies van der Rohe, Scharoun and Daniel Libeskind all have communicated deviation. Even the trademark of the city, the Brandenburg Gate, was at the time of its construction without precedence in Berlin. The Gate was a foreign body and a drastic deviation from the dominant late baroque style of that period. While the Brandenburg Gate is currently a monument that contributes to the identity of both the city and the nation, it would not have been built 200 years ago if identity had been merely equated with conformity.

Example: Martin-Gropius-Bau

Back to the present: let me begin with an example of building renovation that typifies what is going on in Berlin. The Martin-Gropius-Bau (Building), named after its architect – the great-uncle of Walter Gropius – is the most important exhibition space in Berlin. This structure is located on Niederkirchnerstrasse, across from the current City Parliament building which is the former Prussian State Parliament. Diagonally across the street is the former Air Ministry of Göring, which later became the GDR House of Ministries, and which is presently the new Federal Finance Ministry.[2] Niederkirchnerstrasse, formerly Prinz-Albrecht-Strasse, is named after Käthe Niederkirchner who because of her resistance as a communist was executed by the SS. The Prinz Albrecht name had become a synonym for the Gestapo base and other command centres of the Nazi regime found at Prinz-Albrecht-Strasse 8 and in the Prinz-Albrecht-Palais on an adjacent lot. The ruins of these buildings have been removed and in their place a historical Information and Documentation Centre 'The Topography of Terror' is being built. Through chance, the Martin-Gropius-Bau has survived this century's traumas and has been renovated. The Berlin Wall ran right through this historically charged topography and along Niederkirchnerstrasse, and sections of the Wall are still standing here. Until the Wall was opened it was not possible to use either this street or the main entrance to the Martin-Gropius-Bau.

In the restoration of this building in the 1970s as West Berlin's primary exhibition centre, it was necessary to modify and use the south entrance that was accessed through the former garden which leads off Stresemannstrasse. The narrow steps of the south wing were never really sufficient as a main entrance, while the deactivated but more meaningful vestibule and historic main steps on the north were only reached after a journey through the entire building.

For the renovation work in 1998–99 it was at first debated whether the building's functional arrangements that had been forced by the Berlin Wall should be reversed. Exhibition producers and visitors from the West had become used to the building's arrangement. Some of them understood the abnormal situation that they had become familiar with over twenty years as the normal, if not as the historically valid.

Fig. 11.1 Martin-Gropius-Bau

The view of the building's southern façade was popularised over the years in countless illustrations, catalogues and brochures, and exhibition banners were generally hung on this 'back' side: exhibition publications almost never showed the building's forgotten true front that was facing the Berlin Wall. With the restoration of the original entrance, the building interior was redeveloped to be oriented once again toward the public space of Niederkirchnerstraße and surrounding Friedrichstadt. With this we see not only an especially valuable rehabilitation of a historical landmark but also a successful project for Berlin in terms of mental reunification.

This example is an appropriate one for a discussion of city marketing, and not only because of its fortunate outcome. More important with this episode is the footnote that the so-called internal Berlin positions and arguments concerning this conflict over the main entrance are really not of interest to anyone except a few in Berlin. Questions related to city marketing are the same, however, all around the world: What is it about this city that distinguishes it from others? What is this city's profile, and what makes it different? This suggests that marketing arguments should be developed in a comparative way through interaction with the outside world, and not through narrow introspection.

The now abandoned notion that one of the most important cultural institutions in the city would continue to be accessed from its rear – because of historical arguments and even though there was once again an accessible street at its front – would thus have been an announcement provoking no more than a shrug of the shoulders. While only a modest development, it is nonetheless significant that with the first exhibition after renovation in May 1999 the main entrance was reinstated, and with that a piece of Berlin.

Diversity of identities

It is essential for Berlin marketing that many of the city's facets are presented instead of reducing Berlin to one aspect or characteristic and the creation of a single slogan. Such reductionism is insufficient for communicating great and complex compositions, except at the cost of concealing and repressing rather than propagating information.

While Berlin marketing has work to do within the city to correct some self-images that are strangely defended in the guise of identity, there is also much to be done externally against tired but ingrained Berlin clichés. An image of a new and different Berlin must be presented that is in the process of claiming a position in a different and changed Germany as well as a different and changed Europe. Whereas clichés are important and necessary for communication, they have the disadvantage of tending over time to distance themselves from reality. Thus clichés can get in the way of the sending of current reality-based messages and can negatively limit people's understanding and decrease their interest in the city. For these reasons Partner für Berlin[3] is working to establish new images in people's heads that will replace or at least complement the old stereotypes of the 'Roaring Twenties', Berlin as a 'Front City', and the nightclub district which never closes.

In 1991 it was said by a sociologist that Berlin had no Berliners, but rather only East and West Berliners. The Berliners – meaning those that identify with the entire city – were yet to be born and raised. In a similar way we can say that the view from the outside also needs to be concentrated on the Berlin that is currently forming.

Berlin's strong profile

Four points are illustrated below by which Berlin distinguishes itself not in terms of degree but fundamentally from other German and

European cities. These four distinguishing characteristics outline Berlin's new identity:

The *transition* and *new beginning* that Berlin finds itself caught up in will go on and continue to positively attract attention. Much of Berlin is being newly defined and renewed, from the city's appearance to its infrastructure and local business community, the academic and research institutions and much of the cultural sector. No other metropolis is currently experiencing such a comprehensive wave of modernisation. In other cities such aspects have, generally speaking, long since formed and solidified.

Berlin's *location* in a growing Europe along with its competence in East–West affairs is leading to an interweaving of the city into new geographic, political, cultural and economic networks. Now at the eastern edge of the EU, Berlin will be moved into a central position through the planned eastward expansions. Berlin – as no other comparable actor – is in a position to assume new roles for the EU regarding an integration of the new EU states to the east. After the Turkish population, Poles are now the second largest immigrant group in Berlin.

Berlin, after years of isolation, is rediscovering itself in the new European geography, and this is also impacting on the city's internal agenda. Berlin is the only European city that belongs equally to the East and West, equally able to draw on experiences from both worlds. It would be wise to see this not as a burden but rather to greet it as an advantage and to learn to work with it. The unique East–West capacities found in Berlin are certain to be of value in the newly emerging central and eastern Europe. We will in any case not be asked too many times if we welcome these changes. Polish, Russian, and other people from the Baltic States are increasingly making Berlin their main destination and starting-point in the West.

As Berlin takes on the role as *Germany's capital*, the city becomes a centre for political decision making in Europe's most populated country. And as Europe is in the process of both uniting and expanding, Berlin assumes a position of international importance and gains new connections in many different areas, concerning everything from economics and media to tourism and culture. While it is interesting that the Bonn politicians have come to Berlin, it is more significant that Berlin is changing its relationships with the rest of Germany and that Berlin is once again playing a significant role relative to the rest of the German States. As a capital city, Berlin takes on a new agenda and Berlin's internal understanding is also altered in the process. Berliners no longer have Berlin 'for themselves', and this is important for their view toward the future. Intensive and ongoing exchanges with the rest of the country serve to sharpen the eyes for new opportunities and alternatives. Thus the opinions and feelings of Berlin residents are modified and influenced by outside forces.

As Germany's largest city, Berlin has a considerable *urban density* and a large internationally mixed population, representing a great potential for a cross-fertilisation of information and ideas. Contributing to this are the city's public spaces that are again growing together, and a newly forming information and communication infrastructure. Further supporting this is the increasing number of institutions and organisations that work with international exchange programmes (Wissenschaftskolleg, American Academy, Einstein-Forum, Aspen Institute, European Academy, Goethe Institute, Science Centre Berlin, universities, associations, party foundations, cultural institutions, and so on). The large number of immigrants and the differentiation of social groups and cultures in Berlin mean that many different life styles are expressed in this city. These groups are often large enough to form the critical mass necessary to build stable subcultures. Throughout its modern history Berlin has been characterised as a cosmopolitan city of immigrants, attracting German-speaking people but also many others. Due to demographic trends of a declining and ageing population, Berlin must actively work to continue to attract new immigrants. We also see that this is necessary when we combine Berlin with the surrounding region of Brandenburg – which contains some of the most sparsely populated areas in Europe – and realise that Berlin is quantitatively at the lower range of being a functioning metropolis. Berlin must already import demand for its cultural productions, even though the Berlin population displays one of the highest levels of demand in the world.

All of this means that Berlin should be able to develop a new self-image through its interactions with the world, as the city repositions itself both regionally and globally. It is worth noting that a global view can serve as a good corrective in which it is a useful exercise to ask oneself such questions as: How do I explain Berlin to someone from India? Such a perspective helps to separate the essential from the unessential, and to clarify one's view of the variety of identities found in this large city.

Conclusion

I offer below a few examples to illustrate how Berlin's city marketing is disseminating images of a new Berlin that are a great distance from the

Fig. 11.2 Brandenburg Gate placed in a new context

entrenched clichés. The so often stereotyped Brandenburg Gate is not taken out of circulation but is instead placed in a new context (Fig. 11.2); the cliché of 'fast-paced' Berlin is reframed in terms of irony and satire (Fig. 11.3). Well-known museum highlights such as

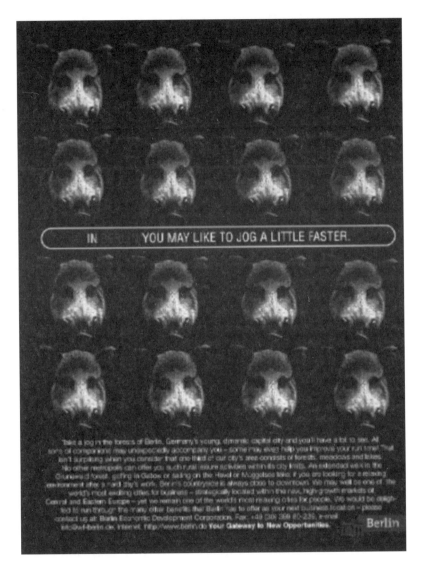

Fig. 11.3 Wild boars and the pace of Berlin

Warhol works or Pergamon exhibits are not used. Instead, the new Painting Gallery (Gemäldegalerie), for example, is related to new urban design concepts, and the quantitative breadth of Berlin's museums is related to local meteorological statistics (Fig. 11.4). Finally, an image

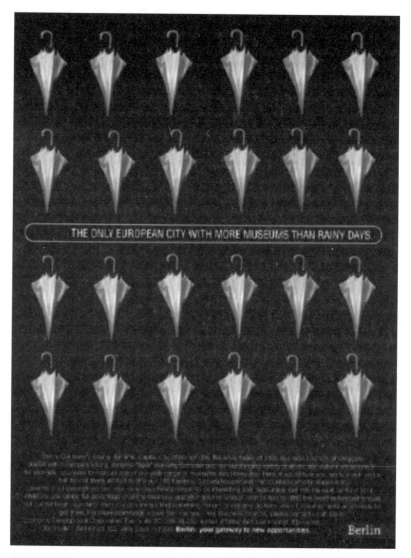

Fig. 11.4 More museums than rainy days

that has surprised many in its rapid ascent to being an icon for the new Berlin is the Reichstag's new dome with its glass skin (Fig. 11.5).

The image of the Reichstag's new dome is suddenly to be found in countless variations and from the widest range of photographers, dis-

Fig. 11.5 The Reichstag's new dome

played in advertisements and wall calendars, in brochures and on television, in photographic reports on Berlin, in newspapers and on postcards, in night-time views and at every other time of day. This technical and architectural wonder by Norman Foster, in connection with the Quadriga, is well on its way to establishing itself as Berlin's new trademark. The publicly accessible dome enables new and unfamiliar views into the Parliamentary Chamber as well as out into the city. This could become a trademark for the whole country, beyond already being one for Berlin: an observatory that is the eye of the capital city on the Federal Parliament.

Notes

1   L. Wieseltier, 'Against Identity: Wider das Identitätsgetue', *Die Zeit* (17 February 1995).

2   This structure was built by Ernst Sagebiel who was also the architect of Tempelhof Airport.

3   The name 'Partner für Berlin', Gesellschaft für Hauptstadtmarketing ('Partners for Berlin', Company for Capital City Marketing) refers to the fact that the company does not merely engage in advertising for tourism and its work is uniquely organised. The company is financed and controlled by its partners, including over 100 private, national and international firms who themselves are interested in promoting Berlin. In addition to many Berlin firms are Deutsche Bahn AG and Lufthansa, British Petroleum BP, *Time Magazine*, *Newsweek* and *Business Week*, DaimlerChrysler, Siemens AG and the Dutch service company Randstad. The Berlin Senat is neither a partner nor is it represented on the board, but it does finance advertising and PR campaigns which it contracts out to Partner für Berlin.

   The company's mission is to further develop a profile of Berlin's particular strengths and to communicate this profile both internally and externally. This is done, for example, through events and initiatives that positively bring both the local population and visitors into contact with current situations in Berlin. So, for example, the otherwise upsetting problems caused by the city's many construction sites (noise, dust, traffic jams, and so on) have been – with the support of private and public developers – successfully reframed for Berliners and visiting tourists as the birthing process of a new Berlin. Thousands of visitors came to the 'Show Sites', where unnerving construction sites have been reinterpreted as attractions, as shows and as symbols of an emerging lifestyle. This approach is not based on any form of nostalgia, but does see history as a factor than can be used positively as an important element in the profile of the new Berlin of today and tomorrow. This is evidenced in the new Reichstag and the Brandenburg Gate. Annoyance can thus be replaced over time with curiosity, interest and pride. This process is strengthened by the growing positive interest outside the city that is increasingly directing attention to Berlin's development.

12

Building a Shared Future: the Laganside Initiative in Belfast

Mike Smith and Kyle Alexander

Belfast, a maritime city straddling the River Lagan, has in the last decade responded to the challenge of a derelict waterfront. It has done so against a backcloth of conflict and violence. Today a transformed waterfront is an integral aspect of a city promoting itself with confidence. Whilst the scale of development is not that of Berlin's Potsdamer Platz Belfast's Laganside initiative is now attracting international interest as an example of how to implement regeneration. This is in a context where it is increasingly recognised that issues of social exclusion and cultural diversity must also be addressed. In Berlin and Belfast the challenge is to build a shared future. How is this to be achieved? Does new development accentuate or accommodate diversity? Can a balance be achieved between promoting an international image for the city and respecting local history and culture?

Redefining what is possible

Richard Needham, then Parliamentary Under-Secretary of State for the Environment in Northern Ireland, set out the hopes for the Laganside initiative in March 1987. In a foreword to the Laganside Study he wrote:

> Belfast's vibrancy and friendliness have always been evident to those who know the city well. But to people who have never been to Belfast their image of the place is often far removed from the reality. (This study of Laganside) describes the potential which exists to transform completely the environmental quality of a vital part of the city and by this means to help transform perceptions of Belfast at an international level.
>
> The proposals are ... visionary ... ambitious ... but also pragmatic.

> They will be of interest to private investors, businesses, public agencies, voluntary groups or individuals whose co-operation will be vital if the plan is to succeed.[1]

The objective of government was clearly to transform international perceptions (the absence of reference to the reality of a city centre and an economy suffering from twenty years of conflict is noteworthy). The methods were to be visionary, pragmatic and inclusive.

Thirteen years after Richard Needham championed the cause his optimism is rewarded in the findings of an evaluation of the Laganside initiative by the Organisation for Economic Cooperation and Development (OECD). The evaluation, presented at an international conference in Belfast in June 1999, validates what has been accomplished as an example of infrastructure-led development to address environmental, social and economic problems in building a sustainable city in every sense. OECD conclude:

> Laganside has redefined a sense of what is possible in Belfast. Sustainable development as a concept and as a process captures this vision. The economic, social and environmental aspects of development are widely recognised as components of sustainability; ... the pursuit of regional cohesion is emerging as a fourth dimension in Belfast. Because each dimension involves a different time frame only a broadly shared vision can hold the actors and institutions together and inspire public trust and commitment. The achievements of the past decade can become the basis for future efforts to ensure that Belfast has a sustainable future.[2]

The extent to which Laganside has achieved these four dimensions of sustainable regeneration is now examined, preceded by an overview of the task faced and the process employed.

Rediscovering the waterfront: the task

Belfast grew up around its river, the Lagan, its finest natural asset. The river was the focus of transport, trade and industry with the port and shipyard of international repute. Upstream a cycle of industrial growth was followed in recent decades by one of decline. The city turned its back on the river leaving a derelict and neglected river corridor. Uses were low key and contributed little to the urban economy or adjacent communities. Environmental problems included contamination whilst the tidal range of the river led to exposed mudflats at low tide. The layering of fresh water over a saline wedge led to anaerobic conditions. Access along or to the river was limited and recreational activity restricted to an area upstream of the McConnell Weir.

Confidence in the adjacent city centre was low as a result of a sustained terrorist bombing campaign. Private sector investment was dependent on public sector office accommodation and government grant-supported initiatives such as CastleCourt shopping centre. By early evening, the retreat of shoppers and office workers to suburbs left deserted streets.

Inner city communities had benefited from a major housing redevelopment programme but the single aspect housing agency was not sufficiently complemented by a holistic approach tackling other aspects of social deprivation. Tenant selection procedures both reflected and reinforced territorial separation of nationalist and unionist communities and social and owner-occupied accommodation.

The preparation of the Belfast Urban Area Plan in the late 1980s provided the context for the proposal to regenerate the river corridor, drawing on the inspiration of waterfront development in cities such as Baltimore and Boston. The Laganside Concept Plan provided the vision; but how was it to be achieved? It was recognised that coordinated implementation would be difficult within existing organisational and administrative structures and with a spread of responsibilities, interests and property ownership across public and private sectors. A focused area-based approach was proposed with a small, single-minded organisation to be created. Thus Laganside Corporation was established in May 1989 as a non-departmental government agency modelled on UK urban development corporations. Laganside would have a single objective. This was to 'secure the regeneration of the designated area', an expanse of some 140 hectares along a 4.8 kilometre river corridor. This would be achieved by:

- Bringing land and buildings into effective use.
- Encouraging public and private investment and the development of existing industry and commerce.
- Creating an attractive environment.
- Ensuring that housing, social, recreational and cultural facilities are available to encourage people to live and work in the area.[3]

The Laganside partnership approach: the process

During an early visit to London Docklands Development Corporation, their representatives explained that the key to LDDC's success was that

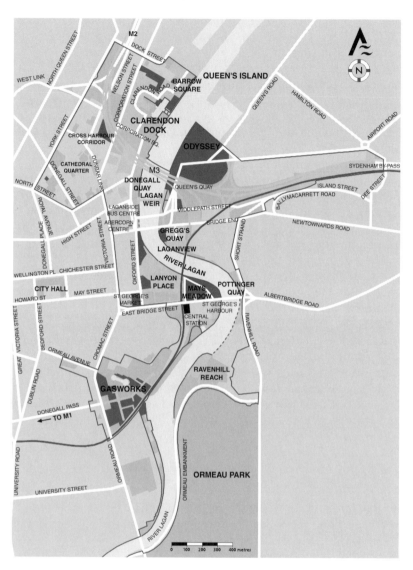

Map 12.1 Laganside boundary in relation to the city centre

'they owned all the land and had statutory planning power to control development'. Significantly, unlike most other UDCs, Laganside had neither of these 'advantages'. As local authorities in N. Ireland lacked planning and development powers, Laganside was not seen as such an imposition or intervention as other UDCs. Much of the land was in public ownership. Whilst vesting powers were available, to date these have not been used aggressively. As a result of these circumstances the essence of Laganside's approach has been cooperation and partnership, its role to facilitate and promote development and undertake physical infrastructure works within the framework of the overall concept plan. A good working relationship has developed with Belfast City Council, fostered by the successful development of the Waterfront Hall, St George's Market and the former Gasworks site. Laganside is a vehicle for implementation apart from the political process but working closely with elected representatives and statutory bodies. Thus whilst emerging from the same ethos as the UDCs with a similar emphasis on levering private sector investment a distinctive agency has evolved a way of working which, with its emphasis on partnerships and co-operation, is appropriate in an urban planning context featuring cultural/political diversity.

The organisation remains streamlined with a total staff of 25 covering development, marketing, finance and river management activities. It is recognised that where an autonomous body is set up as a vehicle for achieving regeneration its relationship to local governance systems is critical to its acceptance and effectiveness. In Belfast, in the current absence of a regional assembly, the role of Belfast City Council is central. Laganside's relationship with the Council has several aspects. A City Council representative sits on Laganside's Board and the Council's Chief Executive is an advisor to the Board. Other Councillors are Board members although not as nominated Council representatives. The Board also includes representatives of the major landowners such as Belfast Harbour Commissioners. However, successful regeneration requires more than formal relationships. Laganside respects the role and authority of the Council as the body of democratically elected representatives, reflecting the range of cultural diversity and political opinion within the city and with civic responsibility for the whole city of which Laganside forms a part. Laganside is primarily a vehicle for implementation, which seeks to work within the context of the city's vision for the future. In promoting the city and in developing strategies and initiatives, both recognise the need for a 'Belfast plc' team approach rather than a disparate and disjointed collection of institutions and agencies. Hence OECD in seeking lessons from elsewhere comment:

> Out of 'The Troubles' has emerged a model/strategy for regeneration ... which has broader relevance. The strategy implemented proved

to be flexible, adaptable and innovative ... A multi-agency partnership approach ... The Corporation understood its context within the City of Belfast.[4]

Environmental and economic dimensions

The foundation of success was an infrastructure-led approach. Focusing initially on physical aspects of regeneration has enabled social and economic aspects to be addressed. Such infrastructure works overcame environmental constraints and created the setting, confidence and commitment to attract private sector investment. The construction of a weir created impoundment of water upstream which together with aeration and dredging has improved water quality to the extent that salmon are returning to the river in increasing numbers. Riverside pathways for pedestrians and cyclists created access along the river whilst provision of slipways and landing facilities have encouraged water-based recreational activities, a river boat and river bus.

With the river environment transformed, a similar infrastructure-led approach has been undertaken on key development sites. The approach involves working in partnership with landowners and local communities to prepare a site masterplan which provides the framework for infrastructure projects and the selection of private developers, based on a development brief. Mixed use and accessible high quality public realm are key ingredients.

The outputs have been impressive. Investment of some £90 million mainly in infrastructure had levered £219 million investment by March 1999. Some 50 hectares of land has been cleared for commercial use. Sixty thousand square metres of new office development, ten thousand square metres of retail/leisure development and 330 residential units have been created. Public/private leverage will have reached 1:3 by March 2000. Ten thousand permanent jobs will be located in the area by 2002.[5]

In the early 1990s the Laganbank area comprised disused markets, bus station and maintenance yard, car parking and auction halls where sheep and cattle could be bought. It overlooked mudflats at low tide. Now renamed Lanyon Place after a famous Belfast architect of the Victorian era it comprises Ireland's largest development project. The magnificent Waterfront Hall concert and conference centre was the catalyst. This new landmark building is the jewel in the crown on the waterfront. Alongside are the 5-star Belfast Hilton hotel and British Telecom Headquarters. Confidence is such that a developer has commenced speculatively a £21 million office block and an impressive terraced building where restaurants will overlook the river.

The former town gasworks has been reclaimed and now provides an attractive landscaped setting for a mix of commercial and community uses. A major call centre for Halifax plc will create 1500 jobs, in terms of jobs the largest inward investment project ever to come to Northern Ireland. At Clarendon Dock disused port land is again the setting for commercial, residential and leisure activity. Across the river the £100 million Odyssey development is the region's Millennium landmark project with an innovative combination of Science Museum, 10 000-seat indoor area, IMAX theatre, multiplex cinema and leisure mall.

The return of residential accommodation to the city centre and waterfront has been a remarkable success. Whilst at first estate agents, building societies and purchasers were hesitant, as the vision started to become a reality with completion of the weir, walkways and in particular the commitment to build the Waterfront Hall, apartments were sold off the plan and resale prices rapidly escalated. But as in other aspects

Fig. 12.1 Belfast's new Waterfront Hall, Hilton Hotel and British Telecom Tower

of Laganside the need to respect social inclusion was recognised. Twenty-five per cent of units to date provide social housing and are adjacent to private accommodation.

As the success of Laganside became established, private sector initiatives are now undertaking new build and in-fill development of fringe areas without public sector incentive or grant support.

Physical integration

As new quarters emerge within Laganside, a linkages strategy seeks to ensure that they are fully integrated into the surrounding city. An urban design and streetscape strategy is addressing these issues ensuring attractive connections between river, city and community. Riverside pathways and pedestrian/cycle friendly linkages encourage access for the general public and local marginalised communities, creating a healthier living environment. The National Cycle route follows the riverside paths and offers accessible longer distance linkage between the inner city and the surrounding countryside.

Fig. 12.2 Nightlife on Laganside

Respecting the past

New development and investment has created the opportunity to restore historic buildings, which provide continuity and character and create that vital sense of uniqueness of place. Restoration of familiar landmarks ensures that residents can identify and locate the emerging quarters in the city.

The discovery that a building due for demolition was in fact Belfast's oldest building, once situated on the now filled-in quayside, was the opportunity for an imaginative restoration with McHugh's Bar now a focus of vitality. Similar discoveries of a cotton warehouse and archaeological investigations of a Belfast pottery enrich the sense of history.

Beside the modern Lanyon Place, the restored Victorian St George's Market is a 'people place'. The Custom House, Harbour Office and Harbour Master's House represent the City's maritime tradition whilst restoration of the Gas Office, Meter House, and Klondyke House keep alive the memory of the town gasworks.

Place names link new developments with former citizens (Lanyon, Pottinger and Gregg) and localities (Lagan Village and Cromac Springs walkways). Councillors insisted that the name Gasworks is retained for the new Business Park despite private sector preference for Cromac Woods, a place name which pre-dated the town gasworks.

Urban design

On all development sites Laganside has sought to achieve a high quality public realm, accessible to all and the setting for private investment. The extensive use of natural stone is noteworthy. This has set new and high standards for the city and created attractive destination places. The quality of infrastructure and public realm sets the standard for new buildings.

A site masterplan provides the context for buildings, sets urban design guidelines and ensures respect for surroundings. Selection of development schemes based on a development brief ensures that appropriateness of use and quality of design are key criteria alongside the financial offer. The scale of development is appropriate to the waterfront location. Only on Lanyon Place have two taller buildings been permitted. These are important landmarks for the city, reflecting the scale and intensity of investment required on this major site and the new-found confidence in the city as prestigious and established end-users Hilton and BT led the way in responding to the government and City Council commitment to Lanyon Place. Remarkably Hilton's decision to invest was pre-cease-fire. Design to some extent reflected the security requirements in this pre-cease-fire context. The continuing commitment to design quality is illustrated in the current invitation to prominent European architects to develop design concepts for a proposed building adjacent to the Waterfront Hall.

Cultural quarter

In 1997 Laganside was given a fresh challenge, moving from the waterfront into a run-down historic area on the fringe of the City Centre surrounding St Anne's Cathedral. Laganside's vision statement for its regeneration strategy is that: 'Cathedral Quarter will become a dynamic and distinctive mixed use, historical and cultural quarter within the centre of Belfast.'[6]

The aim is to develop a regional and international reputation as a cultural and entrepreneurial quarter embracing cultural production, performance, exhibition and retail venues. Cathedral Quarter will have a specialist retail area with emphasis on design, fashion, heritage and the arts. It will be a tourist and visitor destination, a residential area and will be a unique example of urban conservation and regeneration with attractive townscape, streetscape and public realm.

Regeneration in the new Cathedral Quarter seeks to integrate North and West Belfast communities to the City Centre. The opportunity exists for cross-community interaction in a neutral environment.

The challenge is, without significant land ownership by the public sector, to work with the private sector business and arts community to ensure that emerging development is inclusive of both major cultural traditions in Belfast. There is a focus on community involvement and a diversity of activity with arts, culture, training and access to employment initiatives. A balance is being sought between stimulating higher value business, commercial and residential uses whilst ensuring the continued availability of accommodation for arts/cultural activity. A Ladder of Provision Support Scheme seeks to provide a range of rental accommodation with affordable rents and managed workspace.

Connecting people, places and art

The potential of art to function as a vital and energising element in the regeneration process is recognised by the Laganside Corporation. The following observation by Gooding is endorsed:

> Public art serves many purposes but none can have more point and dignity than that of investing a public space with a renewed vitality,

Fig. 12.3 A wall mural in Cathedral Quarter

extending its availability as a place to be in with a sense of identity and where the possibilities of the civil life are enhanced.[7]

Art works have been an integral part of the public realm design or the subject of special commissions improving public appreciation of and identification with these new urban spaces.

The art pieces to date reflect the place, its past or present. 'Sheep on the Road' are a reminder of sheep markets at Lanyon Place. 'Industry past and future' is depicted on sculptured columns at the entrance to the Gasworks. 'The Salmon of Knowledge' near the Lagan Weir marks the location of the River Farset, a now culverted tributary of the Lagan but also signifies the transformation of the Lagan. A cross-community project involving communities on the line of the Farset created mosaics depicting the history of the area. Community arts are encouraged, again encouraging local ownership of riverside walkways.

The introduction of temporary art pieces by international artists, performance art and creation of murals increases the awareness of art and public interaction with new places and broadens the horizons of those involved.

Fig. 12.4 Belfast's new 'Salmon of Knowledge'

The social dimension

From the outset there was scepticism about the Laganside initiative. Was this a vehicle solely for private sector benefit, a quango outside the political process more interested in self-promotion than engaging with local communities with high levels of social deprivation?

Laganside's role was deliberately sharply focused. Its designated boundary was drawn tightly around the vacant waterfront. A deliberate decision was taken not to include community areas within the designated area. Pragmatically this ensured the speedy introduction of legislation establishing the Corporation. More importantly it ensured a single-minded approach focusing on the challenge of vacant sites. Responsibility for surrounding communities remained with existing agencies and mainstream policies. The communities' relationship to Laganside is thus one of 'next door neighbours' who should be consulted, involved and benefit from adjacent development. Initial scepticism was gradually overcome as communities recognised the commitment to engage was genuine. One community worker commented following consultation: 'what impressed us was that Laganside approached us, came out to meet us and seek our views and then came back to show how our concerns were being addressed'.

Development of the Gasworks and more recently Cathedral Quarter involved intensive and ongoing community involvement.

A quinquennial review of Laganside in 1994 by the Department of the Environment for Northern Ireland confirmed the effectiveness of the approach but recognised the need for a widening of objectives to ensure benefits were widely spread amongst residents of local communities and in Belfast as a whole.

Subsequently a community strategy has been formulated and a community officer appointed, ensuring a greater focus on community involvement and in particular on job creation and training initiatives. As new employers move into Laganside, pre-recruitment training programmes, in the hospitality industry for example, have been set up, resulting in local people finding jobs in new hotels and restaurants. Experience has shown that intensive effort is required at a grass-roots level. Laganside has joined with the South Belfast Partnership Board and Training and Employment Agency to work closely with local community groups to encourage and mentor young unemployed people through the selection process. This involves a 'Laganside Roadshow' touring the various communities and interview technique workshops for potential trainees. Realistic targets are set. It is recognised that in areas where unemployment is the norm, even one or two young people moving into employment will begin to influence peer group perceptions.

Laganside is cooperating with existing economic development organisations to encourage enterprise, self-help and job creation. An employability project is currently being developed to increase local access to employment. It will involve an employer–community link scheme, specific sectoral training courses, a schools based awareness initiative and a core skills programme.

Laganside encourages groups to hold events within the area and supports these through a Community Events Grant Fund. Hundreds of events have been assisted to date bringing thousands of people from a wide cross-section of communities to the area. Events assisted include community arts projects, educational projects, community festivals and boat trips. A water safety programme is combined with education about the river, its wildlife and its history. An education officer based at the Lagan Lookout Visitors Centre offers educational visits for school groups.

The new public realm and the river itself provide the setting for major events making Laganside a destination and meeting place, a shared space in a city known for territorial division. River festivals, carnivals and music festivals together with arts festivals bring colour and vitality to the waterfront.

The fourth dimension: the pursuit of cohesion

OECD's evaluation highlighted the fourth dimension of sustainability as the pursuit of cohesion. How have the achievements and strategies outlined above contributed to cohesion, and inclusiveness, respected cultural diversity and dealt with the impact of a divided society?

Richard Needham's original hopes were of transforming international perceptions. A new more positive and confident image of Belfast is being portrayed across the world. The Waterfront Hall and its riverside setting is rapidly becoming a familiar Belfast landmark and backdrop for international press reports, presidential visits, international conferences and celebrity concerts. Locally, within Belfast, development is as OECD describes 'redefining the sense of what is possible'. The Waterfront Hall itself is a shared venue for a diverse range of cultural activities. The decision to build the hall was a result of an alignment of unionist and nationalist parties in the face of opposition from other groups. Development initiatives involving Belfast City Council have been based on cross-party support.

Most of the brownfield development sites along the river are located on or close to an interface between community areas, with a history of segregation and sectarian conflict. Sites such as the Gasworks, Clarendon Dock, and Sirocco were island sites with little public access. The river and its banks were inaccessible and a barrier to movement. Laganside's emphasis in regeneration has been on integration and accessibility creating new mixed-use quarters within the city centre yet respecting their relationships with local communities and seeking to establish a shared ownership.

Local nationalist and unionist communities adjacent to the Gasworks have a shared objective of job creation and community benefit. At an early stage representatives of both communities and several political parties came together to form a Gasworks Trust to lobby for implementation of development. On the night that the Canary Wharf bomb exploded in London, bringing to an end the first IRA cease-fire, Laganside staff were meeting with members of the Gasworks Trust. Around the table sat members of the Unionist, SDLP and Alliance political parties and representatives of both communities including a father whose son had been killed by loyalists at the entrance of the Gasworks, and a loyalist who recalled republican terrorist attacks on his community. As news of the explosion which shattered hopes for peace came through, there was a shared resolve to work together to intensify efforts to ensure that the development on the Gasworks addressed the deprivation of their respective communities and provided an alternative way forward. Was it the experience of working together in local initiatives that started to build a level of trust to seek partnership in government?

The physical demarcation of territory by flags, graffiti, painted kerbstones and murals is a familiar feature in Belfast. At Bridge End, political and community pressure in the 1980s during redevelopment had resulted in the provision of public sector housing for some 56 households – a small isolated residential area turning its back on the river and surrounded by industry. This was a Protestant enclave separated from the East Belfast community by the Catholic Short Strand. The allegiance of Bridge End residents was evident in the red, white and blue painted kerbstones on streets within the area. Residents were active in protecting their area, at times blocking streets in protest against commuter car parking on the residential streets.

Under Laganside, Bridge End has been transformed. Local residents have been involved during the development process. It is now a mixed tenure residential area of some 140 dwellings. New expensive riverside apartments are accessed through the existing housing area. An environmental enhancement scheme upgraded the streetscape and enabled the provision of a children's play area, to which the developer contributed. The red, white and blue paint was removed from the kerbstones and has never reappeared. A riverside walkway has created an attractive amenity. It also opened up access between Bridge End and the Short Strand. Whilst some sought to exploit the potential for conflict, incidents have been minimised as a result of contact between Laganside, local communities and the police. Owner occupation has been introduced into the existing housing area, through the housing authority's 'right to buy scheme'.

Elsewhere new walkways or completed developments provide the opportunity for communities to seek to establish ownership of the new territory through flags and graffiti. The reality of the division remains on the ground. On one bridge across the Lagan it is said you can tell which community people belong to by the side of the bridge they cross. However, with the range of activity now being introduced along the river the territorial division is less apparent as a wide cross-section of the city's population come to live, work and enjoy leisure.

During the housing redevelopment of earlier decades, single-issue groups representing their immediate locality emerged, inevitably reflecting and reinforcing territorial aspects of division. More recently holistic regeneration initiatives have encouraged cross-community multi-dimensional partnerships to be created also bringing together private, public and voluntary sectors. Laganside has also achieved mixed tenure residential development with 25 per cent of the new units providing social accommodation.

The creation of mixed-use quarters in the city centre and Belfast's waterfront provides the opportunity for meeting and mixing beyond defined 'territories'. The linkage of these areas with easy attractive public access encourages interaction. Many cross-community activities are seeking to locate in the Cathedral Quarter. The return of city centre residential accommodation and 'night life' is fostering an urban lifestyle free from the constraints and traditions of existing communities. For the first time a more cosmopolitan lifestyle is emerging in Belfast reflected in 24-hour activity in the city centre. The development of commerce and leisure activities also raises the level of interaction with Dublin, UK and European cities. Private sector housing also allows a mixing of residents from various backgrounds.

The public realm settings have enabled the promotion of carnivals, festivals and outdoor performances in contrast to traditional 'parades'. At the launch of Cathedral Quarter a community artist commented: 'For too long Belfast has been a grey city. Now it is becoming colourful'. The signs of optimism and confidence generated by the success of new development thus not only transforms the city's international image but creates the opportunity for promotion and acceptance of diversity within the city.

Ten years ago Lanyon Place was a derelict and depressing place on a neglected river front. Last summer it was a thrill to mingle with thousands of people at the river festival as people from across Belfast mixed together in a relaxed atmosphere to enjoy festival and fireworks. The setting was impressive against the backdrop of new buildings representing substantial investment. However, the lasting impression is of overhearing bystanders comment: 'Tonight Belfast can be proud of itself.'

Whilst regeneration is often measured in terms of physical and economic outputs it is in the dimension of the quality of life, the achievement of cohesion and the response of the city's residents in terms of confidence, self-image and acceptance of diversity that the seeds of a shared sustainable urban society are beginning to emerge.

Notes

1   Department of the Environment (N.I.), 'Laganside Study' (Belfast: 1997) March.
2   OECD, 'Infrastructure, Investment and Community Development: Laganside Corporation Summary Report' (Belfast: 1999) June.
3   The Laganside Development (Northern Ireland) Order (1989), No. 490(N.I.2).
4   OECD, op. cit.
5   Laganside Corporation, 'Laganside Annual Report' (Belfast: 1998–99).
6   Laganside Corporation, 'Cathedral Quarter Regeneration Strategy' (Belfast: 1998) June.
7   M. Gooding, 'Public Art and Space: Introductory Essay', in *A Decade of Public Art 1987–1997*, London: Merrill Robertson (1998).

13

The Culturally Inclusive City: the Belfast Potential

Bill Morrison

I cannot claim to be in a position to offer detached comment on cultural inclusion. I am a Protestant. I am perceived to possess power, working as I do for the administration appointed by the British Government. I don't see myself as holding values that contribute to division in our society, but the fact is – I was brought up a Protestant. I am not a Catholic. In some quarters, therefore, I cannot hope to be regarded as neutral.

But I have lived in Belfast all my life. This is *my* city. Like everyone else who was born and bred in this city, I have reason to feel proud of the place. If I had been born a Catholic, would I have felt any different? I suppose in one respect I might. I might have wondered if it would have evolved differently – more inclusively – under a different administration. But wherever I might have come from, I am bound to regard the city as home. It is my city, too – and I have a job to do.

I am a planner, and I want to preserve what I know to be precious. But I am also an architect, trained to create something. I *want* to do more than merely preside over a reactive system of development control. There has to be a positive goal. And that goal has to emerge from a shared vision for the future.

That vision is of an inclusive city; a shared city; a city thriving on the proud fact that both communities have an equal stake in its prosperity.

Now of course my vision is no different from that of the public service as a whole. Nor is it a vision just for Belfast: it is a vision for the whole of Northern Ireland. Indeed that has now been loudly proclaimed as the collective aspiration of the entire community.

So there can be little argument, then, about what we want. There are, however, fundamental questions about what is actually meant by a culturally pluralist city; how we might get there – and, of intense interest to me, whether town planning and urban design can make a constructive contribution towards attainment of this objective.

Accommodating differences

Before considering the potential for promoting Belfast as a culturally inclusive city I would like to make some general observations about the things that divide our community, and the issues that have had to be addressed in planning the city over the past twenty-five years.

A former Secretary of State for Northern Ireland identified four characteristics that divide society in Northern Ireland. The first, and probably the issue that perpetuates the problem of how the North of Ireland is to be governed, is *national identity*. The others are *religion, cultural tradition*, and *social inequality*. Whatever policy-makers might say or do in an effort to play down these four differences in pursuit of community cohesion, development policies should certainly ensure that one of them – the element of cultural tradition – is heightened and not diminished. The French have a phrase for it – *'Vive la différence!'* Cultural diversity is to be celebrated.

Despite the nationalist community being described as more Irish than the Irish, and the loyalist community more British than the British, the people of Northern Ireland actually have more in common with one another than they do with the people of either Great Britain or the Republic of Ireland. And we do have a common inheritance in the natural environment, and in the built heritage of our towns and cities, especially Belfast. So there is a connection here, tenuous though it may seem at first. Maintaining that sense of place, and ownership of that place, has something to do with understanding how to accommodate differences.

Our common inheritance

From my experience, I would suggest that the urban planner in Belfast must draw a distinction between what I would call *shared places, contested places*, and *uncontested places*. The most obvious *shared place* is the city centre, and the grounds of the City Hall. A less obvious *shared place*, perhaps, might be the Parliament Buildings and grounds at Stormont – but I will return to that later. In addressing shared places, the urban planner has scope to heighten awareness of the built heritage. There is every opportunity for the exercise of urban design skills and the introduction of public art that will give expression to the common inheritance.

The *uncontested spaces* lie within, for example, the nationalist heartlands of West Belfast – or along the loyalist Shankill Road. These areas have the potential to be presented as cultural quarters, and this certainly would be in line with the wishes of the respective communities, who would oppose any development that would diminish local distinctiveness.

Planning for development in *contested places*, on the other hand, raises a much more fundamental issue. Fear. Fear for personal security translates directly into a threat to community stability. The urban planner enters this arena at his peril.

There are parts of the city that have been derelict for years and can only be described as no-man's land. There are flashpoints, some of which have existed for 150 years – and indeed many of us expect them to still exist in another 150 years. There are other parts of the city where contested places have been eliminated through the planned introduction of a neutral land use or some other form of physical separation. Mistakes have been made, and lessons learnt.

But it also needs to be understood that population movement plays a big part in the establishment and perpetuation of contested space. This is not the occasion to present a study of demographic trends, but in the planning of Belfast, in particular, it is important to understand why people are moving; how the complexion of areas is changing, and what are the expected consequences. The role for the urban planner is to understand this process, not to interfere with it.

Marketing Belfast

It is obvious that Belfast is an interesting place. It is interesting to both investors and tourists because they have read about it. They hear frequent mention of Belfast on radio and television. They see images of violence and destruction; of parades and mass rallies. They learn of political developments from commentators standing at the steps of the familiar Stormont – the building that depicts the image of Belfast to the world outside Northern Ireland.

It is doubtful if any other city in the world has been in the news as frequently over such a long period. In terms of capturing the attention of visitors and investors, Belfast has had a head start. Publicity is not a problem.

The point is that there is a real opportunity here. Not just an opportunity to attract visitor income in support of much-needed economic development, but to give the community a stake in the process of marketing the city. The city can only be marketed successfully as a place to visit, when it can be presented proudly by the citizens of Belfast as a great place to live – and a place to share.

For those who visit Northern Ireland, Belfast is a culturally interesting place. To explore community differences is compelling for the visitor. What places can he or she visit that symbolise those differences? What places are representative of inclusiveness and reconciliation?

I am not suggesting that we hype up divisive differences – nor indeed that we should whitewash over them. In fact we would need to be careful not to do so. But there is scope for place marketing in Belfast and we should acknowledge that urban design could be a valued economic instrument here.

Let me take you on a picture tour of Belfast. We will start at Stormont. Right away a major question arises. Is this building, sitting aloof on a hill in the heart of Protestant East Belfast, a symbol of division? Is this a place with representational meaning only for the unionist community – a symbol of defiance against the ideal of Irish nationalism? Some might say so, and that as such, its use as the seat of government should be consigned to history and the building and grounds put to new use – a theme park or a hotel, perhaps.

Others might say Stormont was built as a symbol of permanent regional governance in defiance of the British who regarded the partition settlement of 1921 as a staging post in a process of constitutional transition. As the sharing of power becomes a reality, it has at least the potential to symbolise reconciliation and inclusion. For the minority, it can be a case of *'our Stormont, too'*.

Let us move on to the Shankill and the Falls. Here again, we have places that tourists want to visit to see for themselves the different traditions that prevail. In recent years both Shankill and Falls have witnessed massive redevelopment of social housing. The housing was sensitively and even-handedly delivered, but redevelopment has visibly diluted those place characteristics that distinguished them for both resident and visitor. Many of the traditional street patterns behind the street frontages have been lost forever. The retention of the street frontages was at the time controversial, and more was left on the Shankill than on the Falls. Although run-down and undistinguished architecturally, the Shankill street frontage remains a vital reference for the citizens who belong to that community.

Peace walls

The visitor to Belfast will always want to see what are euphemistically called the 'peace walls'. There are 13 of them, and it must be understood that these walls are perceived in the community to be necessary – and they will remain in place as long as this is so. They have a serious purpose, and are nothing to celebrate. But they do represent a poignant symbol of what perpetuates the deep divisions in our society and should be openly acknowledged as such. And the fact is they serve a vital function. There is an old Arab saying: 'Live as one – but keep your tents apart'.

Fig. 13.1 A door remains tentatively open on one of Belfast's peacelines

Flashpoints are historically fascinating and over the years have raised issues for urban planning and social housing management that will always be profoundly interesting to the visitor. These stories should be told.

But while we can focus on differences, we must also build upon the positive image of progress towards reconciliation. Here Belfast can learn from the City of Derry/Londonderry. The statue that greets the visitor on arrival in the centre of the town shows two figures reaching to each other across the divide. It is an image that sums up the self-

Fig. 13.2 Reaching across the divide in Derry/Londonderry

image of a city that likes to present itself not just as the place where the struggle started, but the place where the Troubles ended.

America's President Clinton recently cut the turf at Springvale Educational Village – a hugely symbolic project to develop an innovative tertiary education campus on no-man's land between the Shankill and the Falls. This development will need to be handled with extreme sensitivity, but the concept is exciting in terms of both place creation and cultural inclusion.

The city centre

The centre of Belfast has long been regarded as belonging to both communities. The territory is neither claimed nor contested. The city centre is a major centre of employment accessed by both communities – offering around 10 per cent of all the jobs in Northern Ireland. And the city centre has been well supported by urban planning policy in the past. In a planned and managed drive to turn around the fortunes of a city centre devastated by terrorist bombing in the early 1970s, we have seen a major retail investment at CastleCourt underwritten by government subsidy. We have seen the setting up of a development corporation to promote development on the river frontage, and the introduction of regulatory control to prevent commercial office development from drifting to the more affluent suburbs.

There have been some interesting challenges for urban design. It has been argued by others that something of the essential place character has been lost because the planning authority was not more prescriptive in regulating building design, height, siting and use of materials. I disagree. My colleagues and I have worked hard to identify what is essential to the character of Belfast as a place and to protect what is acknowledged to be precious.

I cite one example. The CastleCourt development referred to above had the potential to destroy forever the place we treasure as Royal Avenue. The proposal for major development in this part of the city was crucially important in the process of resuscitating the city centre, and the administration could be forgiven for welcoming it with open arms.

The coherence of this grand Victorian thoroughfare, built a hundred years previously, was, however, seriously threatened by the new development, which involved loss through demolition of buildings which at the time did not enjoy the protection of being within what is now a Conservation Area.

Initially, the designers sought to meet the planners' contextual concerns through the use of matching materials (mainly red brick) and neo-Victorian detailing – seeking to patch into the street façade a building vastly out of scale with the carefully regulated height and rhythm of the buildings of Royal Avenue. After rejection of successive

Fig. 13.3 Royal Avenue: Belfast's major Victorian thoroughfare, circa 1908

schemes, programme pressures brought the case to the desk of the Minister. After careful deliberation the Minister, Richard Needham MP, boldly supported the planners in their call for a completely fresh approach.

What emerged was a contrasting modern design using glass and steel, but one which set back the upper floors and took the essential reference from the Victorian standard cornice height and vertical rhythm of the street. The loss of the original Victorian buildings was lamentable, but the coherence of the thoroughfare, valued by the citizens as a place that identifies Belfast, was restored.

However, the important point is that Belfast city centre, and the buildings and places represented there, belong without question to both communities. Protestant and Catholic – loyalist and nationalist – feel no sense of difference or alienation as they shop together, work together and immerse themselves in the culturally inclusive nightlife at the heart of the city. Here again we have a phenomenon of interest and comfort to the visitor.

But there are big questions about the future of Belfast's centre. The centre is not strong and may suffer – perhaps as an unwanted consequence of new policies to clamp down on central area parking. There is

Fig. 13.4 The CastleCourt Shopping Centre on Belfast's Royal Avenue, circa 1994

no immediate prospect of major investment in the kind of rapid transport systems that could make a difference to modes of travel. District centres may gain advantage in attracting the car-based shopper. Employment may decline as car-based business interests choose to disperse to surrounding towns and teleworking from home becomes commonplace. We must guard against losing the fragile vitality of our shared and valued city centre.

Engaging the community

Moving away from place for the moment, can we celebrate the fact that we in Belfast have a dynamic community sector actively engaged in the planning process? I believe we can.

Under the Direct Rule of the last twenty-five years, many assume that development decisions were delivered with the efficiency and cold determination of a development corporation. The reality has been very different. Nothing was delivered other than through community consensus. In fact virtually any development project I can think of since the 1970s has had the seal of community approval. Westlink, an important road link skirting the city centre, and Poleglass, an overspill housing project for Catholic West Belfast, were the last two projects that were driven through in the face of local opposition.

It has to be stated that some development opportunities may have been lost as the non-elected administration was obliged to retreat from hard choices over the last twenty years. Communities have, however, been strengthened by their active participation in development projects across Northern Ireland.

We in Northern Ireland are only beginning to gain the confidence to celebrate cultural diversity. The publication in January 1996 of an urban planning document entitled 'The Belfast City Region: towards and beyond the Millennium' was the first tentative step outside the sterile boundaries of land use planning.[1] It began a process of engaging the community 'beyond land use planning' in a debate about shaping a shared future.

In December last, the Department of the Environment for Northern Ireland published *Shaping Our Future* – a Draft Regional Strategic Framework for Northern Ireland.[2] The Regional Strategy presents Belfast as a 'gateway' and a 'shop window' which embodies both the Region's troubles, as seen in the effects of the civil unrest, and its potential as witnessed by significant economic successes. But the real significance of this publication is in what it symbolises. It was published following the most extensive public participation imaginable. Almost 600 separate bodies were drawn into the process to ensure that this project would be community-owned.

The community, then, has come up with a regional strategic framework for sustainable development – a strategy that demonstrates commitment to inclusion and regional accountability. The strategy is referred to in the Good Friday Agreement and will be offered for adoption by the new democratically elected Assembly. The new Assembly, working within the framework, will be particularly interested in promoting economic development. Along with the Scottish and Welsh Assemblies, the Northern Ireland elected politicians will be looking to emulate the success of the Republic of Ireland. In this competitive world, the presentation of Belfast as a culturally inclusive city will not merely be seen as beneficial and desirable as I have suggested. It is bound to be regarded as an essential ingredient of any strategy to attract visitors and investors to Northern Ireland.

A civic identity for Belfast

I find it fascinating to observe first hand how democratically elected councillors, despite their political differences, share passion for the city as a whole, and for the city centre in particular. In the year in which we have a Unionist Lord Mayor and, for the first time, a Sinn Fein Deputy Mayor, there is every reason to believe that this is the moment for the Council collectively to promote awareness of what comprises the civic identity of Belfast.

We can learn from Glasgow how to market a city. At the heart of Glasgow's economic development strategy, largely focused on the city centre, was a concerted partnership effort to provide accommodation, festivals and attractions for visitors. Glasgow presented itself as a place with a story to tell. That story is about place – but it is also about the dignity and self-esteem of the citizens. It would have been impossible to re-image Glasgow as being *Miles Better* if the citizens themselves did not believe it.

We in Belfast have just as much reason to believe in our city. The place which represents the centre city has a civic identity which transcends the two ethnic identities. We can make much of that.

To summarise, then, we can learn from Glasgow; we can learn from the Irish Republic; we can learn from Berlin – but in the last analysis we learn most from partnership and engagement with the community. It is my submission that there is potential in the concept of representing Belfast as a culturally inclusive city – a city proud of the fact that it can celebrate and accommodate its differences. The link to urban planning is in the challenge of preserving and enhancing the local distinctiveness that constitutes the substance of place marketing.

Conclusion

The next major planning exercise for Belfast starts in the year 2000. Following adoption of the regional strategy, work will begin on a statutory development plan for the Metropolitan Area of Belfast. What we are doing now is engaging the community in what should be the core objectives of this plan – the positive goal that is to be achieved by means of the plan. The function of the statutory plan is not to set the goal but to secure the means of delivery.

The community has been animated by the regional strategic exercise, and by the work of the Urban Institute and the Belfast Vision Partnership.[3] Never before have I witnessed so many focus groups excited by the challenge of articulating a vision for the future. It is important to recognise the significance of cultural inclusion in this exercise.

Out of the vision of Belfast as an inclusive city; a shared city; a city thriving on the proud fact that both communities have an equal stake in its prosperity – will emerge the planning goal.

Notes

1   Department of the Environment (NI), 'Belfast City Region: towards and beyond the Millennium' (Belfast: HMSO, 1996).
2   Department of the Environment (NI), 'Shaping Our Future: a Draft Regional Strategic Framework for Northern Ireland' (Belfast: HMSO, 1998).
3   Belfast City Partnership Board , 'Our City Our Future, Vision Partnership Statement' (Belfast: 1998).

Part V
Conclusion

14

Planning with an Ethic of Cultural Inclusion: Lessons from Berlin and Belfast

William J.V. Neill and Hanns-Uve Schwedler

The cities of Berlin and Belfast are both desperately seeking normality. Given their fractured histories in the twentieth century the aspiration of returning to the 'common European fold' will only be realised if urban planning in the broadest sense takes place with an ethic of cultural inclusion. This chapter, reflecting on the lessons to be learnt from the contributions to this volume, considers what this means, and the contribution which planners can provide in 'making it happen'. However some cautionary lessons on the limitations of planning in the face of power should be acknowledged at the outset.

The limits of planning

The power of the market over cities can create economic exclusion and thereby exacerbate cultural division. Economic exclusion, for example, in West Belfast, has added to a sense of cultural separation. A major educational village (the Springvale Project) presently under construction in the area is a major planning response. Likewise planning responses to environmentally upgrade pre-fabricated housing developments (Plattenbauten) in East Berlin offset the danger of these becoming economically marginalised 'sink' estates. Creative urban planning responses tackling economic and cultural exclusion illustrate that while localities are not masters of their own destiny they are not impotent in the face of the market either. On the other hand the global market itself is a force for a degree of cultural unity. It has the power to constitute itself in new large-scale place-making projects whether with Sony and DaimlerChrysler in Potsdamer Platz in Berlin or the more modest British Telecom and Hilton Laganside developments in Belfast.

However the suspicion must remain that the allure of commercially driven universalising cosmopolitan culture can provide but a shallow sense of cultural identity. It would be unrealistic to expect, for example, that a new 'loft living' culture taking hold in Belfast could substitute for more deeply felt ethnic identifications. It would be equally naive to expect that new apartment dwellers in Potsdamer Platz could float placelessly free of the genius loci of the reinstated centre of Berlin.

Planning with an ethic of cultural pluralism must also recognise the reality of political power. All cultural traditions and experiences are not equal. In Berlin, as Hain describes, a western hegemony is persistently erasing an eastern experience and identity. And as Heine and Müller make clear, Turkish identity struggles to stake its claim as a part of the legitimate civic life of the city. Here the accepted 'German Way' can appear inflexible to outsiders whether it be restrictions on barbecuing in the Tiergarten or restrictions limiting the minarets and adornments on public mosques. In Belfast a past unionist cultural hegemony made itself felt in the public realm with control over parades, symbols, monuments, public art, place naming and civic design. With the institutionalisation of cultural pluralism in the wake of the 'Belfast Agreement', tension over such affairs will hopefully in the future be a matter of creative cultural coexistence.

Seven lessons

In the face of economic and political power what can planners do then in negotiating difference and plurality within the respective cities of Berlin and Belfast? Seven important lessons emerge from the contributions to this volume. Planning with an ethic of cultural pluralism must:

- Take place within a civic culture of inclusiveness. The planning *process* is important.
- Respect the need for spatial equity.
- Enable cultural *difference* to exist where this is desired.
- Facilitate cultural *integration* and contact where this is desired.
- Respect the contribution of organic development.
- Be open to the introduction of new and novel differences within the city.
- Recognise the unavoidability of marketing the difference in place promotion.

Civic culture of inclusiveness

Ideally planning can contribute to an inclusive civic identity building process. Given the urgency of the political issues at hand it is not surprising that many of the Belfast authors endorse this approach. The planning process in a context of cultural division is as important as the content. The chapter by Hain, in contrast, demonstrates the alienation which a perceived top-down planning process can engender. Planners rather need to be mediators in a planning process which seeks inclusion and where they do not hide behind legalistic and technocratic planning competencies. This can escalate conflict in the spoken domain and become de facto planning for exclusion.[1] Moreover in both Berlin and Belfast the question presents itself whether difference can more easily coexist in relation to the civic identity of a city than in the concept of a nation. Certainly it is possible to be a Belfaster without considering oneself British or perversely even Irish.[2] It is not so clear that it is possible to be a Berliner without being German.

Spatial equity

Although not always considered directly by the contributing authors, it is clear that fairness in relation to locational decisions (schools, hospitals, jobs, leisure facilities and so on) and resource allocation is a *sine qua non* for making a feeling of cultural inclusion possible. Ironically in Berlin it is now West Berliners who sometimes feel a sense of disadvantage in relation to perceived expenditure in the east. In Belfast the concept of ethnic impact assessments[3] has been mooted as a way of making explicit the effect of new planning and investment decisions on the two major traditions. Planning which ignores this dimension of policy is certainly not neutral. Here, in parallel with Berlin, unionist communities can now sometimes feel a sense of perceived disadvantage in relation to spatial equity matters. Tackling this issue directly and transparently can offset brooding resentment.

Planning for cultural difference

Planning with an ethic of cultural inclusion means acknowledging that it is acceptable to be different. It means planning for difference, in recognition that separation is not necessarily bad. This can relate to nurturing cultural quarters in cities (W. Belfast, Kreuzberg); the need for a certain degree of residential segregation for community solidarity (Kreuzberg) and even security (Belfast),[4] the acceptance of overt symbols of difference (Irish place names in Belfast, Moslem minarets in

Berlin); the need to respect and bring into planning discourse the different representational landscapes of the city and the collective memory invested there (the Palast der Republik in Berlin and Stormont in Belfast, for example); and the need to understand the role of spatial practices in the constitution of identity whether this is as innocuous as Turkish cafés or tearooms which are focal social places for men only or the contentious issue of unionist parades in Belfast.

Planning for integration

Planning for cultural inclusion means planning for civic spaces where heterogeneity can be shared and with which different cultural groups can commonly identify. Belfast city centre with changes to rules on parades and demonstrations has moved in this direction. New urban spaces in Belfast, as described in the chapter by Smith and Alexander, strive to provide shared space for mixed cultural living and socialising alongside new civic spaces and public art seeking cross-ethnic identification. Whether this is too bland or innocuous is a matter of debate. In Berlin the Planwerk Innenstadt, a design plan with an integrating aesthetic drawing on pre-Second World War common memory, might be having the opposite effect to its desired intent. It might be fostering, in other words, division and conflict. Certainly the area around the Kaiser Wilhelm Gedächtnis Kirche on the Kurfürstendamm remains a major common civic space and a platform for varied and dissenting cultural voices.

Organic development

Planning for cultural inclusion means resisting the impulse to overplan. People can relate to space in unexpected and novel ways. There would be few middle-aged people in Belfast who did not lament the closing of the old Smithfield Market after fire damage in the early 1970s. Making way for the planned, controlled and monitored environment of the CastleCourt Shopping Centre, the rambling chaos and unplanned nature of Smithfield, for many, represented the soul of the city which has somehow been lost. In Berlin, for example, many of the roadside snack bars, open cafés with bar tables and street markets which shot up like mushrooms after the political changes in Germany have by now disappeared again – not only due to lack of demand, but also because of restrictions and bans based on local regulations or planning grounds.

Openness to the new and novel

Planning with an ethic of cultural inclusion also means being open to the new and novel which over time can induce a sense of identity with a place and even come to symbolise that place's identity. It means not suppressing the 'NIKE' architectural impulse of 'just doing it'. The Brandenburg Gate was novel on its erection. The new Daniel Libeskind Jewish museum in Berlin dares to be different now. Here it must be regarded as disappointing that Belfast's more recent public realm is notable rather for the brutalism of terrorist-proof buildings diluted with mediocre postmodernism than for anything architecturally adventurous or distinctive. New statues of salmon and sheep on Belfast's waterfront underscore the point. Rather, in early 2000, Belfast is distinctive for tourists from around the world writing messages of hope for the peace process on the peace wall at Cupar Way in West Belfast.

Marketing the difference

Berlin and Belfast in the past have both attracted visitors fascinated by compelling images of ideological division on the one hand and ethnic division on the other. While Cold War tourism is now over and terror tourism in Belfast hopefully an endangered activity, both places have, nevertheless, interesting stories to tell. The cosmetic papering over of past conflict, whether in the Planwerk Innenstadt or the search for 'made in Brussels', off the rack, Euro-spatial planning solutions in the case of Belfast, seems misplaced. It remains sad, moreover, at the time of writing, in March 2000, that more revenue can probably be generated in the city of Belfast by marketing the history of the native company (Harland and Wolff) which built the world's most famous ship, the *Titanic*, than by saving this Belfast shipyard and its living heritage from extinction. The negative economic impact in particular on unionist communities in East Belfast is likely to further a sense of cultural exclusion.

Planners and cultural inclusion in Belfast

Because planning for cultural pluralism is on the political agenda in Belfast and Northern Ireland this does not imply that all planners know what this means, feel comfortable with such an agenda or have the knowledge and skills to address it. A questionnaire survey carried out in November 1998 of senior members of the planning profession in Northern Ireland[5] clearly indicated that not all in the profession are in agreement on how to even delineate a cultural identity agenda, let alone to chart a *modus operandi* for proceeding. Those within the Department of the Environment (NI) Planning Service were the most conservative in their responses tending to define the purview of the profession in quite narrow terms. Planners should not get involved in such controversy was a typical response. The field of legitimate concern for planners (as opposed to 'just' being administrators of a statutory land use planning system) opened out in the responses of the private sector, voluntary sector and academic based planners. Even here, however, the view was expressed that planners may presently not have enough knowledge and background to 'thrust' themselves into cultural identity issues. Such responses are in accord with the recent verdict of an American planning academic who suggests that in Northern Ireland 'the profession has retreated from its potential role in creating a strategic and comprehensive framework for ethnic manage-ment'.[6] However, in defence it can be said that the gap between theory and practice looms large for planners endeavouring to 'mainstream' cultural pluralism issues. In moving to be 're-solvers' of cultural conflict, no easy procedural normative template is immediately avail-able. The dominant procedural paradigm in Anglo-American planning theory, that of communicative or discursive collaborative planning which draws heavily on the work of the German sociologist-philoso-pher Jürgen Habermas, has been criticised as utopian.[7] The consensus which such planning through debate seeks may simply not be possible (the cultural terrain can be a battleground of competing identities in Belfast) and there is the question of ensuring the neutrality and inde-pendence of the planner as facilitator (planners are typically from one ethnic tradition or the other in Belfast).[8] Recent plan-making activities affecting Belfast (a Belfast Metropolitan Area discussion document,[9] a draft Strategic Plan for Northern Ireland[10] and a City Vision for Belfast)[11] do, in a search for legitimacy, espouse collaborative planning. Extensive voices have been heard through public consultation. Resulting documents have striven for consensus by producing plans at a high level of generality and aspirational idealism. However, as Tewdwr-Jones and Allmendinger put it, including 'voices' is not the same as pursuing the public interest where the activities of the 'power-ful' are harnessed with democracy.[12] Ideals are more difficult to imple-ment in practice. With this in mind, planners in Belfast, it would seem, are left with the challenging task of forging for themselves a more rig-orous *modus operandi* for an inclusive discursive planning process incorporating cultural difference. The retreat to the generalities produced so far is not enough. Here Habermas's call for a 'civilised dispute of convictions'[13] where none of the participating groups clings fundamentally to its position would seem the appropriate goal.

Planning and the exclusion of history in Berlin

In addition to the intentions of Berlin urban planners to interpret the spatial structure of the pre-war city in a modern fashion and to in-fill spaces with new construction, there is also a further political motif involved in current urban development in Berlin. Planning principles can be presented by politicians as not just a return to a normal past somewhere pre-Second World War but as a new beginning. Since this has serious implications for the collective history of the German people, some words, albeit brief, on this question are in order.

The slogan 'Berlin as the construction site of German reunification' refers, in this context, not only to the importance of developing the city in terms of 'East' and 'West' integration. Rather, on many occasions the attempt is baldly made to use the motif of German unity as a guiding political symbol for capital city planning in Germany thus implanting a second 'zero hour' (tabula rasa) as an identity-creating theme in people's minds. However, in this way layers in history are repressed. In the final analysis history is being falsified. For example, the new Chancellory Office (Kanzleramt) and the parliamentarians' office building span the two banks of the River Spree near the Reichstag and are called 'the Federal ribbon' (Band des Bundes). They thus join former East Berlin with the western part and are interpreted as a physical built symbol of bringing together the two halves of Berlin or even the original and five new Federal states (Länder). A closer look, however, reveals that the two architects Schultes and Frank had already used the basic concept in the 1980s for the Bonn museum complex, at the time simply for formal urban design and aesthetic reasons. It was only a political and media interpretation to describe it as the 'Federal ribbon'.[14]

It may be regarded as symptomatic that a different interpretation was scarcely present in discussions: the west–east orientation of the complex of buildings could be seen as a counter-image to the National Socialist urban design axis which ran in a north–south direction. This selective historical amnesia was present in speeches given by a number of German political figures. When former Chancellor Kohl gave a speech at the formal laying of the foundation stone of the Chancellory building, at no time did he mention the history of the site as one of the crucial locations in the run-up to two world wars.

Several additional instances could be listed of attempts to throw the magic cloak of German unity over Berlin places and buildings and in so doing to attempt to bring about a common symbolic landscape for East and West alike. Even if these attempts prove successful in creating something resembling a common identity for East Germans and West Germans, they nevertheless, will deprive the buildings in question of their history. In so doing the Germans will be denied their shared past, which does not consist exclusively of Goethe and the 'Golden Twenties'. Max Welch Guerra is correct when he states that the function of 'the motif of German unity' is to permit 'the Germans to appear to be the victims, not the perpetrators, of 20th century history'.[15] The point is expanded by Detlev Lücke: 'Anyone who, for whatever reason, suppresses these memories is not adequately appreciating the "aura" of this city which is to be defined essentially in terms of historical contradictions.'[16]

A virtually exclusive association of the city by Berlin urban planners with the built structures of 1920s Berlin adds to and underpins, perhaps subconsciously, the de-historising which emanates from politically motivated interpretations of the city's buildings and places. By these methods a period of over fifty years of tyranny and the rule of force which was so characteristic of the history of Berlin in the twentieth century has been deleted from the physical and spatial memory of the city. In this way identity-creating political gesturing associates itself with spatial planning and results in a loss of individual (that is, personally experienced) and collective (that is, inherited) history. Both of these should be a component part of German identity and of German identities.

Notes

1 Bodenschatz states that Planwerk is structured in a far from process style … It is oriented towards the complete picture, a final position. (H Bodenschatz, 'Planwerk Innenstadt Berlin: eine Bestandsaufnahme', Arkitektenkammer Berlin (ed.), *Planwerk Innenstadt Berlin Provokation* (Berlin: published by the Architektenhammer, 1997) p. 112.

2 Building on this theme, a proposal is presently under active consideration to build a museum of citizenship in Belfast's Crumlin Road jail thus rebranding a major and contentious city site.

3 B. Murtagh, 'Segregated Space in Northern Ireland: Principles and Practice' (Belfast: Community Relations Council, 1996).

4 The social functions of segregation have been closely studied by social scientists. In Middle Eastern towns and cities, *see* for example, H.U. Schwedler, *Arbeitsmigration und urbaner Wandel. Eine Studie über Arbeitskräftewanderung und räumliche Segregation in orientalischen Städten* (Berlin: Reimer, 1985).

5 W.J.V. Neill, 'Cultural Pluralism, Identity and the Role of Planners in Belfast and Northern Ireland: a Report to the Royal Town Planning Institute Irish Branch (Northern Section)', Belfast: School of Environmental Planning, Queen's University Belfast, 1999) p. 34.

6 S. Bollens, quoted in F.W. Boal and B. Murtagh, *Planning and Ethnicity in Northern Ireland: Comparative Experiences* (Belfast, unpublished manuscript, 1998) p. 18.

7 M. Tewdwr-Jones and P. Allmendinger, 'Deconstructing Communicative Rationality: a Critique of Habermasian Collaborative Planning', *Environment and Planning* A, Vol. 30, (1998) pp. 1975–89.

8 Cultural tension is reflected in the fact that while the Royal Town Planning Institute has one Irish Branch this fractured into a Northern and Southern section in the 1970s. The Irish Planning Institute likewise recruits on an all-Ireland basis but has few Protestant members in the North.

9 Department of the Environment (NI), *Belfast City – Region: Public Voices* (Belfast, HMSO, 1997).

10 Department of the Environment (NI), *Draft Regional Strategic Framework for Northern Ireland* (Belfast, HMSO, 1998).

11 Belfast City Partnership Board, *Belfast City Vision: Our City Our Future* (Belfast: 1998).

12 Op. cit., p. 1988.

13 Habermas, quoted in A. Treibel, 'Theory of Communicative Action, Discourse Ethics and Political Practice: notes on recent developments in Habermas', *Soziologie*, Journal of the Deutsche Gesellschaft für Soziologie, Special Edition 3 (1994) pp. 135–48, p. 144.

14 M. Welch Guerra, 'Hauptstadtplanung als Medium einer städtischen Identitätsfindung', *69th Stadtforum* (Berlin: unpublished manuscript, 1998).

15 Ibid.

16 D. Lücke, 'Die mentale Wiedervereinigung Berlins', *67th Stadtforum* (Berlin: unpublished manuscript, 1998).

Bibliography

Abel, C., *Architecture and Identity: towards a Global Eco-culture* (Oxford: Architectural Press, 1997).

Anson, B., Response to 'Architecture of No-Man's Land', *Architect's Journal*, No. 37, Vol. 180 (1984).

Ascherson, N., 'Why Heritage is Right-Wing', *The Observer* (November 8, 1987).

Ashworth, G.J. and P.J. Larkham (eds), *Building a New Heritage: Tourism, Culture and Identity in the New Europe* (London: Routledge, 1994).

Banghard, A., 'Berlin – Transformation einer Metropole' in W. Süß (ed.), *Hauptstadt Berlin, Bd. 2 – Berlin im vereinten Deutschland* (Berlin Verlag, 1995).

Bardon, J., *Belfast: an Illustrated History* (Belfast: Blackstaff Press, 1982).

Barnekov, T., R. Boyle and D. Rich, *Privatism and Urban Policy in Britain and the United States* (New York: Oxford University Press, 1989).

Barth, F. (ed.), *Ethnic Groups and Boundaries: the Social Organization of Cultural Difference* (London: George Allen and Unwin, 1969).

Beckett, J. *et al* (eds), *Belfast: the Making of the City* (Belfast: Appletree Press, 1988).

Belfast Chamber of Trade, Department of the Environment (Northern Ireland) and Belfast City Council, Report on the Belfast City Centre: The Way Forward Seminar (1983).

Belfast City Partnership Board, 'Our City Our Future, Vision Partnership Statement' (Belfast: 1998).

Belfast City Council, 'Towards and beyond the Millennium: Vision Response' (Belfast: 1997).

Belfast City Partnership Board, 'What the People Said' (Belfast: 1998).

Belfast Development Office, 'Belfast? Belfast!: Communications' (Belfast: Department of the Environment (NI), undated).

Birrell, D. and A. Murie, *Policy and Government in N. Ireland: Lessons of Devolution* (Dublin: Gill and Macmillan, 1980).

Blackman, T., *Planning Belfast: a Case Study of Urban Policy and Community Action* (Aldershot: Avebury, 1991).

Blau, S., '*Das Instrument Stadtforum und die Demokratisierung der Planung*', Diplomarbeit (Master's Thesis) at Geographische Institut der ETH Zürich (Zürich: unpublished manuscript, 1977).

Boal, F.W. and B. Murtagh, 'Planning and Ethnicity in Northern Ireland: Comparative Experiences' (Belfast, unpublished manuscript, 1998).

Bodemann, M., *Jew, Germans, Memory: Reconstructions of Jewish Life in Germany* (Ann Arbor: University of Michigan Press, 1996).

Bodemann, M., 'Terrains of Violence, Terrains of Memory: German and Israeli Varieties'. Paper delivered at Time and Value Conference, University of Lancaster, Institute of Cultural Research (1997).

Bodenschatz, H., *Berlin. Auf der Suche nach dem verlorenen Zentrum* (Hamburg: Junius Verlag, 1995).

Bouchet, D., 'Information Technology, the Social Bond and the City: Georg Simmel Updated: about the changing relationship between identity and the city'?, *Built Environment*, Vol. 24, Nos. 2/3 (1998).

Boyer, C., 'The Return of Aesthetics to City Planning', *SOCIETY* (May/June 1988).

Brett, C.E.B., *Buildings of Belfast* (Belfast: Friars Bush Press, 1985).

Brett, C.E.B., 'Conservation amidst Conflict', *Icomos Information* (Oct/Dec 1986).

Brown, S., 'Central Belfast's Shopping Centre', *Estates Gazette*, 19 October (1985).

Buckland, P., *A History of Northern Ireland* (Dublin: Gill and Macmillan, 1981).

Burg, A. and S. Redecke (eds) *Chancellery and Office of the President of the Federal Republic of Germany: International Architectural Competitions for the Capital Berlin* (Bonn: Birkhäuser Publishers, 1995).

Buruma, I., 'From Hirohito to Heimat', *New York Review of Books*, 26 October (1989).

Casey, E.S., *Getting Back into Place: toward a Renewed Understanding of the Place World* (Indianapolis: Indiana University Press, 1993).

Castells, M., *The Power of Identity* (Oxford: Blackwell, 1997).

Comedia, 'Within Reach: a Strategy for Community-based Arts Activities in Belfast', Belfast City Council (Belfast: 1995).

Community Relations Council, Interface Project (Belfast: 1998).

Cooke, P., *Back to the Future: Modernity and Locality* (London: Unwin Hyman, 1990).

Coopers and Lybrand Deloitte, The N.I. Economy: Review and Prospects (Belfast: 1990) January.

Crawford, H., *Industries of the North 100 Years ago: Industrial and Commercial Life in the North of Ireland 1981–91* (Belfast: Friars Bush Press, 1986).

Darby, J. and G. Morris, 'Intimidation in Housing', *Community Forum* 111, No. 2 (1973) pp. 7–11.

Davies, M., *City of Quartz: Excavating the Future in Los Angeles* (London: Vintage, 1990).

Department of the Environment (NI), *The Heart of the City Conference Report* (November 1980).

Department of the Environment (NI), *Belfast City Centre – the Way Forward*, Seminar Report (October 1983).

Department of the Environment (NI), *Belfast Urban Area Plan 2001* (Belfast, HMSO, 1990).

Department of the Environment (NI), *Belfast City Region: towards and beyond the Millennium* (Belfast: HMSO, 1996).

Department of the Environment (NI), *Belfast City – Region: Public Voices* (Belfast, HMSO, 1997).

Department of the Environment (NI), *Laganside Study* (Belfast: HMSO, 1997) March.

Department of the Environment (NI), *Draft Regional Strategic Framework for Northern Ireland* (Belfast, HMSO, 1998).

Department of the Environment (NI), *Shaping Our Future: a Draft Regional Strategic Framework for Northern Ireland* (Belfast: HMSO, 1998).

Easthope, A., 'The Peculiar Temporality of the National Narrative', Paper delivered at Time and Value Conference, University of Lancaster, Institute for Cultural Research (10–13 April 1997).

English, R. and G. Walker (eds) *Unionism in Modern Ireland, New Perspectives on Politics and Culture* (London: Gill and Macmillan, 1996).

Ersöz, A., 'Türkische Ökonomie nach der Wende in Berlin', in R. Amann and B. von Neumann-Cosel (eds), *Berlin. Eine Stadt im Zeichen der Migration* (Darmstadt: Verlag für wissenschaftliche Publikationen, 1997).

Fassbinder, H., 'Stadtforum Berlin', *Harburger Berichte zur Stadtplanung*, Bd.8 (Hamburg, 1997).

Faulkner, B., *Memoirs of a Statesman* (London: Weidenfeld and Nicolson, 1978).

Federal State of Berlin, *Berlin in Brief* (Berlin: Presse- und Informationsant, 1995).

Feldmann, V., 'Grundlagen des Planungs- und Baurechts in der BRD und Rechtsanforderungen an den Umweltschutz', Senatsverwaltung für Bau- und Wohnungswesen (ed.), *Kongreßbericht. Erste Stadtkonferenz Berlin. Planen, Bauen, Wohnen* (Berlin: Kulturbuch-Verlag, 1990).

Foy, M., 'Belfast 1991', *Belfast Telegraph*, 28 December (1991).

Friedan, B. and L. Sagalyn, *Downtown Inc. How America Rebuilds Cities* (Cambridge, MA: MIT Press, 1989).

Ganser, K., 'Instrumente von gestern für die Städte von morgen? in K. Ganser, J. Hesse and C. Zöpel (eds), *Die Zukunft der Städte* (Baden-Baden: Verlagsgesellschaft, 1991).

Habermas, J., *A Berlin Republic: Writings on Germany* (Cambridge Polity Press, 1998).

Haerdter, M., 'Mythos Mitte', *Positionen*, 1 (1998).

Hagemann, L. and A.T. Khoury, Dürfen Muslime auf Dauer in einem nicht-islamischen Land leben? *Zu einer Dimension der Integration muslimischer Mitbürger in eine nicht-islamische Gesellschaftsordnung* (Altenberge: Echter Verlag, 1997).

Hall Report, Report of the Joint Working Party on the Economy of N. Ireland, Cmnd 446 (Belfast: HMSO, 1962).

Hamilton, D., 'Foreign Direct Investment and Industrial Development in N. Ireland' in P. Teague (ed.), *The Economy of N. Ireland: Perspectives for Structural Change* (London: Lawrence and Wishart, 1993).

Hansen, M., 'Dossier on Heimat', *New German Critique*, 36 (1985).

Hartung, K., 'Berliner Ungleichzeitigkeiten', *Kommune*, 4 (1997).

Harvey, D., *The Condition of Postmodernity* (Oxford: Blackwell, 1990).

Harvey, D., *Justice, Nature and the Geography of Difference* (Oxford: Blackwell, 1996).

Hassemer, V., 'Strategic Planning and Development Programme of Berlin', European Academy of the Urban Environment (ed.), *Strategies of Development for Central European Metropolises* (Berlin: published by E.A.U.E, 1993).

Häussermann, H. and R. Neef, *Stadtentwicklung in Ostdeutschland. Soziale and räumliche Tendenzen* (Opladen: Westdeutscher Verlag, 1996).

Healy, P., 'Planning for the 1990's', Department of Town and Country Planning, University of Newcastle-upon-Tyne, *Working Paper Series*, No. 7, (1989).

Heine, P., 'Verbreitungsgebiet der islamischen Religion: Zahlen und Information in der Gegenwart' in W. Ende and U. Steinbach (eds), *Der Islam in der Gegenwart* (München: Beck, 1996).

Hendry, J. and J.M. McEldowney, *Conservation in Belfast*, Report to the Department of the Environment for N. Ireland, Department of Architecture and Planning, Queen's University of Belfast (1987).

Hewison, R., *The Heritage Industry* (London: Methuen, 1987).

HMSO, *Parliament Buildings Stormont* (Belfast: undated).

Hodgkiss, R., 'The Bitter Tears of Fassbinder's Women', *Guardian*, 8 January (1998).

Hoffmann-Axthelm, D., 'Das Berliner Planwerk Innenstadt und seine Kritiker', *Kommune*, 12 (1997).

Institut für Regionalentwicklung and Strukturplanung IRS (ed.): *Archäeologie und Aneignung. Ideen, Pläne und Stadtfiguration. Aufsätze zur Ostberliner Stadtentwicklung nach 1945* (Erkner: published by IRS, 1996).

Jencks, C., 'Post-Modernism and Discontinuity', *Journal of Architectural Design*, Special Edition (1987).

Jenkins, R., *Social Identity* (London: Routledge, 1996).

Jonker, G. and A. Kapphan (eds), *Moscheen und islamisches Leben in Berlin* (Berlin: published by Ausländerbeauftragte des Senats von Berlin, 1999).

Kapphan, A., 'Zuwanderung and Stadtkultur. Die Verteilung ausländischer Bevölkerung in Berlin', in R. Amann and B. von Neumann-Cosel (eds), *Eine Stadt im Zeichen der Migration* (Darmstadt: Verlag für wissenschaftliche Publikationen, 1997).

Karakasoglu, Y., 'Die Bestattung von Muslimen in der Bundesrepublik Deutschland aus der Sicht türkische-islamischer Organisationen', in Höpp and Jonker (eds), In fremder Erde. Zur Geschichte und Gegenwart der islamischen Bestattung in Deutschland, *Arbeitshefte Zentrum Moderner Orient*, Vol. 11 (Berlin, 1996).

Kil, W., 'Würde, Idylle, Segregation. Wie ein "Planwerk" versucht, die Metropole zu bändigen', *Kommune*, 2 (1997).

Kokkelink, G., 'Islamische Bestattung auf kommunalen Friedhöfen', in G. Höpp and G. Jonker (eds), In fremder Erde. Zur Geschichte und Gegenwart der islamischen Bestattung in Deutschland, *Arbeitshefte Zentrum Moderner Orient*, Vol. 11 (Berlin, 1996).

Kramer, J., 'The Politics of Memory', *The New Yorker*, 14 August (1995).

Laganside Corporation, 'Cathedral Quarter Regeneration Strategy' (Belfast, 1998) June.

Laganside Corporation, 'Laganside Annual Report' (Belfast: 1999).

Larmour, P., *Belfast: an Illustrated Architectural Guide* (Belfast: Friar's Bush Press, 1987).

Lash, S. and J. Urry, *The End of Organised Capitalism* (London: Polity Press, 1993).

Lavery Report, *Belfast Urban Area Plan: Review of Transportation Strategy* (Belfast: HMSO, 1978).

Lefebvre, H., *The Production of Space* (Oxford: Blackwell, 1991).

Liggett, H. and D.C. Perry, *Spatial Practices: Critical Explorations in Social/Spatial Theory* (London: Sage, 1995).

Lynch, K., *The Image of the City* (Cambridge, MA, MIT Press, 1960).

Mandani-Pour, A., *Design of Urban Space* (Chichester, John Wiley, 1997).

Matthew Report, *Belfast Regional Survey and Plan: Recommendations and Conclusions* (Belfast: HMSO, 1963).

McDonagh, R., *A Partnership Approach to Regeneration: Some Guiding Principles* (Belfast: Department of the Environment (NI) 1995).

McEldowney, J.M. and J. Hendry, 'Protection and Neutrality in a Divided City', *Journal of European Spatial Research and Policy*, No. 1, Vol. 2 (1995).

Meuser, P., 'Wie demokratisch ist das Planwerk? Die Form der Stadt als soziale Angelegenheit', *Stadtforum – Zukunft des Zentrums* (29 April 1998).

Mooney, S. and F. Gaffikin, *Reshaping Space and Society: a Critical Review of the Belfast Urban Area Plan* (Belfast: Centre of the Unemployed, 1988).

Morley, D. and K. Robins, *Spaces of Identity: Global Media, Electronic Landscapes and Cultural Boundaries* (London: Routledge, 1995).

Morrison, B., 'Making Belfast Work', *The Planner*, December (1990).

Moss, M., 'A Strategic Vision for Belfast' (Belfast: Department of the Environment (NI), 1995).

Moss, M., Opening Remarks to a Meeting of Belfast City Council, 11 May (1995).

Moss, M. and J. Hume, *Shipbuilders to the World: 125 years of Harland and Wolff 1869–1986* (Belfast: Appletree Press 1986).

Murtagh, B., *Segregated Space in Northern Ireland: Principals and Practice* (Belfast: Community Relations Council, 1996).

Myerscough, J., *The Arts and the Northern Ireland Economy* (Belfast: Northern Ireland Economic Council, 1996).

Needham, R., 'Battling for Peace' (Belfast: Blackstaff Press, 1998).

Needham, R., 'Gods' Smile on Belfast', Letter to *Belfast Telegraph*, 8 August (1991).

Neill, W.J.V., 'The New Plan for Belfast: a Model for the Future or Dancing on a Volcano', Pleanail, *Journal of the Irish Planning Institute*, No. 7, (1987) pp. 45–55.

Neill, W.J.V., 'Anywhere and Nowhere: Reimaging Belfast', in D. Smyth (ed.), *Whose City? The Shaping of Belfast*: A two-day Seminar organised by Community Technical Aid, Fortnight Educational Trust and Royal Town Planning Institute (Conference Proceedings, Fortnight Educational Trust, June 1992).

Neill, W.J.V., 'Physical Planning and Image Enhancement: Recent Developments in Belfast', *International Journal of Urban and Regional Research*, Vol. 17, No. 4 (1993).

Neill, W.J.V., D. Fitzsimons and B. Murtagh, *Reimaging the Pariah City: Urban Development in Belfast and Detroit* (Aldershot: Avebury, 1995).

Neill, W.J.V., 'Memory, Collective Identity and Urban Design: the Future of Berlin's Palast der Republik', *Journal of Urban Design*, Vol. 2, No. 2 (1997) pp. 179–92.

Neill, W.J.V., *Cultural Pluralism, Identity and the Role of Planners in Belfast and Northern Ireland: a Report to the Royal Town Planning Institute, Irish Branch* (Northern Section) (Belfast: School of Environmental Planning, Queen's University, 1999).

Neue Gesellschaft für Bildende Kunst (ed.), *Dokumentation der Ausstellung und Aktionen vom 28.8–11.10.98* (Berlin: published by the Neue Gesellschaft für Bildende Kunst, 1998).

Neuman, M., Planning, Governing and the Image of the City', *Journal of Planning Education and Research*, Vol. 18, No. 1 (1998) pp. 61–71.

N.I. Information Service, 'Nine Point Package to Spell Rebirth of Belfast' (Belfast: 1978).

Norberg-Schulz, C., *Genius Loci: towards a Phenomenology of Architecture* (London: Academy Editions, 1980).

Oc, T. and S. Tiesdall, *Safer City Centres* (London: Paul Chapman, 1998).

O'Connor, F., *In Search of a State: Catholics in N. Ireland* (Belfast: Blackstaff Press, 1993).

OECD, 'Infrastructure, Investment and Community Development: Laganside Corporation Summary Report' (Belfast: 1999) June.

Patton, M., 'Looking Back in Anger', *Ulster Architect* (June 1985) pp. 2–5.

Pauley, *Terminal Architecture* (London: Reakteon Books, 1998).

Pfeiffer, U., 'Berlin vor dem Boom?', *Bauwelt*, 36 (1990), p. 1840ff.

Planning Advisory Board, Housing in N. Ireland: Interim Report of the Planning Advisory Board, Cmnd 224 (Belfast: HMSO, 1944).

Press Release, New City Centre Forum Launched (Belfast: Northern Ireland Information Service, 15 October, 1992).

Purdy, M., 'DUP in "Lundy" Jibe over Ormeau', *Belfast Telegraph*, 2 April (1997).

Rodwell, B., *Elevating Belfast, Omnibus, Autumn* (Belfast: N.I. Information Office, 1993).

Rogers, R., *Cities for a Small Planet* (London: Faber, 1998).

Samuel, R., *Theatres of Memory* (London: Verso, 1996).

Savage, M. and A. Warde, *Urban Sociology, Capitalism and Modernity* (London: Macmillan, 1993).

Schaefer, R. and P. Dehne, *Aktuelles Planungshandbuch zur Stadt- und Dorferneuerung* (Augsburg: WEKA, 1994).

Schiffauer, W., 'Der Weg zum Gottesstaat, Die fundamentalistischen Gemeinden türkischer Arbeitsmigranten in der Bundesrepublik', *Historische Anthropologie*, I (1993).

Scholz, F. (ed.), 'Türkische Bevölkerung in Kreuzberg. Gewerbe – Handel – Wohnen. Kreuzberg-Projekt Sommersemester 1996, Institut für Geographische Occasional Paper *Geographie*, H. 8 (Berlin: Freie Universität, Berlin/Institut für Geographische Wissenschaften/ZELF, 1996).

Scholz, F. (ed), 'Räumliche Ausbreitung türkischer Wirtschaftsaktivitäten in Berlin', B. Hofmeister *et al.* (eds), *Berlin, Beiträge zur Geographie eines Großstadtraumes. Festschrift zum 45. Deutschen Geographentag in Berlin* (Berlin: Reimer, 1985).

Schümer-Strucksberg, M., 'The Berlin Strategy for Further Development of Large Housing Estates: Statement of Position', European Academy of the Urban Environment (ed.), *A Future for Large Housing Estates* (Berlin: published by EA.UE, 1998).

Schusterman, R., *Pragmatic Aesthetics: Living Beauty Rethinking Art* (London: Blackwell Press, 1992).

Schwedler, H.-U., *Arbeitsmigration und urbaner Wandel. Eine Studie über Arbeitskräftewanderung und räumliche Segregation in orientalischen Städten am Beispiel Kuwaits* (Berlin: Reimer, 1985).

Seidel-Pielen, E., *Aufgespießt – Wie der Döner über die Deutschen kam* (Hamburg: Rotbuch Verlag, 1996).

Senatsverwaltung für Stadtentwicklung, Umweltschutz und Technologie (ed.), *Flächennutzungsplan Berlin, FNP Erläuterungsbericht* (Berlin: published by Senatsverwaltung, 1994).

Senatsverwaltung für Stadtentwicklung, Umweltschutz und Technologie (ed.), *Planwerk Innenstadt Berlin – Ein erster Entwurf* (Berlin: Kulturbuchverlag, 1997).

Senatsverwaltung für Stadtentwicklung, Umweltschutz und Technologie (ed.), *Planwerk – Next Generation: Internationale Hochschulprojekte zum Planwerk Innenstadt Berlin* (Berlin: Kulturbuchverlag, 1998).

Senatsverwaltung für Stadtentwicklung, Umweltschutz und Technologie (ed.), *Planwerk Innenstadt: Machbarkeitsstudien für den instrumentellen Bereich* (Berlin: Kulturbuchverlag, 1998).

Senatsverwaltung für Stadtentwicklung, Umweltschutz und Technologie, *Planwerk Innenstadt Berlin. Ergebnis, Prozess, Sektorale Planung und Werkstätten* (Berlin: Kulturbuchverlag, 1999).

Sennett, R., *The Conscience of the Eye* (New York: Norton, 1992).

Simpson, B., 'Belfast – the Great Revival', *Belfast Telegraph*, 13 May (1985).

Skeffington Report, People and Planning: Report of the Committee on Public Participation in Planning (London: HMSO, 1969).

Smith, N., *New Urban Frontier. Gentrification and the Revanchist City* (London: Routledge & Kegan Paul, 1996).

Spies, U.B. 'Der Türkenmarkt am Maybachufer (Kreuzberg/Neukölln)', *Occasional Paper Geographie: Türkische Wirtschaftsaktivitäten in Berlin*, H.3 (Berlin: Freie Universität Berlin/Institut für Geographische Wissenschaften/ZELF, 1998).

Squires, G. (ed.), *Unequal Partnerships: the Political Economy of Urban Redevelopment in Post War America* (New Brunswick: Rutgers University Press, 1989).

StadtRat (ed.), *Umkämpfte Räume: Strategien in der Stadt* (Hamburg, Berlin, Göttingen: Libertäre Assoziation, 1998).

Stimmann, H., 'Discussion Paper Presented at the Trade Fair Constructa 92 in Hannover on 8 February 1992', Senatsverwaltung für Bau- und Wohnungswesen (ed.) *Pro Bauakademie. Argumente für eine Neugründung* (Berlin: by Senatsverwaltung, 1992).

Stimmann, H., 'Was nützt uns die Geschichte? Der historische Stadtgrundriß als Ressource für die Zukunft', *Stadtforum – Zukunft des Zentrums* (29 April 1998).

Stollard, P., 'The Architecture of No-Mans Land', *Architects Journal*, No. 31, Vol. 180 (1984).

Strieder, P., 'Welche Stadt wollen wir? Das Planwerk als Wegweiser jenseits der Architekturmoden', *Stadtforum – Zukunft des Zentrums* (29 April 1998).

Temple Bar Properties, *Temple Bar Shopping and Temple Bar Living* (Dublin: undated).

Temple Bar Properties, *Development Programme for Temple Bar* (Dublin: 1992).

Tewdwr-Jones, M. and P. Allmendinger, 'Deconstructing Communicative Rationality: a Critique of Habermasian Collaborative Planning', *Environment and Planning*, A, Vol. 30 (1998) pp. 1975–89.

Treibel, A., 'Theory of Communicative Action, Discourse Ethics and Political Practice: Notes on Recent Developments in Habermas', *Soziologie*, Journal of the Deutsche Gesellschaft für Soziologie, Special Edition 3 (1994) pp. 135–48.

Trimble, D., Statement as reported in *Belfast Telegraph*, 16 November (1999).

Trippel, K., 'Der Stadtumbau im historischen Zentrum Berlins. Planungspolitik in der Nachwendezeit', *HSP-Papers*, 4/98, Arbeitsschwerpunkt Hauptstadt Berlin, Freie Universität Berlin (1998).

Walker, B. and H. Dixon, *No Mean City: Belfast 1880–1914* (Belfast: Friars Bush Press, 1983).

Weiner, R., *The Rape and Plunder of the Shankill* (Belfast: Farset Co-operative Press, 1978).

Wilson Report, *Economic Development in N. Ireland*, Cmnd 479 (Belfast, HMSO, 1965).

Wilson, R., 'Putting the Gloss on Belfast', *New Society*, 13 May 1988.

Young, J.E., *The Art of Memory: Holocaust Memorials in History* (Munich: Prestel-Verlag, 1994).

Zukin, S., *The Cultures of Cities* (Cambridge, MA: Blackwell, 1995).

Index

Figures/table/maps are indicated by *italics*, where there is no related text on the same page.